The Philosophy of Mario Perniola

Also Available From Bloomsbury

The Sex Appeal of the Inorganic: Philosophies of Desire in the Modern World, Mario Perniola
20th Century Aesthetics: Towards A Theory of Feeling, Mario Perniola
The Bloomsbury Italian Philosophy Reader, eds Michael Lewis and David Edward Rose
Benjamin on Fashion, Philipp Ekardt
Art, Politics and Rancière: Broken Perceptions, Tina Chanter

The Philosophy of Mario Perniola

From Aesthetics to Dandyism

Enea Bianchi

BLOOMSBURY ACADEMIC
LONDON • NEW YORK • OXFORD • NEW DELHI • SYDNEY

BLOOMSBURY ACADEMIC
Bloomsbury Publishing Plc
50 Bedford Square, London, WC1B 3DP, UK
1385 Broadway, New York, NY 10018, USA
29 Earlsfort Terrace, Dublin 2, Ireland

BLOOMSBURY, BLOOMSBURY ACADEMIC and the Diana logo are trademarks of
Bloomsbury Publishing Plc

First published in Great Britain 2022
This paperback edition published 2024

Copyright © Enea Bianchi, 2022

Enea Bianchi has asserted his right under the Copyright, Designs and Patents Act,
1988, to be identified as Author of this work.

For legal purposes the Acknowledgements on p. xii constitute an
extension of this copyright page.

Cover design by Charlotte Daniels
Cover image: Mario Perniola / The Visionary Academy of Ocular Mentality (© Luca Del Baldo)

All rights reserved. No part of this publication may be reproduced or transmitted
in any form or by any means, electronic or mechanical, including photocopying,
recording, or any information storage or retrieval system, without prior
permission in writing from the publishers.

Bloomsbury Publishing Plc does not have any control over, or responsibility for, any
third-party websites referred to or in this book. All internet addresses given
in this book were correct at the time of going to press. The author and publisher
regret any inconvenience caused if addresses have changed or sites have ceased
to exist, but can accept no responsibility for any such changes.

A catalogue record for this book is available from the British Library.

A catalog record for this book is available from the Library of Congress.

ISBN: HB: 978-1-3502-8147-9
PB: 978-1-3502-8151-6
ePDF: 978-1-3502-8148-6
eBook: 978-1-3502-8149-3

Typeset by RefineCatch Limited, Bungay, Suffolk

To find out more about our authors and books visit www.bloomsbury.com
and sign up for our newsletters.

*Dedicated to my mother Daniela Margutti
and to my father Giuseppe Bianchi Papetto*

Contents

Preface		x
Acknowledgments		xii
Abbreviations of Perniola's Works		xiv
Introduction		1

Part 1

1	The Suicide of Literature	11
	Perniola's youthful manifesto: towards a strong feeling	11
	The Metanovel	14
	The dogma of spontaneity: social media and the culmination of the Romantic project	23
	Perniola's *storiette*, or, literature after death	26
2	To Love or Smash Images? The Dimension of the Simulacrum	33
	The Roman aesthetics of simulacra	33
	Guy Debord and fake news	38
	The Jesuit-Baroque tradition and the Internet of Things	41
3	Action at the End of Action: Rituals without Myths	49
	Against the anti-ritual tradition	49
	Perniola's expanded *epoché*	51
	The ritual in ancient Roman religion	53
	The difference of the Catholic feeling	55
	Perniola versus Heidegger and weak thought	62
4	George Bryan Brummell: the Ritual Clothing	69
	Brummell's assault on fashion	69
	Sprezzatura, je ne sais quoi, subtlety	72
	Neither aristocracy nor the bourgeoisie	74
	Romantic history versus dandy *storietta*	76
	Dandyism and the simulacrum of death	78

Part 2

5	What Is It Like to Be a Thing?	83
	Our relationship with things	84
	Neutral dimensions, vibrating stones	87
	Turning oneself into a mirror	91
	Uncanny, radiating and intense things	95
6	A Queering Agency: Perniola's *The Sex Appeal of the Inorganic*	99
	The sexual Big Bang and the limits of orgasm	99
	Post-rock, suspended entities, perversions	104
	The transit or how to endlessly multiply genders and sexes	112
7	Beauty is Like a Blade: Towards a Strategic Theory of Aesthetics	123
	Stoicism or beauty as action	123
	Making unlawful matches between things: Baltasar Gracián's Baroque	128
8	Charles Baudelaire: Greatness without Convictions	135
	To each age its beauty	135
	Perniola's aesthetic horizon and Baudelaire's anti-aesthetics	138
	Dandies, mirrors, blackness	142
	Getting rid of nature	145
	The dandies between stoics and samurai	147

Part 3

9	The Artistic Alienation and the Situationist International	153
	Art must be killed	153
	Guy Debord's dandyism	165
10	A Shadow and Its Art	171
	Art and psychosis	171
	The excessive remainder of the artwork	176
11	Oscar Wilde: the In-Between Dandy	187
	Recurrent dandy ideas in Oscar Wilde	187
	The subversion of writing	193
	Dandyism and queerness	198
	Mona Lisa vamp	200

Conclusion 207

Notes 211
References 223
Index 237

Preface

You died on a January night and you left with a golden dragon on a red tie and an inscription on your grave: 'Neither Living Here, Nor Dead There', as if life has always been a simulacrum of death to you, a detached participation in the great theatre of the world. While I was working on my PhD thesis on your thought, from which this book stems, suddenly I could not discuss anything with you anymore.

Maybe I should have returned to Itamaracá, the island off the coast of Pernambuco, where you said you used to feel surrounded by a present in standstill and enclosed within a quiet wildness. Perhaps I should have revisited the ruins of Cuzco, because the Inca, like the dandies, despised money but still imbued their lives with the enchantment of objects. But I needn't have travelled so far. I could have strolled the old streets of Rome and its forgotten quarters, let the questions fade in the alleys of Trastevere, below the façade of the Basilica of Santa Maria, where every morning you walked by to get the newspaper and visit the small bookstore at the corner. I could have swum in the waters of Lake Nemi, above sunken Roman ships, where you used to spend every summer, resting your eyes on the trees to take a pause from writing. In the end I could not discuss anything with you anymore but I could constantly turn back to these memories, to try to reconstruct you, fashioning a silhouette that would keep you in a state of suspended presence, like the mannequin of Metaphysical paintings.

The pages of this book select, cut and sew up the landscapes and the fabrics of your world, trying to tailor a suit that would fit your inorganic body. I don't think you would agree with one of the main arguments of this book: that your philosophy is essentially a dandy's philosophy. You have never paid too much attention to this phenomenon; on several occasions you referred to it casually, the one exception being an article in which two pages revolve upon it. You have always expressed an admiration for Baudelaire, though: in your opinion he was one of those individuals who broadened the aesthetic horizon, including marginal, fringe, psychopathological experiences, but above all someone who clothed the things of the world with unexpected, brilliant and uncanny intensities. However, you never wrote or said anything about the other two exemplar dandies I chose to put side by side with you, Brummell and Wilde. Yet there is so much of you in them and so much of them in the current world: from the subversion of normativity to a post-natural attitude towards things; from the osmosis between organic and inorganic up to the stingy, witty, strategic beauty; from the endless multiplications of genders to a never-ending flow of feeling and excitement.

Many would not consider yours a dandy philosophy – perhaps they still associate you with the Situationists, after all, you and they have never had too much in common. There is no triumphalist vitalism, anarchic subjectivity or sectarianism in your path. In the burning streets of the 1960s and 1970s, you valued the detached and cold style, typical of the artificial, baroque and dandyish humanity which you recognized in the person of Guy Debord.

You would probably not consider your philosophy to be essentially dandy, yet in the years I met you and became your student, I constantly witnessed an aesthetic lifestyle, oriented towards elegance and witticism, but above all intimately connected to a challenge issued to the world. Perhaps the greatest challenge: opening up to this very world, transforming it by making even what is necessary beautiful, at war with the world but always keeping a light heart. An *amor fati* that has never meant passivity and fatalism, or an unhappy escape into a nostalgic past, but first and foremost an acceptance of what is given, even at the cost of being part of a commodified arena, of a declining institution, of a society of spectacle – taking a subversive, *oppositional* stance.

To become mirrors as wide as the world, so that the world can reflect itself in us and not the other way around, against all narcissisms. Because only what is real can become beautiful, while what is possible or ideal will never have the strength to become so. It is then a matter of working on what has had the opportunity to be brought to life, to exist, to be, and which through rituals, simulacra, transits, enigmas and *storiette* is transmitted, propagated, persisting constantly beyond itself.

Because dying is not an infinite alternation between days and darkness, it is not a slow fading from embers to embers, but becoming-something-else, in some other place and in someone else, blooming.

Acknowledgments

This book stems from my PhD dissertation written between 2016 and 2020 at the National University of Ireland, Galway. Throughout its writing I have received a great deal of support and assistance.

I would first like to thank the Italian Department at NUI Galway, especially Prof. Paolo Bartoloni, whose expertise on the subject matter was invaluable. Thank you for your consistent support and guidance.

I would like to acknowledge Ivelise Perniola for allowing me to examine Mario Perniola's private archive, which opened this book to newer and larger territories. I would also like to thank Luigi A. Manfreda and Massimo Di Felice for their precious advice.

Many thanks to my editor at Bloomsbury, Lucy Russell, for championing my book and accompanying it through the editorial process. Thanks also to the Bloomsbury team for their work. I am also grateful to the anonymous reviewers who provided insightful recommendations and criticism.

Thanks to my parents, Daniela Margutti and Giuseppe Bianchi, to whom this book is dedicated, for their never-ending encouragement and patience which gave me a vital freedom to develop this book. Also, my thankfulness goes to my grandmother, Rossana Micacchi, for her unwavering care.

Furthermore, to my friend and colleague Paolo Santori, my gratitude for all the hours listening to and discussing my academic concerns, hopes and future projects. Although there are clouds above, the sea has never been this open, and we are on the same vessel.

In addition, I could not have completed this book without the crucial help of my friends, relatives and colleagues. I would like to single out all those who in any way had a beneficial impact on me and the writing of this book throughout the years, be it reading and commenting on my project, assisting me during some troubling moments or raising a pint for all the good moments shared: Matteo M. Paolucci, Arianna Pagliara, Simone Mencherini, Zsuzsanna Balázs, Cian O'Brien, Oliver Milne, Vittorio Dinca, Giada Lagana, Eli Borges Junior, Fernando Batista, Giulia Peverelli, Flaviano Petrucca, Giulia Viaggi, Michela Dianetti, Mattia Cestonaro, Tatiana Chadourko, Giacomo De Luca, Aris Tsoullos, Anastasia Beltramello, Andrea Ciribuco, Anna Gasperini, Richard Jeffery,

Manolo De Persis, Sara Bucci, Paolo Bangrazi, Sara Pelagaggi, Sara Falchetti, Elena Nordio, Wang Jianjiang, Andrew Ó Donnghaile, Sandro Perna, Pietro Chiumbuto, Maša Uzelac, Laura Britton, Síomha Mc Garry, João Andrade, Tasos Matopoulos, Agata Joanna Lag, Mario Inglese, Shi Wenxuan, Emanuele Occhialini, Mirko Papella, Luca C. Palmas, Andrea Quintiliani, Emanuele Curcio, Martina Cesaretti, Joshua Tammaro, Michele Carosi, Albino Lucarelli, Takafumi Kato, Ryan Dennis, Alessandra La Gioia, Gabriele Corsetti, Maraiza Pereira, Luca Salis, Michelangelo Moffa, Alessio Biancalana, Ayumi Rosa Filippone, Roberto Urbani, Igor Bangrazi, Clara Polisini, Sara Bianchi, Palmiro Margutti, Emanuela Spalla, Luciano Micacchi, Alessandra Margutti, Monica Margutti, Giuseppe De Carolis, Oriana Bologna, Angì Perniola, Alberto, Adriano e Graziella Della Scala, Giuliano Compagno, Nadja Tawfiq, Francesca Pirisi, Hi Dee, Fabiana Bartuccelli. Thank you, every one of you is an inspiration to me, you made this journey intense and unforgettable.

Finally, my deepest gratitude goes to B. Irene Perin and her love.

Abbreviations of Perniola's Works

AA	(1971), *L'alienazione artistica*, Milan: Mursia.
AC	(1982), 'Arte e carcere', in L. Russo (ed.), *Oggi l'arte è un carcere?* 11–24, Bologna: Il Mulino.
ACT	(2007), 'Del arte como transgresión al arte como profesión', trans. S.J. Castro, *Estudios filosóficos*, LVI, 181: 17–29.
AE	(2016), *L'arte espansa*, Turin: Einaudi.
AGS	(1999), 'An Aesthetic of the "Grand Style": Guy Debord', trans. O. Vasile, *Substance*, 28 (3): 89–101.
AH	(2014), 'Araki's Hells', trans. J. Hayne, in N. Araki, *Photography for the Afterlife. Nobuyoshi Araki,* 314–22, Tokyo: Heibonsha.
AI	(1969), 'Arte immaginazione e ricupero culturale', *Quindici*, 19: 12.
AIS	(2004), *Art and Its Shadow*, trans. M. Verdicchio, London and New York: Continuum.
AMN	(1995), 'L'art comme mutant neutre'. Available online: http://www.marioperniola.it/site/index.php/my-books/french/item/372-l-art-un-mutant-neutre (accessed 3 September 2021).
AOS	(1966), 'Artaud e l'origine della scrittura', *Tempo presente*, 2: 48–52.
AR	(1966), 'Arte e rivoluzione', *Tempo presente*, 12: 69–74.
AS	(2013), *L'avventura situazionista. Storia critica dell'ultima avanguardia del XX secolo*, Milan-Udine: Mimesis.
ASC	(2017), 'L'avventura situazionista. Conversazione con il filosofo Mario Perniola', interview conducted by I. Carozzi, *Linus*, 5: 12–15.
AT	ed. (1994), *L'aria si fa tesa. Per una filosofia del sentire presente*, Genoa: Costa & Nolan.

BCN	(2009), 'Between Clothing and Nudity', in P. McNeil (ed.), *Classic and Modern Writings on Fashion* [eBook edn], London and New York: Bloomsbury.
BD	(2019), 'Becoming Deleuzian?', *Deleuze and Guattari Studies*, 13 (1): 482–94.
BI	(1977), 'Bataille e l'Italia', *L'erba voglio*, 29/30: 16.
BN	(1977), *Bataille e il negativo*, Milan: Feltrinelli.
BR	(2011), *Berlusconi o il '68 realizzato*, Milan-Udine: Mimesis.
BSE	(1961), 'Beckett e la scrittura esistenziale', *Tempo presente*, 9/10: 727–33.
CA	(2013), *20th Century Aesthetics. Towards a Theory of Feeling*, trans. M. Verdicchio, London and New York: Bloomsbury Academic.
CC	(2004), *Contro la comunicazione*, Turin: Einaudi.
CD	(1984), 'Entretien avec Mario Perniola', interview conducted by C. Descamps, in *Entretiens avec Le Monde*, Paris: La Découverte: 141–8.
CDP	(1987), 'Carlo Michelstaedter. La conquista del presente', *Mondo operaio* (April): 108–9.
CLC	(1994), 'Celebrare la città', *Millepiani*, 2: 53–62.
COA	(1988), 'The Comeback of Aesthetics', *Estetica News*, 1: 1.
CR	(1970), 'Critica e realizzazione dell'arte in Dadà', *Agaragar*, 1: 42–77.
CTA	(2007), 'Cultural Turns in Aesthetics and Anti-Aesthetics', *Filozofski vestnik*, 23 (2): 39–51.
CTC	(2007), 'The Cultural Turn of Catholicism', in H. Laugerud and L.K. Skinnebach (eds), *Instruments of Devotion: The Practices and Objects of Religious Piety from the Late Middle Ages to the 20th Century*, 45–60, Aarhus: Aarhus Universitetsforlag.
CTP	(2002), 'Cultural Turning Points in Art: Art Between Parasitism and Admiration', trans. M. Verdicchio, *Res*, 41: 127–35.
CV	(2010), 'Arte vida e meio. O sex-appeal do inorgãnico na Vale do Côa', trans. S. Azzoni, in *A arte antes e depois da arte*, 85–9, M.-T. Cruz: Côa Museum.

D	(1998), *Disgusti. Le nuove tendenze estetiche*, Genoa: Costa & Nolan.
DA	(1983), 'Una dea dell'abbondanza', *La Gola*, 2 (6): 22.
DH	(1982), *Dopo Heidegger. Filosofia e organizzazione della cultura*, Milan: Feltrinelli.
DI	(1976), 'La differenza italiana', *L'Erba Voglio*, 27: 11–16.
DIP	(1984), 'The Difference of the Italian Philosophical Culture', trans. R. Friedman, *Graduate Faculty Philosophy Journal*, 10 (1): 103–15.
DS	(1991), *Del sentire*, Turin: Einaudi.
E	(1995), *Enigmas. The Egyptian Moment in Society and Art*, trans. C. Woodall, London: Verso.
EAI	(2012), 'L'enigme de l'amour en Italie: *in viva morte morta vita vivo*', *Les Cahiers européens de l'imaginare*, 4: 184–93.
EC	(1994), 'Eccitazione', in M. Perniola (ed.), *L'aria si fa tesa. Per una filosofia del sentire presente*, 87–94, Genoa: Costa & Nolan.
EE	(2011), 'Expanded Epoché', *Iris. European Journal of Philosophy and Public Debate*, III (6): 157–70.
EFH	(2006), 'Expansão e fragmentação do horizonte estético', trans. V. Moura, *Diacrítica, Filosofia e cultura*, 20 (2): 107–18.
EIC	(2017), *Estetica italiana contemporanea*, Milan: Bompiani.
EIN	(2015), 'L'esthétique italienne, du *Novecento* au XXIe siècle. Entretien avec Mario Perniola', interview conducted and trans. by P. Quintili, *Collège international de Philosophie*, 4 (87): 101–27.
FA	(1992), 'La filosofia dell'arte', in E. Agazzi (ed.), *Filosofia e filosofia di*, 75–84, Brescia: La Scuola.
FS	(1987), 'Il forte sentire di Carlo Michelstaedter', *Alfabeta*, 102: 24–5.
HE	(2003), 'L'horizon esthétique et la beauté interlope', *Bulletin de la societé française d'esthétique* (April): 1–8.
I	(1977), 'Introduzione', in F. Nietzsche, *L'Anticristo*, 7–14, Rome: Newton Compton.

IB	(1973), 'Interpretazioni di Bataille', *Rivista di estetica*, XVIII (2): 138–76.
IE	(2015), 'Italy the Enigma. Italian Contemporary Aesthetics', *Studi Culturali*, 3: 317–24.
IEB	(1979), 'L'iconoclasma erotico di Bataille', in G. Bataille, *Le lacrime di Eros*, 7–21, Rome: Arcana.
II	(2013), 'La Internacional Indeterminada', trans. M. Huernos, in F. Davis (ed.), *Horacio Zabala, desde 1972*, 38–40, Buenos Aires: UNTREF.
IMP	(1999), 'Intervista a Mario Perniola', interview conducted by L. Pratesi, *Artel*, 1: 76–81.
IS	(1968), 'L'Internazionale Situazionista e i fatti francesi di maggio', *Nuovi argomenti*, 11: 129–40.
IVS	(1978), 'Icones, visions, simulacres', *Traverses*, 10: 39–49.
IYR	(2011), 'Impossible, yet real', *Cultura*, 8 (1): 187–212.
JJ	(2006), 'The Japanese Juxtaposition', *European Review*, 1: 129–34.
KP	(2013), 'Knowledge, Power and Politic-Cultural Civilization', *Cultura*, 10 (2): 41–8.
LC	(n.d.), 'Libertini e camerati', preparatory studies on *The Sex Appeal of the Inorganic*, in Mario Perniola's private archive, Rome.
LEC	(2009), 'L'eterno Confucio', *Il Manifesto*, January 22: 13.
LPD	(1984), 'Lettera sul pensiero debole', *Alfabeta*, 58: 24–35.
LR	(2011), 'Literati and Revolutionaries in Rome between 1968 and 1970', *Annali d'Italianistica*, 29: 315–24.
LTC	(2009), 'Lente trasformazioni all'ombra di Confucio', *Il Manifesto*, September 29: 11.
M	(1966), *Il metaromanzo*, Milan: Silva.
MAT	(1965), 'Manierismo e autenticità in Tommaso Landolfi', *Tempo presente*, 9/10: 68–72.

MBM	(1969), 'Maurice Blanchot o il masochismo delle lettere', *Nuovi argomenti*, 15: 268–83.
MC	(2005), 'Editoriale. Magic corporation', *Ágalma*, 9: 5–6.
MN	(2012), 'L'artiste, monnaie vivante', interview conducted by C. Margat, *Arearevue)s(*, 26: 21–4.
MTC	(2009), *Miracoli e traumi della comunicazione*, Turin: Einaudi.
NO	(1975), 'Nietzsche e l'opposizione eccessiva', *Il verri*, 9: 17–67.
NP	(1971), 'Il negativo e la poesia in Georges Bataille', *Rivista di estetica*, XVI (3): 342–70.
NSC	(2001), 'La natura del "sentire cattolico"', interview conducted by T. Danese, *Conquiste del Lavoro*, 24 November: 7.
NVP	(1989), 'Neoantique Versus Postmodernism', *Estetica News*, 6: 1.
OMP	(2014), 'Obsolescenza del mito politico', *Filosofia politica*, 3: 425–34.
OR	(1969), 'Origine della reificazione poetica nella Grecia antica', *Rivista di estetica*, XIV (3): 336–60.
OS	(1969), 'Origine storica della reificazione artistica nell'età moderna', *Rivista di estetica*, XIV (2): 226–55.
PC	(1968), review of P. Cabanne, *Entretiens avec Marcel Duchamp*, in *Rivista di estetica*, XIII (1): 129–31.
PD	(2012), *Presa diretta. Estetica e politica. Da Nietzsche a Breivik*, Milan-Udine: Mimesis.
PF	(2002), 'Prova di forza o prova di grandezza? Considerazioni sull'ágalma', *Ágalma*, 3: 62–79.
PM	(1959), *Programma Manifesto*, self-published.
PNA	ed. (1995), *Il pensiero neo-antico. Tecniche e possessione nell'arte e nel sapere del mondo contemporaneo*, Milan-Udine: Mimesis.
PNM	(n.a.), 'Nota preparatoria per la seconda edizione de *Il metaromanzo*', in Mario Perniola's private archive, Rome.
PP	(2010), *Più-che-sacro, più-che-profano*, Milan-Udine: Mimesis.

PS	(1998), *Philosophia sexualis. Scritti su Georges Bataille*, Verona: Ombre Corte.
PSN	(1999), 'Per una sessualità neutra. A colloquio con Mario Perniola', interview conducted by E. Tavani and G. Gravina, *Almanacchi Nuovi*, 2/3: 107–15.
QC	(2008), 'Il quarto corpo', *Ágalma*, 16: 8–15.
RIE	(1995), 'Rituals in Exhibition', in I. Gianelli and G. Verzotti (eds), *Heim Steinbach. Catalogo della mostra 1995 (Rivoli)*, 21–9, Milan: Charta.
RC	(1983), 'Mario Perniola et les rites contemporains', interview conducted by C. Descamps, *Le Monde Dimanche*, 7 August: XI–XII.
RNP	(2013), 'Per una rivalutazione della nozione di profondità', *Ágalma*, 25: 93–101.
RT	(2001), *Ritual Thinking. Sexuality, Death, World*, trans. M. Verdicchio, Amherst NY: Humanity Books.
SA	(1991), 'Il superamento dell'arte e l'Internazionale Situazionista', in V. Valentini (ed.), *Dissensi*, 257–65, Palermo: Sellerio.
SAI	(2017), *The Sex Appeal of the Inorganic*, trans. M. Verdicchio, London and New York: Bloomsbury Academic.
SAIA	(n.d.), 'Il sex appeal dell'inorganico. Conoscenza e sessualità', preparatory notes on *The Sex Appeal of the Inorganic*, in Mario Perniola's private archive, Rome.
SAIC	(1997), 'The Sex Appeal of the Inorganic: A Conversation between Sergio Contardi and Mario Perniola', *Journal of European Psychoanalysis*, 3/4. Available online: http://www.psychomedia.it/jep/number3-4/contpern.htm (accessed 3 September 2021).
SC	(2001), *Del sentire cattolico. La forma culturale di una religione universale*, Bologna: Il Mulino.
SISV	(2016), 'Del sentir inorgánico al sentir vegetal', trans. F. Consiglio, *Disputatio. Philosophical Research Bulletin*, 5 (6): 307–34.
SO	(1966), 'Il surrealismo oggi', *Tempo presente*, 9/10: 69–72.

SPB	(2014), *Sobre el pensar barroco*, Lima: Instituto Italiano de Cultura de Lima.
SRM	(1970), 'Il surrealismo e la realizzazione del meraviglioso', *Agaragar*, 2: 62–79.
SS	(2011), *La società dei simulacri*, Milan-Udine: Mimesis.
SSA	(n.d.), 'Il Settantasette e i Situazionisti (titolo provvisorio). Autointervista', in Mario Perniola's private archive, Rome.
SSF	(1978), 'Sogno e società in Freud', *Il verri*, 12: 119–37.
SSI	(1979), 'Scambio simbolico, iperrealismo, simulacro', *Aut aut*, 170/171: 67–70.
T	(1985), *Transiti. Come si va dallo stesso allo stesso*, Bologna: Cappelli.
TBA	(2015), *Del terrorismo come una delle belle arti*, Milan-Udine: Mimesis.
TCE	(2021), *Tiresia contro Edipo. Vite di un intellettuale disorganico*, Genoa: Il Nuovo Melangolo.
TP	(1971), 'Teoria e pratica nel Rinascimento', *Agaragar*, 3: 53–83.
TR	(1968), *Tiresia*, Milan: Silva.
TS	(2010), 'Teoria della storietta', in C. Terrile (ed.), *La filosofia spontanea*, 143–53, Florence: Le Lettere.
UAP	(1978), 'Umanismo, anti-umanismo, pseudo-umanismo', *Nuovi argomenti* (January): 216–32.
USS	(2005), 'Un sesto senso: la sessualità?', keynote lecture presented at *Festivalfilosofia*, 16 September (Modena, Carpi e Sassuolo).
VB	(1995), 'Verità e bellezza in Heidegger', in A. Pieretti (ed.), *Estraneità e testimonianza interiore*, 209–17, Naples: Edizioni Scientifiche Italiane.
WE	(1976), 'Il Witz come elusione del conflitto', *Il verri*, 3: 7–21.

Note on translations

All quotations from sources in languages other than English are translated by the author.

Introduction

Mario Perniola's philosophical trajectory made him a leading representative of contemporary Italian philosophy worldwide. On the one hand, he was associated with Italian and international academic institutions, and on the other, he was also involved in non-academic milieus, starting with Guy Debord and the Situationists in the late 1960s; his engagement ranged from Afro-Brazilian rituals to the experimental theatre of the *Societas Raffaello Sanzio*. He was a thinker on and off the beaten track, an insider and an outsider all at the same time (Gasquet 2018). His bibliography includes *20th Century Aesthetics* and *Estetica Italiana contemporanea* (Italian Contemporary Aesthetics), which are two volumes devoted to the most significant aestheticians of the era, and *The Sex Appeal of the Inorganic* and *L'avventura situazionista* (The Situationist Adventure). The former explores the relationship between material culture, sexuality and perversions in the postmodern era, and the latter presents a historical account of Situationist International, a revolutionary movement of the 1960s. In addition to conducting research on traditional aesthetics, he developed theories and concepts by investigating fringe, alternative and uncanny phenomena. Influenced by several streams of thought and traditions from the Western, Eastern and Southern worlds, including Roman ritualism, Stoicism, Jesuit-Baroque thought, twentieth-century avant-gardes, Brazilian culture, Japanese aesthetics and Chinese polemology, Perniola gained popularity in both academia and the broader public. Interested in more than just canonical objects in the study of aesthetics, namely art, the beautiful, the sublime, taste and sensitive knowledge, Perniola understands aesthetics as a wider horizon that also includes lifestyles, manners, politics, extreme and alternative experiences and, broadly speaking, the realm of 'feeling' (*sentire*). The originality of his perspectives lies in the unusual combination of heterogeneous thinkers and experiences that he merged and developed alongside a philosophy-based, rigorous and coherent theoretical framework.

This book compares Perniola's work with the phenomenon of dandyism. It focuses on Perniola's aesthetic and philosophical thought to develop and explore its affinity with three exemplar dandies, namely George Bryan Brummell (1778–1840), Charles Baudelaire (1821–67) and Oscar Wilde (1854–1900), aiming to represent how Perniola's philosophy can be considered a 'dandy' philosophy.

Perniola was born in Asti on 20 May 1941, and he died in Rome on 9 January 2018. His theoretical achievements range from aesthetics to art theory, sociology of communication, literary and political theory, cinema and urban studies, among others. Philosophically honed at the University of Turin under Luigi Pareyson's supervision, his first book, *Il metaromanzo*, was reviewed by Nobel laureate Eugenio Montale in *Corriere della Sera* (Montale 1966), enhancing Perniola's reputation among Italian intellectuals and thinkers. In fact, starting from the 1960s, Perniola became acquainted with figures such as Alberto Moravia, Gianni Vattimo, Umberto Eco, Ignazio Silone, Nicola Chiaromonte, Guy Debord, Jacques Derrida, Jean Baudrillard, Michel Maffesoli, Pierre Klossowski (he was also the polemic object of a poem written by Pier Paolo Pasolini in 1972). In this fertile and dynamic intellectual milieu, Perniola gained professorships at the University of Salerno first (1970–83) and then at the University of Rome Tor Vergata, where he taught from 1983 to 2011. Over the decades, he founded four journals – *Agaragar* (1970–2), *Clinamen* (1988–92), *Estetica News* (1988–95) and *Ágalma* (2000–18) – which comprised multifaceted areas of study, from critical theory to aesthetics, cultural studies, philosophy of art, Eastern thought and literature.

Despite the number of articles, reviews, essays and special issues published on Perniola's thought (see, for instance, Vogt 2019a; Ryynänen 2021; Bartoloni 2011, 2019; Duarte 2021), no comprehensive monograph on his overall reflections has been produced to date. The scholarly literature on Perniola mostly covers specific areas of his research and does not scrutinize it as a whole. The only research that brings together multiple aspects of his work was published by Massimo Verdicchio (2001) as the introduction to Perniola's collection of essays in *Ritual Thinking. Sexuality, Death, World*. Nonetheless, it presents a limited view of Perniola's publications, mostly only concerned with his output during the 1980s and 1990s; it does not include the fundamental books and articles published in the previous as well as subsequent decades. This book, in contrast, takes into account both youthful and mature writings, providing a comprehensive enquiry into Perniola's reflection.

To write this book, a critical comparative investigation of the connections between Perniola and dandyism was undertaken. When drawing on Perniola's own works, I focus specifically on nine concepts that he has elaborated over the years – the metanovel, *storiette*, the simulacrum, the ritual without myth, the sex appeal of the inorganic, the transit, strategic beauty, artistic alienation and the artistic shadow – which represent the philosophical and aesthetic core of his thought. At the same time, these ideas resonate and share key aspects with the aesthetically oriented lifestyles of dandies. I have chosen the three exemplar dandies for one primary reason. Having collected information on numerous other dandies before embarking on the journey of this book, I have found that although a dandyish attitude can be found rather uniformly within the phenomenon of dandyism (elegance and witticism being two central and recurrent aspects of it; see Montandon 2016), a variety of perspectives, standpoints and behaviours have arisen within the phenomenon. From my preparatory enquiry, I found that the three dandies I have chosen present particularly deep and significant affinities with Perniola's thought. As I will explain in the following pages, Brummell established what I define as 'ritual clothing', close to Perniola's idea of 'ritual thinking', wherein Stoic detachment and Roman religiosity meet the dandy aesthetic; Baudelaire, in his praise of artificiality and exteriority, echoes the theory of the 'inorganic' and the notion of 'specularism' elaborated by Perniola; finally, the theory of the artwork as a 'living thing', proposed by Wilde in *The Critic as Artist*, can be compared to the concept of 'artistic shadow', presented by Perniola to explain the role and value of the artistic object within mass societies. Taken together, these three dandies allowed me to follow Perniola's trajectory in its entirety.

Although the book engages with Perniola's key philosophical notions, in an attempt to invite the reader to venture into the originality of his thought, it is not intended as a summary of all his writings. Therefore, I had to bracket off several areas of study in which Perniola intervened throughout the decades from this discussion, especially his work on Georges Bataille, Italian contemporary aestheticians, contemporary politics and various non-Western traditions of thought.[1]

This approach to Perniola's philosophy informs the structure and the order of the book, comprising three main parts. Part One is divided into four chapters. The first three explore specific concepts elaborated by Perniola, while the last is devoted to Brummell's dandyism. The notions I have chosen to explore in this section – the metanovel, the *storiette*, the simulacrum and the ritual without myth – despite their irreducibility and heterogeneity, display a common and recurrent thread within Perniola's thought. Specifically, they involve a series of experiences and phenomena, including forms, appearances and manners, and entail the possibility for a plethora of other concepts, including difference, suspension and effectuality, emerging precisely from exteriority and formal discourses.

I start with Perniola's youthful research on the theory of literature, when he explored the relationship between authorship and writing in the works of a selection of writers, including Joseph Conrad, André Gide, Michel Leiris and Samuel Beckett. In his first book, *Il metaromanzo*, Perniola, in the wake of an increasingly developing field of metatheory in the 1960s, discusses the self-referential attitude of several writers, which he categorizes under the umbrella concept of metanovelists. Loathing the traditional novel with its canonical categories, such as the omniscient narrator, these writers developed a writing style heavily oriented towards experimentation and 'work in progress', all within the aesthetic horizon of self-reference and metafiction. Perniola draws a unifying thread that, starting from the Romantic idea of spontaneity, sincerity and return to nature (exemplified by Rousseau's *Confessions*) as well as metanovelists' search for authentic writing, arrives at the current social media context: in believing that immediate and spontaneous writing can adequately express the 'I', the users are the culminating point of 200 years of literature.

Against this cultural landscape, Perniola praises a minor literary genre that he traces back to the late seventeenth century France: the *storiette* (roughly translated as 'short stories'). He published a collection of eight *storiette* with the title *Del terrorismo come una delle belle arti* (Of Terrorism as One of the Fine Arts), which feature several recurrent and key ideas of his overall philosophy, namely desubjectivation, transit and aesthetic detachment. Moreover, Perniola himself declares his *storiette* beyond the categories of truth and falsity, closely related to the logics of the simulacrum.

The chapter following that on the *storiette* concerns Perniola's conception of the simulacrum, which he does not view in derogatory terms. While the simulacrum is often understood as a deceptive dissimulation, Perniola views it as a useful concept for interpreting the contemporary world with its virtual and digital simulations as well as the numerous experiences and traditions of thought that have emerged in the West in the past centuries (such as ancient Roman religiosity and the Jesuit–Baroque tradition). The connection between suspension, simulation and difference links the simulacrum to the ritual without myth. The latter comprises a ritual performance in which the accent is not put on a myth (that is, a meaning, a moral goal, an ideology) but on the formal performance itself. In these sections, I show how in both Roman and Jesuit ritualism, there is a crucial connection between aesthetics, appearances and manners on one side and effectuality, action and openness to the world on another. Perniola transposes this religious idea into the philosophical realm by elaborating ritual thinking, a non-ideological practice oriented towards effectiveness. Ritual thinking is connected to an epochistic reduction of the self, which implies the suspension of one's own judgement and beliefs. In fact, for Perniola, only by dissolving one's desires, impulses and identity can they assimilate the external world, with its manifestations and endless possibilities.

The concepts that I discuss in the first chapters are useful to outline Brummell's figure as well as to show in which terms the dandy's lifestyle embodies Perniola's philosophy. Specifically, I discuss what I describe as Brummell's everyday ritual clothing, which exhibits several essential aspects of Perniola's ritual thinking. Where Perniola praised an idea of the ritual against myth, Brummell likewise moved against the myths of his time (especially those of the emerging middle class with its bourgeois mindset and normativity). In addition, the English dandy grounded his life on the daily repetition of an actual dressing ritual, oriented towards the suspension of his identity and subjectivity. Paradoxically however, although he spent up to three hours a day in front of the mirror, Brummell meticulously worked on the disappearance of himself in the folds of his clothes and fabrics, slowly becoming a simulacrum, an artificial image with a suspended ego, and nonetheless managed to become an acclaimed and recognized *arbiter elegantiarum* in the fashion-conscious London of the time.

In Part Two, Perniola's philosophy and Baudelaire's dandyism are discussed. Chapters 5 and 6 are devoted to Perniola's thing theory and inorganic sexuality, respectively, while chapter 7 is dedicated to his peculiar conception of beauty, which he terms 'strategic beauty'. One of the main sources for chapters 5 and 6 is *The Sex Appeal of the Inorganic*, complemented by other scholarly literature on Perniola's understanding of thingness. I distinguish Perniola's interpretation of the notion of thing from the Marxist one. The latter sees the thing as the reifying product of human work within mass society. Perniola, in contrast, traces the experience of the thing back to Palaeolithic engravings, to Egyptian architecture, Baroque aesthetics, Freudian psychoanalysis and contemporary phenomena, such as art installations, sci-fi literature and drug addictions, just to name a few. Holding these heterogeneous realities together is the understanding of the inorganic realm in a non-metaphysical way. While traditional metaphysics divides the organic and the inorganic, privileging the first over the latter, Perniola elaborates on a peculiar idea of the thing instead, which possesses three main aspects: the 'neutral', the 'external' and the 'radiative'. The neutral dimension implies osmosis between the organic and the inorganic, owing to which the boundaries between what is inert and what is alive collapse. Instead of conveying the idea of a neutralization of feelings, it means opening up to what was left behind by traditional metaphysics: the inorganic realm.

I investigate exteriority through Perniola's discussion of Zen philosophy and Baroque literature by underlining a process that the Italian philosopher refers to as 'specularism'. Specularism refers to the acceptance of one's own present in order to allow what is external, what comes from outside, to find space within oneself. Like the mirror surface, which reflects the world around itself, Perniola praises the idea of becoming a thing, specifically the mirror, as a means to enter the neutral dimension. Against Marxist and spiritualist theories, which polarize human and non-human, natural and artificial, Perniola – by drawing from thinkers such as Poe, Baudelaire, Wittgenstein and Freud – elaborates thingness under the sign of a philosophic, aesthetic, uncanny and perverse intensity.

This finally brings me to Perniola's most famous book, *The Sex Appeal of the Inorganic*. With its almost pornographic prose, the Italian thinker ponders on the union between philosophy, perversions and sexuality by conceptualizing the so-called 'thing that feels', which implies a suspended feeling in the horizon of a permanent, anti-hedonist, anti-orgasm excitement that goes beyond pleasure. This paradoxical experience also allows me to set out Perniola's queer standpoint, which, starting from his youthful first novel *Tiresia* up to his posthumous autobiography *Tiresia contro Edipo*, always sought to transgress the boundaries of biological sex through the subversion of ideological and heteronormative mindsets.

In chapter 7, I discuss the notion of strategic beauty elaborated by Perniola, which is influenced by several pivotal elements from Stoic and Baroque traditions. Against objectivist and subjectivist aesthetic theories, Perniola highlights the connection between aesthetics, forms and rituals on the one hand and effectuality, tangible results and tactics on the other. Hence, his idea of beauty entails close attention to the present and its manifestations.

In chapter 8 I explore Baudelaire's dandyism, which shares two main aspects with Perniola's discourse. First, the French dandy links beauty with modernity – that is, the contingent and transient aspect of one's own contemporaneity. In doing so, he does not favour any essentialist or idealistic conception of beauty but rather a more plastic one, and it falls on the dandy to extract and explore it. Thus, he shares the idea of a strategic beauty as well as a welcoming disposition towards one's own time, as evinced in Perniola's notions of specularism. Baudelaire, in fact, invites the dandy to become a mirror as large as the entire metropolis in order to welcome what comes from outside. Second, Baudelaire praises the idea of an artificial and suspended life against nature and vitalism – two other polemic objects of Perniola's research. Instead of spontaneous, ardent and passionate subjectivity, he praises an artificial individual who dissolves their identity in clothes and make-up, fostering the idea of an epochistic personality in the midst of urban environments.

In Part Three, I investigate Perniola's theory of art, focusing first on his early writings and then on his mature thought. Chapter 9 covers the period from 1966 to 1972, which condenses his overall perspective on art and society in those years. The articles I discuss, alongside his major work on the subject, *L'alienazione artistica*, are influenced by the counterculture of the 1960s (especially the Situationist movement) and the historical avant-gardes (especially Dadaism and Surrealism).

Perniola indicates that art, throughout Western history, has provided merely a halved and impoverished manifestation of human creativity, backing it up with two main justifications. On the one hand, he argues that art practices have not been independent and are actually subjugated to ideological political diktats. On the other hand, art could have meant creative freedom only for a small number of individuals and never for the community as a whole, resulting in a separation between a few 'actors' and a mass of 'spectators'. Perniola's conclusion is paradoxical. Provided that art in the Western world has always been accompanied by this alienation of creativity, he claims that the two terms are inseparable: art *is* alienation. Therefore, to change the status quo, that is, to overcome artistic alienation, the very concept of art itself should be overcome as well. Thus, his main point is not about the realization of art within the Western world but the realization of creativity. In other words, creativity must be realized beyond art, as art has never managed to allow individuals to express creativity authentically.

In the following pages, I discuss Perniola's subsequent remarks on the Situationist International and Guy Debord's figure. Specifically, I discuss both Perniola's critical remarks on the Situationist movement, and I highlight a shift in Perniola's art theory. I describe this shift as the transition from a 'more-than-life' to a 'more-than-form' theory. Whilst, in his early writings, Perniola's goal was to develop theoretical and practical possibilities for the re-appropriation of everyday life, in his later reflections he does not cast questions on the mass or 'spectacular' society. Rather, he focuses on the role and the value that artwork possesses precisely within the contemporary consumerist and capitalist world. It is a shift from the centrality of life to the centrality of form: the revolutionary practice of the counterculture movement makes way for the 'enigma' and the 'shadow' of the artistic object. Perniola explores the thingly nature of artworks to show that, regardless of any market or commercial appropriations, it is still possible for artistic forms to convey ideas, meanings and values that resist and subvert economic homogenization. He compares the economic and promotional realms to a 'light' that invests the artworks. To avoid a complete commodification of the art world, he claims that it is necessary to protect and guard the enigmatic and mysterious characteristics of artworks themselves. Perniola calls this aspect 'shadow', precisely because they resist, so to speak, the investment of light produced by art institutions and apparatuses.

Finally, chapter 11 on Wilde was written with two main objectives in mind. On the one hand, it aims to show how the Irish dandy's lifestyle is aligned with that of Brummell and Baudelaire. Specifically, I discuss the essays in which Wilde argues for dandyism and aesthetic-oriented lifestyles, focusing particularly on four core themes: the relationship between beauty and contemporaneity; the praise of artificiality against nature; the privilege accorded to exteriority and elegance; and, finally, the critique of bourgeois society. The subsequent pages underline both the peculiarity of Wilde's path and its connections with Perniola's philosophy. Drawing on Regenia Gagnier's research on Wilde and the Victorian public (1987), I claim that the Irish dandy's ironic witticism had several shared characteristics with the avant-garde practice of the *détournement* (diversion), praised both by the Situationists and Perniola. As I will clarify, Wilde's aim was to use new technological tools – the press, large-scale editions, trendy magazines and journals – to subvert them from within and make art possible regardless of the growing commodification of culture and tastes. In addition, the chapter investigates Wilde's art theory contained in the essay *The Critic as Artist*, in which he claims that the artwork can be considered a 'living thing' or an ever-changing aesthetic form, which is echoed, I argue, by Perniola's theory of the 'inorganic' and his notion of the 'shadow'.

In conclusion, this book is based on the hypothesis that the core idea emerging from both Perniola and the dandies is that of 'challenge'. The figures investigated share the essential characteristic of engaging in a continuous aesthetic challenge towards their own lives and times. Several polemic objects of this challenge are examined – from the bourgeois mindset to romantic idealism; from vitalism to nature; from metaphysics to spiritualism; and from heteronormativity to the 'racism' of objective beauty. Perniola and the dandies have elaborated a philosophy and practice *in opposition*, which accept reality with its multiple aspects and possibilities. 'Opposition', 'challenge', and *amor fati* (love of fate) are at the heart of the figures I discuss. Brummell, Baudelaire, Wilde as well as Perniola are united by a common thread that weaves the aesthetic and practical domains together. The aesthetics of challenge in relation to the status quo, the philosophy and practice against normativity and ideology indicate a choice favouring the present and its not-yet-uncovered enigmas and possibilities.

Part One

1

The Suicide of Literature

Perniola's thought is first and foremost about aesthetics, counterculture, communication and art theory. Simultaneously, another significant aspect of his intellectual path involved literature, and not just from a theoretical perspective: Perniola himself wrote one novel, a collection of short stories and an autobiography, and it is precisely with literature that my journey into his thought begins.

Interestingly enough, Perniola ended his writings precisely where he started them: his first and last efforts, respectively – *Il metaromanzo* (The Metanovel) and *Tiresia contro Edipo* (Tiresias Against Oedipus) – deal with the same theme, namely the relationship between authorship, literature and life. His second and second-to-last works, respectively – *Tiresia* (Tiresias) and *Del terrorismo come una delle belle arti* (On Terrorism as One of the Fine Arts) – are experimental and subversive writings that question forms, normativity and the literary tradition of the novel itself. In an almost-palindromic fashion, one can start reading Perniola's works from the end to get an understanding of his initial concerns, and vice versa. Therefore, Perniola's literature during his formative years at the University of Turin and his more mature endeavours intersect with and inform his overall philosophical and aesthetic perspective. In this chapter, I specifically examine Perniola's reflections on the theory of literature alongside his collection of *storiette*, leaving any discussion of his work's queer and subversive dimensions for a later stage.

Perniola's youthful manifesto: towards a strong feeling

Perniola's very early foray into literature entailed a short collection of poems, unknown to the public, which he self-published in 1959 at the age of seventeen, printing just fifty copies at his own expense. Even with this early poetic debut – titled *Programma Manifesto* (Manifest Program) – it is possible to get a glimpse of several themes that recur through Perniola's literary journey. The epigraphs, taken from Dante and Machiavelli, indicate that Perniola was particularly concerned with themes such as destiny, fate and chance. Although he does not explicitly state it, the teenage Perniola seems to be fascinated with issues such as how can the individual face powers beyond their control? In what ways should they behave towards the unexpected and the randomness of events? The first three lines of *Programma Manifesto* indicate Perniola's position: 'Today – persuaded – I do not compromise. / I must bend fate to my word / Discreet in the winds of chance' (PM: 1). At least two themes emerge from these lines: the idea of 'persuasion' and the relationship between actions and circumstances. I believe that Perniola draws the first from the work of Carlo Michelstaedter, the Italian philosopher, who in 1910, after submitting his thesis, titled *Persuasion and Rhetoric*, took his own life. Perniola later declared Michelstaedter to be one of Italy's most significant philosophers of the twentieth century, adding that he felt reverberations from Michelstaedter's thought in his own philosophy.

Posthumously published in 1913 and almost unnoticed for decades, *Persuasion and Rhetoric* underwent a revival starting in the 1980s, and it soon became a cult book. Exploring a constellation of ideas and authors ranging from Greek philosophy to the Old and New Testaments, the text revolves around the experience of an enigmatic and extreme feeling grounded upon the idea of turning oneself into a 'flame' (Michelstaedter 2004: 57). To put it briefly, Michelstaedter viewed the natural course of life as a never-ending hunger and craving for something *else*, i.e. humans never seem able to possess anything because as soon as they reach what they thought they wanted, they immediately feel unhappy, empty or dissatisfied and start craving something else, cyclically repeating the process until they die. This natural and spontaneous attitude is at work within most fields of human existence, from society to language and love. We might crave a job, material security, wealth, pleasure, human relationships etc. and in the face of this, Michelstaedter seems to tell us: 'You are studying to obtain a degree, to then hope to get a job, which would, in turn, give you some financial security, hoping to buy a house, get married, have children, cultivate your hobbies ... and then what? Death happens. But where were *you* in all these moments? *What* were you actually doing while hoping, desiring for these things to become real?' I believe that Michelstaedter's answer would be that we always are waiting, waiting for a time yet to come, always procrastinating in hopes of attaining something that eludes our present and presence to escape the thought of death and avoid facing it.

The entire world can be seen through the lens of what Michelstaedter views as rhetoric. 'Rhetoric' is not intended simply to mean 'the art of impressive speaking', but also to describe an insatiable desire, which he understands – echoing Arthur Schopenhauer, Giacomo Leopardi and key themes in Buddhist thought – through its connection with lacking something, i.e. we strive for something that we miss, and we suffer because we believe that by filling this gap, we will become happy. Against this attitudinal backdrop, Michelstaedter outlines the path towards 'persuasion'. Again, the common definition of this word ('move by argument') leads us off the track. For him, persuasion means the conquest of the present precisely against the action of desire and rhetoric. Being persuaded means being in a paradoxical state in which one accepts one's own present and can 'consist' in it, letting the thirst, hunger and striving for the future to fade away. The enigmatic state of freedom from the chains of life generates the feeling of a 'flame'. This perspective should not lead the reader towards viewing *Persuasion and Rhetoric* as a book that rails against the idea of purpose or praises self-destructive vitalism. Treating one's own life as a continuous series of projects means, for Michelstaedter, avoiding a crucial challenge: facing death. If we remove death from the everyday realm, and we view it more and more as something not belonging to us, distant, surrounded by medical devices to prolong one's life and memorial social media accounts that want us always at hand and available, we end up living a crippled life until our final stumble into nothingness: '*He who fears death is already dead*' (Michelstaedter 2004: 39, original emphasis).

Perniola, who would discuss Michelstaedter on several occasions decades after his first youthful reference in *Programma Manifesto*, asserts specifically that 'turning oneself into a flame' means avoiding this predicament by instead entering the realm of a 'strong feeling' (*forte sentire*), which Michelstaedter emphasizes in this sentence by quoting Sophocles' *Electra*: 'Everyone at every point of life ... finds himself where / it is no longer the moment to hesitate, but to act' (2004: 42). The highest point does not comprise an instant that took place in the past or that is awaiting; it is connected inherently to the dimension of the present (on Perniola's interpretation of Michelstaedter, also see Harrison 1999). The highest point is always available to those who can listen and seize the καιρός (*kairos*), i.e., the opportunity. As Perniola points out (FS: 9, CDP, E: 149–53), Michelstaedter distinguishes between those who live before things and those who live within things. The former approaches things in a merely instrumental way, while the latter loves things in themselves: 'The first love the sea because they can swim in it; the second [love] the sea for itself. The first love a friend for their utility, the second [love] friends for themselves' (FS: 9). Therefore, for Perniola, the 'strong feeling' is connected to a welcoming disposition towards what comes from outside and an approach of renewal in relation to things. This is a crucial aspect of Perniola's overall philosophy. The 'strong feeling' implies the abandonment of the instrumental relationship with things. As long as a subjectivist pathos takes things into account only insofar as they can be useful for something, things never can appear in themselves, but only function through *our* projects, *our* goals, *our* desires. To step out of this long historical and metaphysical violence towards things, a new attitude must be adopted. Elaborating on several traditions, schools of thought and outsider figures – such as Michelstaedter – Perniola calls it 'feeling from outside' (*sentire dal di fuori*), which comprises making room in oneself to take in the world's manifestations.[1]

A second relevant element of these perspectives can be discovered in the excerpt from Perniola's early poetry which mentioned: 'discreet in the winds of chance'. Now, this seems to be an oxymoronic statement if we consider that it comes right after 'I must bend fate to my words': how can one bend one's destiny through discretion? Is not discretion too weak to succeed in fulfilling this task? I assert that another tradition that has influenced Perniola's thought emerges here, that of post-Renaissance and Baroque literature, from St. Ignatius to Baltasar Gracián up to Francesco Guicciardini. Despite their heterogeneity they are united by an overall political and aesthetic tonality that views discretion as a fundamental skill. Discretion is the ability to establish, with weighted judgement, a distinction between things, viewing differences and affinities at first unimaginable and knowing how to move between cases and occurrences.

From these very initial remarks I have presented, a recurring aspect of Perniola's philosophy has been highlighted: the link between feeling and strategic thought, i.e. the link between aesthetics, action and lifestyle, which has accompanied Perniola since he was seventeen.

The Metanovel

Perniola's first book, *Il metaromanzo* (The Metanovel) – originally his graduation thesis, supervised by Luigi Pareyson – was published in 1966, when Perniola was twenty-five years old. This text stemmed from five years of research in which Perniola focused on the theme of self-referentiality in authors such as Samuel Beckett, Antonin Artaud, Tommaso Landolfi and Maurice Blanchot (see BSE, AOS, MAT, MBM), as well as other academic and outsider literature on the theory of the novel. In 1961, while still studying law at the University of Turin (before turning to philosophy after less than a year), Perniola wrote an article that he brought to the attention of Nicola Chiaromonte, director of the journal *Tempo presente* at the time. The article, published with the title 'Beckett e la scrittura esistenziale' (Beckett and Existential Writing), displays the conceptual core that Perniola would develop in subsequent years: to investigate literary practice on an aesthetic level, and more specifically, to dwell on the relationship between author and writing. A revised version of this article has been included in *Il metaromanzo*.

This book immediately gained the attention of Italian intellectuals, writers and philosophers (see, e.g. Montale 1966; Sabatini 1966; Eco 1966; Pedullà 1966; Mizzau 1968). It comprises a philosophical investigation of what Perniola calls the 'metanovel'. The prefix *meta-* means 'after', which, followed by 'novel', suggests for Perniola a particular writing style – shared by numerous authors – that leaves behind the canonical understanding of the novel. 'Metanovel' is employed by Perniola as an analogy with metalanguage and metalinguistics, i.e. a language used to describe a given language's formal structure – a language that, in so doing, reflects on language itself. Similarly, the metanovel corresponds to the literary expressions characterized by self-reference, a novel of the novel (M: 22). Perniola's investigation focuses particularly on the first half of the twentieth century, although he is well-aware that Western literary tradition includes writings that could be called *ante litteram* metanovels. From the *Vita Nova* to *One Thousand and One Nights*, up to *Don Quixote* and *Notes from Underground*, the authors often present a self-referential attitude, appreciable in self-critical considerations, reflections on the books themselves, on the reader or even on language. Still, for Perniola, this phenomenon reached its peak starting with Henry James and continuing up until Samuel Beckett. It can be viewed as an aesthetic and literary framework that allows the researcher to interpret and read a thread of authors from a new perspective. However, Perniola was not alone in exploring this trend at the beginning of the 1960s. Above all, he was in the company of French thinkers Maurice Blanchot, Roland Barthes, Jacques Derrida, Maurice Nadeau and Lionel Abel, as well as the milieu revolving around the journals *Tel Quel* and *La Nouvelle Revue Française*. Manifestations of a metaliterary sensibility also can be seen in Federico Fellini and Jean-Luc Godard's films, as well as the plays of Bertold Brecht, Luigi Pirandello and Jean Genet. Therefore, metatheory involves the most disparate fields – philosophy, militancy, theatre, cinema, literature, art etc. – and in the 1960s, it was almost omnipresent in culture. Perniola contributed to this dynamic and multifarious environment through his *Il metaromanzo*.

These preliminary remarks help contextualize Perniola's first book in the broader cultural debate around metatheory, as well as outline the general idea and argument's trajectory. The starting point lies in the loathing that a heterogeneous group of novelists, or rather meta-novelists, feels towards the traditional novel. The outcome is a self-referential writing style in which the novel's theme is the writing of the novel itself. As Perniola points out, the white sheet for these authors is similar to a mirror; thus, their novels end up representing the act of writing that produces them. Influenced by Blanchot's theories on the space of literature (*espace littéraire*), Perniola examines several authors, including Henry James, Joseph Conrad, André Gide, Antonin Artaud, Samuel Beckett, Henry Miller, Lautréamont the circle of writers who gravitated around *La Nouvelle Revue Française*. Among these heterogeneous authors, Perniola identifies common features and shared perspectives in the wake of metaliterature. Through the analysis of essays and novels, Perniola examines passages and excerpts, underlining a primary common attitude that all the authors he highlights share: a strong anti-naturalistic perspective and, more generally, an opposition to the novel's traditional canons, both in terms of content and form. From the content's perspective, the metanovelists are at odds with the edifying, hedonistic, propagandistic or informative concerns that inform traditional literature, particularly Victorian and naturalist novels. From a formal perspective, they condemn the figure of the omniscient narrator, the temporal frame involved and the narrative structure. Traditional novelists put everything into context, providing a rational narration that explains facts and events, creating space-time frameworks that allow the reader to enter an intelligible universe of meanings and conventions. Such a narrator is aware of themselves and of the story they tell. The traditional novel presupposes a world that imposes itself upon the author and determines the work, becoming nothing more than an epiphenomenon of the facts described (M: 74). In a nutshell, the traditional novel comprises the universe of comprehensibility that common language provides us, exemplified well by André Breton in his *Surrealist Manifesto*, which employs the following sentence to point out conventional literary works' triviality and banality: '*La marquise sortit à cinq heures*' ('The marquise went out at five o' clock'). A main argument backs up the metanovelists' critiques. They aim to explore the possibility of an absolute work in which literature and art coincide, a goal betrayed every time works and characters are used only as the means to express something else – e.g. meanings, morals, political statements etc. Absoluteness, in the etymological sense of the word, requires literature to break free from the limits set by concerns extraneous to it.[2] Instead of considering a work as an accomplished jewel made by an author-demiurge, the metanovelists try to grasp the process of writing itself, with no presumed acquisitions or objectives. For metanovelists, the traditional novel is dominated by the author who knows and distinguishes what is important from what is not, what should be said from what should not be said: 'Such novels, even when they express the absurd, they do not destroy anything' (BSE: 727).

Perniola examines several writers emphasizing that we can appreciate a transformation from the writer *as* narrator to the writer as a *work in progress*, leading to literary experiments in which the work is inseparable from its process, i.e., writing project and realization coincide.

Given these initial perspectives, it is now time to focus on the specific cases that Perniola studied. I will inquire into the evolution of what Perniola views as the history of the metanovel, from Conrad to Beckett, to provide an overall picture of the themes discussed. Perniola traces the progression of metanovel theory to three main theoretical steps: in Conrad, the narration is conducted from the character's perspective; in Gide, the 'character as novelist' appears; and in Leiris, Artaud and Beckett, the 'novelist as character' (M: 51) emerges.

Starting with Conrad, Perniola examines the technical procedure that the English writer employs in works such as *Lord Jim* and *Chance*. In these works, Perniola notes that Conrad does not merely relate a fact or a story – as the traditional novelist would do – but rather puts numerous intermediaries between the reader and the fact. In so doing, the fact itself loses its concrete reality and disappears in a house of mirrors. The novel's creators are multiplied, a strategy that resembles Akira Kurosawa's *Rashōmon*, taken from the short stories of Ryūnosuke Akutagawa. *Rashōmon* involves various characters providing alternative accounts of the same events, ending up in a spiral of deception, including self-deception. The same goes for Conrad's *Lord Jim*, in which words are always at the centre of misinterpretations and uncertainty of which the characters are aware: 'There will be no message, unless such as each of us can interpret from the language of facts, that are so often more enigmatic than the craftiest arrangement of words' (2005: 285). For instance, in *Lord Jim*, Marlow, the narrator, talks to the audience about Jim's trials after Jim himself told him about the facts in question. In so doing, Conrad shifts from concrete experiences and facts to focus on the difficulties of storytelling itself through his characters' mouths. Thus, the novel's author is no longer comparable to a divine creator but is himself thrown into the story as a character, talking about the difficulties of writing. Perniola asserts that with Conrad, the novel slowly starts to become a preface of itself, an ongoing process of research whose development coincides with its formulation (M: 64). In this claim lies the metanovel's experimental feature: its authors do not know where they are going, nor where the process ultimately will take them.

Perniola notes that a further step along this path was taken by André Gide, who often tells stories about characters who are novelists themselves and are caught up in thinking, discussing and developing the same ideas that Gide is trying to develop in his books. Perniola cites a striking example in the opening words of Gide's *Marshlands*:

> Around five o'clock, it started to get cold outside; I closed my windows and returned to my writing. At six o'clock, my dear friend Hubert walked in. He was back from riding school.
> 'So!' he said. 'Hard at work?'
> 'I am writing Marshlands', I replied.
> 'What's that?'
> 'A book'.
>
> 2021

The character becomes an alter ego of the author, caught with his pen in his hand, writing about the difficulties encountered while the novel itself is being written.

Perniola asserts that another central aspect of metaliterature is visible in the need to bring to light the life of the writer's consciousness, in its integrity and uniqueness:

> If the character is the transparent image of the author, who has no other interest except for the construction of the work, the whole book becomes the history of its attempts, taken in their transience and in their becoming, realizing a perfect identity between literature and life.
>
> M: 72

Gide, like Conrad, shares an introspective understanding of the novel: for both of them, writing is not a means of investigation into reality, but rather into psychological examination. This spiritualist perspective is at odds with the naturalist and traditional novel, in which social facts inform the work. On the contrary, for Gide, it is precisely the life of the author's consciousness that must be the central focus. Finally freed from the burden of needing to represent the external world with precision and accuracy, the novel becomes a pure, abstract, conceptual work shaped only according to the artistic process.

Alongside Gide and Conrad, a collective effort to combine metaliterary experiments was carried out by the *Nouvelle Revue Française*, a journal founded in 1909 by a group of French intellectuals. Perniola specifically examines Jacques Rivière, who was the journal's director between 1919 and 1925. The metaliterary interest of Rivière and Artaud derives from an exchange of letters between the two after Rivière refused to publish Artaud's poems in his journal (also see AOS). These letters morphed into a fascinating discussion, not so much about the reason for the rejection, but rather for their exchanges on metaliterature, specifically the process of writing and the relationship between literature and life. Significantly, Rivière proposed to Artaud that he publish these letters, an episode also commented upon by Blanchot: '... poems that he Rivière judges insufficient and unworthy of being published, cease to be so when they are complemented by the account of the experience of their insufficiency' (quoted in M: 99). Perniola highlights that the letters' epicentre is exquisitely metatheoretic: the authentic expression of the artistic process in its becoming – the claim to grasp the origin of thought and work in their passage from nothing to being (M: 101).

In addition, Perniola investigates Leiris' *Biffures*. At first glance, *Biffures* is an examination of the author's memories, particularly from childhood, but simultaneously, it is filled with continuous reflections on style, on the book's intentions and on the origins of writing. For example, Leiris often specifies the moments at which he is writing, the places where he is staying, the strolls he takes and the discoveries he makes while writing. Here, too, lies a recurrent idea shared by the metanovelists – namely that the poetic practice does not lie in the unfolding of a pre-established design of which the author is aware, but rather comprises an unceasing work in progress.

But where does this conception of writing *in fieri* lead Leiris? On closer inspection, Perniola points out that the final pages of *Biffures* demonstrate the failure of Leiris' attempt. In fact, Leiris, at the end of the novel, condemns and despises his own writing, attributing this failure to the constitutive impossibility that lies at the heart of the metanovelistic project: 'If I want to give substance to this present moment – to this very presence – here it escapes and fades away. Everything I can say about it to bring it back to reality resolves into the most vain chatter' (quoted in M: 120). Leiris points out that searching for 'authentic writing' that truly can express the author's voice is doomed to failure.

So, from where does this constitutive short-circuit of writing emerge? Perniola clarifies this point by investigating Beckett's novels, focusing particularly on *The Unnamable*, which he views as an existential 'adventure of thought' (M: 133). It is the third volume of a trilogy whose first volume is *Molloy*, followed by *Malone Dies*. This trilogy, Perniola asserts, perfectly exemplifies the metanovelistic technique in action, as it possesses all the aspects examined so far brought to their ultimate end.

First, Beckett, in a Pirandellian fashion, views a story's characters as a mask that the author is forced to wear, in turn alienating and distorting them. The traditional novelist's goal is to develop the 'meaning' of something (be it friendship, love, the misery of the human condition, etc.). To do so, the author assembles what they believe to be proper metaphors and representations, imagines a series of characters who say the right words at the right moment, edits the text by cutting and rewriting passages, and in the end, if they are talented, somebody will read it. In so doing, the author's feelings, experiences and thoughts constantly are manipulated, corrected, shredded and mended back together, so that the writing itself does not represent the author anymore, but rather an abstract, impersonal and atemporal figure.

Beckett – for Perniola – is precisely at odds with this method of writing. His work can be viewed as a thorough critique of the alienating art of writing, in search of a language with which the writer finally can speak about themselves, a language that can involve them properly, instead of making them disappear. Beckett frequently expresses his disappointment and dissatisfaction towards his alienating creations: 'I am neither (I needn't say) Murphy, nor Watt, nor Mercier, nor, (no, I can't even bring myself to name them, nor any of the others whose very names I forget, who told me I was they, who I must have tried to be – under duress, through fear or to avoid acknowledging me): not the slightest connection' (2009: 319). For this reason, he revolts against his own characters, feels oppressed by each of them and relentlessly searches for his own voice:

> Is there a single word of mine in all I say? No, I have no voice (in this matter I have none). That's one of the reasons why I confused myself with Worm. But I have no reasons either, no reason. I'm like Worm, without voice or reason: I'm Worm. No, if I were Worm I wouldn't know it. But I don't say anything, I don't know anything. These voices are not mine, nor these thoughts, but the voices and thoughts of the devils who beset me.
>
> 2009: 341

...

> When I think of the time I've wasted with these bran-dips (beginning with Murphy, who wasn't even the first), when I had me on the premises, within easy reach! Tottering under my own skin and bones (real ones), rotting with solitude and neglect, till I doubted my own existence.
>
> 2009: 390

These passages demonstrate the desperate endeavour which suffocates Beckett's humanity. He fights with these oppressive shadows which do not let him speak about himself, as his voice becomes lost, estranging him. Beckett does not want to provide a picture of reality, nor does he wish to elaborate on edifying claims or set up gnoseological coordinates. He is not interested in imbuing his works with universal significance.

For Perniola, Beckett tries to elaborate on an alternative method of writing that must be distinguished from the traditional one. Perniola calls it 'philosophical and existential' (BSE: 729), but in a different sense than that which describes the typical French existentialism of Jean-Paul Sartre or Albert Camus. In fact, Perniola views them as still imbued with pedagogic and edifying aims, typical of traditional novels, whereas Beckett's existentialism is concerned with the possibility of expressing the 'thought in act' (*pensiero in atto*). Interestingly, Perniola links Giovanni Gentile's neo-Idealism with Beckett's writing by claiming that they both shared a fundamental assumption about reality, namely that it is founded by the 'act' of the subject, who asserts their consciousness *hic et nunc* and independently from the sequence of past, present and future. In so doing, 'what is past, what is not immediately present to consciousness, does not exist' (BSE: 729). Writing becomes the mimesis of one's own *Erlebnis*, i.e. the imitation of one's own experience in the precise moment in which it happens. Beckett's *The Unnamable* appears then as a blooming of spontaneous statements unrestrained from any pre-determined design, testing and stretching the limits of the text itself by striving to bridge experience and writing, life and literature.[3]

In his endeavour, oriented towards grasping what exists *while* it exists, *while* it is in action and ongoing, Beckett meets the constitutive gap between experience, conscience and subjectivity, on one hand, and their representation and expression through the medium of language on the other. From Michel de Montaigne to Blaise Pascal, Marcel Proust and Georges Bataille, an extremely rich body of literature by thinkers and writers already has explored this issue – wondering whether language can communicate and convey one's own inner experience adequately. Referring to desire and hope, Montaigne, in his *Essays*, wrote '*Nous ne sommes jamais chez nous, nous sommes toujours au de-là*' ('We are never at home; we are always beyond'), which exemplifies well the aporetic outcome of Beckett's writings – and those of metanovelists in general. The moment in which we believe we are authentically expressing our 'I' through a spontaneous and immediate writing style, we actually are mystifying it. Perniola, though not quoting Freud explicitly, seems to me an heir to psychoanalytic theory, which asserts that it is the unconscious that contains the keys to the human character, and on these grounds maintains that such literary self-representation easily can betray our expectations of authenticity. If it is the unconscious who is the actual, real autobiographer, then our everyday self is no longer essential, as it appears unreliable and intermittent. Beckett is well aware of this impossibility, according to Perniola, and he lives it in an exasperated way because it implies realizing that alienation is not just the premise of the traditional novel, comprising instrumental rhetorical devices and character/masks: it is also the inevitable outcome of all writing that aspires to the authentic expression of subjectivity (BSE: 731). Therefore, Beckett's writing paradoxically becomes a recording of the difficulty, of the short circuit, of the failure that the author himself experiences: 'It issues from me, it fills me, it clamours against my walls. It is not mine. I can't stop it, I can't prevent it, from tearing me, racking me, assailing me. It is not mine. I have none: I have no voice and must speak; that is all I know' (2009: 301).

Perniola's critique of Beckett is not informed by the anglophone literature on the Irish writer (see, e.g. Esslin 1980), but by that of the French (Blanchot and Bataille). Whereas the former perceives Beckett's work as a great expression of the human condition, particularly in its derelict and absurd aspects, the latter viewed him in a more nihilistic and pessimistic light. For instance, Blanchot claims that in Beckett, there is no literary work, but merely the destruction of forms and styles. As William Marx put it: 'The French saw in Beckett a language that is won by the ruin; the Anglo-Saxons a language that wins over the ruin. For the former, nothingness in spite of the work; for the latter, the work in spite of nothingness' (2005: 176).[4]

Among other commentators on *Il metaromanzo*, Nobel Prize winner Eugenio Montale made a significant impact in inspiring Perniola's research in subsequent years. In his review of the book, Montale states that 'it is undeniable that the trend studied by Perniola exists. . . . But it could also be demonstrated that novels or tales having as the topic themselves, their mechanism rather than their informative side, have always existed' (1966: 14). Even though, as suggested earlier, Perniola was aware of the long history of the metanovel trend within literature, in a preparatory note as part of the second edition of *Il metaromanzo* (which never was published), he writes that the issue of the metanovel is much wider and involves the historical category of art itself, not just twentieth-century literature, adding 'Montale was right' (PNM: 1). Thus, it is only after Montale's remarks that Perniola decides to expand his theory by studying the constitutive alienation of the whole art world. In a later chapter, I will focus on Perniola's *L'alienazione artistica* (The Artistic Alienation), which was published five years after *Il metaromanzo* and can be viewed as a continuation of his first research, and which identifies the notion of alienation as a central aspect of the whole history of Western art.

The dogma of spontaneity: social media and the culmination of the Romantic project

Perniola traces the metanovel's poetic roots back to the Romantic movement, examining several claims elaborated on in both the German and French cultural environments of the late eighteenth-century – specifically in Fichte's idealism; the journal *Athenaeum*, founded by August and Friedrich Schlegel; and Jean-Jacques Rousseau's *Confessions*. Here, I briefly will sum up Perniola's critique of Rousseau, as I believe it is useful to present an unexpected and surprising manifestation of these issues in the contemporary world. Specifically, Perniola singles out a trend from Romanticism and metatheory that still can be relevant in today's social media writings.

Perniola views Rousseau's autobiography *Confessions* as fundamental to understanding the metanovel's origins. The specific aspect of *Confessions* highlighted by Perniola lies in the 'sincerity' and 'spontaneity' with which the author believes he talks about himself and his entire life. The very beginning of Rousseau's autobiography displays a clear declaration of his main goal: 'Here is the only portrait of a man, painted exactly according to nature and in all its truth, that exists and that will probably ever exist' (1990: 3). Thus, Rousseau believed that language – conceived of as pure transparency – actually could provide a faithful picture of the subject matter – in this case, the transference of Rousseau's life. In so doing, Rousseau writes with the presumption of presenting his true nature to his fellow men. However, this claim does not convince Perniola, nor a plethora of theorists and writers of the past two centuries, including Friedrich Nietzsche, Roland Barthes, Maurice Blanchot and Michel Foucault: writing is never a simple transference of the writer's thoughts, ideas and spirit. Those who believe that spontaneity is synonymous with purity and correspondence with oneself wrongly assume that they have at their disposal a whole series of psychic instances that, in reality, always elude the discussion. In this sense, the metanovel, as we have examined it, possesses a key principle of Rousseau's Romanticism: they are both caught in the effort of trying to find an adequate expression of their interiority through self-reference.

Perniola advances the thesis that these assumptions brought the novel, and the literary environment more generally, to a dead end, comprising nothing but immediate protocol sentences (as in Beckett's case) of singular subjective indications or allusions to ongoing experiences that are immediately transferred to the white sheet. In his critique of Romanticism, Perniola focuses only briefly on Rousseau, and the reader might perceive his argument as being only partially developed and investigated. By gathering a plethora of authors and labelling them as those who brought the Romantic perspective to extreme consequences, Perniola risks assimilating heterogeneous concerns and poetics too easily. As Angelo Sabatini pointed out, the intellectualistic introspection of Henry Miller (another author whom Perniola includes among the metanovelists) is not irreducible to the Romantic expression of life. In so doing, it appears that, to a certain extent, Perniola forces these authors under the cluster concept of the metanovel to support his analysis. Simultaneously, it is worth noting that several other scholars and thinkers – such as Jean Paulhan (2006), William Marx (2005) and Giulio Ferroni (1996) – share several basic assumptions. For instance, Marx explores the idea of a transparent language at length, and claims that it (or the attempt at it) can be defined as the characteristic trait of Romantic literature between 1750 and 1850, which is informed by what he calls the 'dogma of spontaneity' (2005: 51). Inspired by the notion of the sublime, Marx adds that philosophers such as Diderot and Boileau, and writers such as Stendhal and Balzac, have privileged a fluid, mysterious and immediate writing style aimed at instantly communicating the whole multitude of sentiments and impressions experienced by the author in the belief that they could have reached a faithful representation of their interiority. Striving for communicative authenticity and transparency, these authors neglected the formal aspects of literary style and language: 'With Stendhal or Balzac, it is a whole civilisation that started to write badly, deliberately and on purpose, refuting the beautiful style' (2005: 50).

Does this not sound familiar to the contemporary everyday social media user? According to Perniola, from Rousseau to James, Conrad, Artaud, Beckett and social media users, there is no break in continuity. Although Perniola is by no means a critic of the Internet and its interaction technologies – a topic I will discuss later – in looking back at his first book four decades later, he draws a parallel between blogs and metanovel theory (TS).

Perniola writes about the blogosphere and personal blog accounts in general, but I believe that his claims find even more poignancy if juxtaposed more specifically with Twitter, Reddit, Twitch, TikTok, Snapchat, Facebook, Instagram etc. Just like Beckett's verbal transference of his flowing consciousness and Rousseau's spontaneity, today's social media users express themselves in immediate, quick and often belligerent posts and tweets online. Perniola believes that social media tends to barbarize cultural and political debate by inviting its users to write in this uninhibited and immediate way. On this topic, Italian studies theorist Paolo Bartoloni notes that Perniola's thought displays an 'open intellectual "hostility" against the superficial emotions of the contemporaneous through the mobilisation of aesthetic acts' (2007: 120). For instance, when Facebook invites us to share our thoughts or what we are doing currently in a post, not only does this lead to confusion between what is public and what should remain private, but it also overcrowds the web with mostly self-referential posts about mundane aspects of life – from one's own achievements to one's failures, from the food one has eaten to a new puppy, from personal outbursts to anger against politicians, the poor, the wealthy etc. For example, several scholars (such as Ussama 2020) now are focusing on how social media, particularly Twitter and Facebook, influenced Donald Trump's victory in 2016's US presidential election, as well as how he expressed himself in his accounts. One finding indicated a significant trend in rising COVID-19 cases in the US alongside Trump's negative sentiments towards the medical community in tweets and posts. Perniola made a similar discovery – although with different methodologies with respect to Ussama – in 2010 regarding blogs and the rise of the *Movimento 5 Stelle* (Five Star Movement), an Italian political party led by activist Beppe Grillo. Perniola asserts that the key aspects of the general emotional tonality on the web include difficulty with social interactions and unseemly reactions – simultaneously hyper-excited and indifferent – accompanied by an omnipresent echolalia (i.e. repetition of what is heard by the subject) in which everything goes 'viral'.

Perniola links Romanticism and metaliterature precisely to the environment just outlined. Both move into the self-referential horizon of supposedly transparent writings. Provocatively, Perniola states: 'Between Beckett's *The Unnamable* and Beppe Grillo, there is no break in continuity: why should one read Beckett if he is not able to recount any actions, any experiences that resonate with other people? The blogger argues this way: "I can do this as well, so I have no need to read Beckett. Why should it just be him talking about himself? Everybody should be able to do so, even if nobody listens to them"' (TS: 147). In another Perniola book, tellingly titled *Berlusconi o il '68 realizzato* (Berlusconi or the '68 Realized), Perniola asserts that this logic has rotted the broader cultural and political debate (cf. Gnoli 2011; Berardi 2012; Friberg 2017). 'Why can't I do it as well?' seems to be one of the most abused vindications of the contemporary citizen, who is at once a photographer through Instagram, a politician through Facebook and Twitter, a porn actor through OnlyFans, a video maker through YouTube, an artist through Pinterest etc.

That being said, this does not mean that no legitimate artists, photographers, politicians or writers exist online. On the contrary, it is precisely the overflow of data and information that makes it more difficult to distinguish – as Roland

Barthes put it in 1960 – *écrivains* (a writer) from *écrivants* (roughly translated as 'one who writes'). Perniola devoted an issue of the journal *Ágalma* precisely to this topic. He views most blog posts as being closer to emotional outpourings, with therapeutic and recreational outcomes, than to pieces of literature. Perniola describes how threads start from the optimistic Romanticism *à la Rousseau*, followed by the metanovelists and today's users, then place the strongest emphasis on the need to express oneself at all costs, fostering the belief that through a spontaneous and immediate outpouring of words, this goal actually can be reached.

Perniola's *storiette*, or, literature after death

A crucial question still needs to be answered: where does Perniola see literature now? Is there any way out from the dead end of the metanovel? How can we step out from a nihilist and populist drift that views writing as a mere recording of one's own moods, for the most part not even read by anyone? Perniola exhumes, so to speak, a minor and underground literary genre that he asserts neither falls within the traditional idea of the novel, grounded on the omniscient narrator, nor within the metanovel's literary self-referential dimension. He calls this minor genre *storietta*, borrowing this term from the so-called *historiettes*, whose progenitor is Gédéon Tallemant des Réaux, who, beginning in 1657, wrote a collection of short stories on the biographies of leading men in French public life during his time. Following his example, Perniola wrote his series of *storiette* and published them in 2016 under the title *Del terrorismo come una delle belle arti* (Of Terrorism as One of the Fine Arts). On a formal and stylistic level, des Réaux's *historiettes* and Perniola's *storiette* are dissimilar, and I would claim that they only share two aspects: each story's short length and the voluntarily reduction of literary ambitions (compared with the traditional novel). Beyond the *historiette* genre, Perniola also asserts that his writing style is influenced by the Japanese *setsuwa*, a literary genre characterized by a combination of myths, legends, folk tales and anecdotes. However, Perniola takes the work of Tallemant des Réaux and the *setsuwa* only as pretexts to advance philosophical and literary claims.

Perniola's *storiette* can be compared more credibly with other cultural phenomena, and not only those belonging to the literature realm. At odds with the metaliterary stance of self-reference and the search for a correspondence between the 'I' and language, Perniola explores an experimental form of writing involving a destabilization of the subjective authorial dimension, similar to the mockumentary, which depicts fictional events while presenting them as a documentary. Specifically, Perniola writes eight *storiette*, which he describes as 'beyond true and false' because they recount events that really happened as if they were fictional and vice versa. For example, the text is accompanied by a series of documents, photos, letters and artworks, both real and fake.

In addition, the writing style is a hybrid between philosophical essay, fiction and autobiography. To put into practice his distancing from the 'I', Perniola resorts to a literary device: he uses the second-person plural in the manner of an interviewer who only speaks and never asks the person on the other side questions. This fictional interviewer does not refer to the interviewed with the standard 'you' (which in Italian is '*tu*', but also can be the formal '*Lei*'), but rather with '*voi*' ('you' plural). Perniola wishes to create a sense of estrangement and uncanniness in the reader, who remains puzzled trying to figure out *who* lies behind the '*voi*': is it Perniola himself, or is it somebody else? Were the stories told actually lived by Perniola, or is he merging them with fictional elements, or events that occurred in somebody else's life? Perniola makes it clear that his objective is to write as impersonally as he possibly can: 'The question that you [*voi*] have been asking yourself since adolescence is the following: *Why you* [*voi*]*?* (in which this pronoun is to be understood as nothing more than a simple imputation, a nominal designation, a pure convention, nothing substantial)' (TBA: 50, emphasis added). It is no coincidence that the book's two epigraphs are Blaise Pascal's *Le moi est haïssable* (The self is hideous) and Arthur Rimbaud's *Je est un autre* (I is another). As Saunders put it, commenting on Rimbaud's famous phrase:

> One reason 'I is another', for Rimbaud at least, is that (as he has just explained in the same letter) 'C'est faux de dire: Je pense: on devrait dire: On me pense' ('It's wrong to say "I think"; one ought to say "I am being thought"'). That could be read as saying that the 'I' isn't experienced as subject of thought, only as the object of thought: and thus that the self that we are aware of when we try to think of ourselves is estranged from the subject doing the thinking, and always appears as 'other' to it. I think therefore I am another.
>
> 2010: 503

In other words, the failed attempts by the metanovelists, and the writers who believed or tried to express themselves through the 'I', can be rethought – for Perniola – in terms of multiplicity of subjectivity by estranging literary devices such as the second-person plural. Perniola never appears in the *storiette*, although for a good part of them, he is actually talking about his life – recounting events that occurred, friends who he met, places he visited etc. The scene is populated by a multifarious array of figures belonging to different space and time frameworks, in which Perniola's self consistently is fluid, elusive and absent.

The *storiette* embrace heterogeneous themes, from the existentialist and terrorist adventures of extreme radical-left armed groups of the 1970s, to the surreal stories of writers, bohemians, philosophers, psychics, publishers, monks, artists and academics. Some of these people were active in Italy, Japan, France and Mexico, while others still belong to otherworldly realms, but are depicted as active subjects on Earth. Still, for the whole narration, we have an unknown storyteller who endlessly refers to a suspended, void, displaced subject. For instance, the narrator devotes several pages to the accurate explanation of several Buddhist precepts, such as that of reincarnation – after which we are told the story of Mario De Carlo, Perniola's real uncle, who tragically died when he was sixteen in a lift accident and of whom Perniola/the narrator claims to be the reincarnation.

Thus, Perniola does not appear to be an author in the traditional sense. He might be viewed almost as a Freudian compromise formation, an oneiric, dreamy, symbolic manifestation that always redirects the eye of the beholder towards something else, in the manner of dreams, forgetfulness and lapses that are always pointing to another meaning, explanation or *raison d'être*. Just as Nietzsche wrote that we should become our own guinea pigs, Perniola did not just theorize on literature: fifty years after *Tiresia* – his 1966 novel that I will focus on later – with his *storiette,* he put his ideas about the possibility/impossibility of literature into practice.

However, after all these considerations, it seems to me that Perniola's *storiette* are informed by two opposing premises. On the one hand, he claims that the novel, the metanovel and the *storiette* can be viewed as historical categories and, thus, dependent on a constellation of unavoidable social, political and cultural contexts. For instance, he asserts that the 1960s counterculture – himself included – did not dramatically or significantly succeed in changing society, nor did they create history or take proper 'action', but only created *storiette* and communication. Perniola asserts that the society of the second half of the twentieth century was 'petrified' by the nations that won the Second World War. Despite the global protest movements that coalesced in 1968, which were followed by years of terrorist attacks and bombings from both left- and right-wing armed groups (at least in Italy, Germany and Japan), for Perniola, no appreciable history was made, but something rather different was: 'Italian history between 1968 and 1977 was not a civil war, but rather the simulacrum of a civil war, conditioned by the karmic remainders of the true civil war of 1943–1945. This latter was a history, yours merely a simulacrum of history, that is, an ensemble of *storiette* whose ultimate meaning is artistic, literary, cultural' (TBA: 54). Here, another significant concept elaborated on by Perniola emerges: the simulacrum. The next chapter will be devoted precisely to this, but for the moment, it is sufficient to say that Perniola considers here the following two opposing sides: the generation of the fathers, those who fought in the Second World War and wanted to maintain the ideological and political system they built, and the younger generation, who wanted the chance to shape their own history and destiny. Still, Perniola believes that the latter, his generation, failed in doing this: 'The generation of Sixty-Eight did not succeed in making history, but only *storiette*; these produce hilarity or drip blood, but are devoid of exemplarity and constitute, in any case, a minor genre' (TBA: 32). Thus, Perniola seems to believe that there are historical periods that can be understood and examined more effectively if they are framed within the logics of the *storietta*, and others in which another literary genre works better.

The second, opposing premise can be detected in another passage, in which Perniola wonders whether history itself is not a *storietta* inflated by historians and writers:

> It can be said that the *storiette* are nonetheless *some things*, that between being and nothingness, behind which many pompous men hide themselves, there still is the τι [*ti*], of which the ancient Stoic philosophers spoke and, moreover, it can be said that the human condition is only made up of *storiette*, transformed into history by the servility and the opportunism of handbooks and schoolbooks' editors.
>
> TBA: 38

Today's literary and social media hyperconsciousness brings Perniola to the realm of the *storiette*. Against the traditional novel's ambitions, the impotence of Beckett's language and the communicative dogma of Romantics and social media users, Perniola does not say farewell to literature, but instead tries to produce a text that is at once more humble and 'minimalist'. In his conclusion to *L'adieu à la littérature*, William Marx asserts that a specific trend in contemporary literature can be taken as a cue: 'Rather than getting out of the crisis from above, that is, by seeking all the azimuths of radical aesthetic solutions, with uncertain results, the minimalists choose an issue from below. . . . The evolution of literature will, thus, take the form of a revolution, in the proper sense, namely a return to the zero point, susceptible of initiating a new cycle of transformation' (2005: 180–1). I believe that Perniola's *storiette* should be understood in precisely these terms. They do not have any nostalgia for the past values and ambitions of the novel, nor do they dismiss literature as an impotent realm. Nonetheless, Marx includes in the minimalist trend authors such as Günter Grass, Salman Rushdie, Ôe Kenzaburô, Gao Xingjian and Bret Easton Ellis, to whom I would not ascribe Perniola's overall anti-subjectivist and anti-normative perspective. In addition, I am not convinced that Perniola himself succeeded in clarifying and exemplifying cognate authors and trends in contemporary literature. His *storiette* are not just fictional developments of things that actually happened in his life, merged with philosophical, aesthetic and artistic research. I believe that more than the Japanese *setsuwa* or des Reaux's *historiette*, they can be ascribed to a specific branch of the autofiction genre, namely the 'autobiografiction'. This *portmanteau* term was coined in 1906 by Stephen Reynolds and researched more recently by Max Saunders in 2010. As Reynolds put it in his article, autobiografiction is that literary genre which 'occupies the point where fiction, autobiography, and the essay meet, and which fades imperceptibly into those forms' (1906: 28), which he exemplified by citing several works from the modernist literature of the time (such as those of James Joyce and Virginia Woolf). Reynolds asserts that autobiografiction is suited in particular to expressing authors' 'spiritual' concerns and inner experiences, namely all the emotions that can intensify one's soul. Therefore, his definition is quite restricted insofar as he believes that autobiografiction – understood as the nexus of fiction, autobiography, documentary and essay – emerges particularly when the author experiences spiritual crises. Thus, fictionalizing one's own autobiography becomes ultimately a psychological consolation for those who write it or for those who read it.

However, Saunders, departing from Reynolds' definition, broadens the notion of autobiografiction to include other fictionalized life writings (such as letters, diaries and biographies), as well as other tones beyond the spiritualistic (e.g. ironic and comic). Perniola himself wrote of his *storiette* that they are 'halfway between the serious and the facetious', accompanied by a general emotional tonality of 'terror and irony'. In addition, Saunders asserts that a significant aspect of autobiografictional works lies in what he calls 'disturbances', i.e. ways to displace the reader through literary devices such as pseudonymity, anonymity, heteronymity, use of the third person and shift of person (2010: 121). I believe that Perniola's use of the second-person plural to fictionalize his autobiography can be ascribed to precisely this idea of a displacement of subjectivity. Perniola uses an uncanny form that problematizes his very subjectivity by paradoxically making it elusive and absent, while simultaneously also producing doubts about the reader's expectations concerning the relationship between the fictional and real author. To this extent, Perniola's *storiette* also can be compared to Henry Adams' autobiography, *The Education of Henry Adams*, which is written in the third person: 'The writing of autobiography in the third person introduces a split between the enunciating voice and the enunciated subject; between the narrator and Adams. This split enacts the multiplicity it describes in the way it constantly wrong-foots the reader, who keeps forgetting that the story of "Henry Adams" is actually being told by Henry Adams' (Saunders 2010: 144). Both Adams and Perniola treat their autobiographies with detachment by estranging authorial devices (third-person singular and second-person plural) and a generally ironic and witty writing tone, which disrupts traditional autobiographical conventions.

Ultimately, Perniola responds to the impasse of the metanovelists – i.e. their literary project's records of failure with their literary project – through a more constructed, multiple and conflicting idea of the autobiographical self, which is multiplied through an increasingly fictional writing style.

2

To Love or Smash Images? The Dimension of the Simulacrum

A core idea within Perniola's philosophy is that of the simulacrum. As suggested, Perniola considers his *storiette* beyond the categories of true and false and closer to the logic of the simulacrum. Almost forty years before the publication of the *storiette*, Perniola's *La società dei simulacri* (The Society of the Simulacra) emerged. This book, which we focus on here, takes into account the notion of a simulacrum from different perspectives: philosophical, aesthetic and political. Therefore, not only has Perniola dwelt on this notion for almost four decades, but it can also be considered a *passepartout* to understand multiple aspects of his entire path.

The Roman aesthetics of simulacra

The simulacrum has been the focus of several interpretations in the twentieth century, which put it at the centre of philosophical and sociological debates (such as Deleuze 1969, 1983; Baudrillard 1978; Klossowski 1981). The term simulacrum derives from the Latin *simulacrum*, which means 'image' or 'representation'. It has the same root (*simul-*) of *simulare*, a verb that can be translated into 'to copy, represent, feign'. In its early use, it indicated, above all, a statue or image of the gods but also a portrait or sculpture representing a person. At first glance, the simulacrum consists of a form or semblance of something else. In this sense, it means 'something that imitates another'. The theory of the simulacrum goes back to Plato's distinction between a real and false world (that of ideas and appearance respectively). Nietzsche, followed by Deleuze and Klossowski in the 1960s and 1970s, put the Platonic metaphysical structure into question by starting to elaborate on a theory of simulacra as images freed from the burden of any 'original'. The fall of metaphysics is connected to the Nietzschean idea of the death of God, which can be understood as the end of the (illegitimate) supremacy of absolute truths. As a result, the world of appearances not only becomes the only actual existing reality, but it also loses its negative and debasing aspects: from the moment at which the metaphysical hierarchy is no longer imposed on appearances, these are freed from the burden of being mere copies. The ideas of origins and originals do not fit in a world devoid of metaphysics: if there are no absolutes and eternal ideas on which things are shaped and modelled, then these very things lose their statuses of being copies and semblances. The circle that holds together the original and copy is broken, and instead of a metaphysical polar opposition, humans are left with simulacra or images that do not refer to an original. Following Nietzsche, Deleuze claimed that the overthrow of Platonism, that is, the negation of the superiority of the 'original', also liberates the simulacra from being 'deceptive copies'.

Another significant interpreter of the notion of the simulacrum was Jean Baudrillard. Perniola's first essay on the simulacrum was published in the journal *Traverses* (IVS) in the same issue as another article on the same subject by Baudrillard (1978: 3–38). The two philosophers knew and commented on each other's standpoints yet reached divergent conclusions. Specifically, as Perniola claims, 'it [the simulacrum] originates from the conceptual horizon opened up by the Nietzschean claim of a simultaneous suppression of the real world and of the apparent one, which is understood as the end of metaphysics' (SSI: 69). The distinction between a real world and apparent world is also investigated by Perniola in *La società dei simulacri*. Here, Perniola, on the one hand, focuses on the critique of metaphysics elaborated by Martin Heidegger and Pierre Klossowski (also see MN; Burch 2002); on the other hand, he develops his theory of the simulacrum by analysing Roman religious rituals and the Jesuit-Baroque tradition (see Aylesworth 2015).

In this chapter, I will concentrate on Perniola's interpretation of several Roman rituals and on St Ignatius's *Spiritual Exercises* for two main reasons. On the one hand, I agree with various scholars (such as Silva 1980; Bukdahl 2017; Capovin 2020) that Perniola's most original insights are precisely the ones devoted to the theory of simulacra in these traditions; on the other hand, keeping this focus allows me to show the affinity between the simulacrum of death and dandy lifestyle, which will be investigated later.

Baudrillard underlines the dumbing down effects of simulations (from Disneyland to TV shows), leading 'reality' to desertification. On the other hand, Perniola explores possible solutions and alternative strategies concerning the relationship between power, knowledge and image within a society of simulacra. He claims that Baudrillard's theory is a significant contribution to the field:

'Baudrillard's originality consists in applying this concept [the simulacrum] to the analysis of social and political phenomena, in which reality seems to be completely dissolved into an infinite spiral of remands, signs devoid of a referent' (SSI: 69). Nonetheless, he criticizes the 'derealization' (*derealizzazione*) implicit in the notion of simulacrum as a deceiving 'hyperreality' for Baudrillard, whereas for Perniola, the opposite holds true. Baudrillard's nostalgia for the 'real' reveals a Platonic approach that is at odds with Perniola's theory:

> The simulacrum is not a recreational spectacle nor a manipulative and mystifying staging, but rather, it is a mimicry implying the discovery of the precariousness of existence and suspension of individual subjectivity: it is a therapy to survive, transforming the feeling of being lost and demoralized into a will to challenge and into a drunkenness close to the experience of a trance.
>
> SS: 8

This passage – which is included in the introduction to the second edition of *La società dei simulacri* – is crucial when trying to grasp Perniola's understanding of the simulacrum. First, he disentangles his view from that of Baudrillard's, claiming that the simulacrum is irreducible to a 'recreational spectacle' (such as Disneyland) or to a 'manipulative and mystifying staging' (such as mass media). Perniola characterizes the simulacrum using a different set of terms: 'suspension of subjectivity', 'survival therapy', 'will to challenge' and 'trance'. Why does Perniola associate the simulacrum with such heterogeneous notions? What does the contemporary digital and informatic society share with a religious ritual? If several scholars have discussed the contemporary pervasiveness of images in terms of narcissism and the cult of the personality (cf. Lasch 1979; Illouz 2013), why does Perniola define our society in terms of 'desubjectivation'?

According to Perniola, it is misleading to think of a 'society of simulacra' as beginning only with the age of the mass media and spread of the internet. The contemporary age is indeed marked by the ubiquitous technical reproducibility of informational content, along with the infinite possibilities provided by its unlimited simulation and repetition through the web and virtual world. However, religious, political, philosophical and ordinary attitudes grounded on the simulacrum long predate these modern media. Perniola first identifies this concept in two ancient Roman religious rituals and then in the religious thought of the Jesuits.

Perniola explores the *Parallel Lives* by Plutarch and the *Saturnalia* by Macrobius. Specifically, he focuses on the *Parallel Lives*' thirteenth section concerning the life of the second King of Rome, Numa Pompilius. He tells the story of the blacksmith Mamurius Veturius, the 'first artist' known to Roman history. The tale goes as follows:

> In the eighth year of his reign a pestilence, which traversed Italy, distracted Rome also. The story goes that while the people were disheartened by this, a bronze buckler fell from heaven, which came into the hands of Numa, and a wonderful account of it was given by the king, which he learned from Egeria and the Muses. The buckler came, he said, for the salvation of the city, and must be carefully preserved by making eleven others of like fashion, size, and shape, in order that the resemblance between them might make it difficult for a thief to distinguish the one that fell from heaven... When Numa showed the buckler to the artificers and bade them do their best to make others like it, they all declined, except Veturius Mamurius, a most excellent workman, who was so happy in his imitation of it, and made all the eleven so exactly like it, that not even Numa himself could distinguish them.
>
> Plutarch 1967: 351–3

Perniola is fascinated by this account; he points out that the operation carried out by Mamurius is situated beyond the Platonic opposition of 'true' and 'false' and 'copy' and 'original'. In doing so, this operation gives a high dignity to what would normally be considered a mere replica. This operation is paradoxical in that the prototype is at once maintained (the original shield is always present among the others) and at once erased (keeping it indistinguishable from the copies). The conceptual implications of this operation are wide ranging: 'Mob rule and fraud require a reference to the truth. Impostors are born in the shadow of the prophets' (RT: 98–9). In other words, because of the unique piece, the exceptional element is multiplied, and deception, fraud and attempted theft from Numa's enemies are no longer feared. By breaking the identity and the unity of the object, that is, by transforming something into a simulacrum, the *becoming* is made innocent. This context opens a 'beyond good and evil' condition (Nietzsche 2003), that is, a dimension in which the metaphysical opposites of true/false, real/apparent and copy/original no longer have a reason to exist. In addition, Numa does not have the eleven copies of the shield produced to subsequently conceal them for fear they may be stolen, he multiplies their visibility by handing them over to the twelve *Salii* (young patricians dressed as archaic warriors) during their sacred processions (set up by Numa himself).[1] Aesthetically speaking, Plato's standpoint on art can be described as metaphysical and spiritualist objectivism (see Tatarkiewicz 1970: 117–18). Following Polykleitos' *Canon*, for instance, a human body is harmonic if the head of the subject is one-eighth of the height, the torso three-eighths, and the legs four-eighths.

Objectivism, within the artistic domain, maintains that something is beautiful if it possesses certain properties and qualities that make it harmonic in its whole. In addition, Plato's objectivism was grounded not only on numbers, proportions and measures, but upon the distinction between a true world, on the one hand, and appearances, on the other. Hence, a thing is beautiful not only if it is harmonic but also if this harmony leads the human soul closer to the world of ideas. In contrast, Mamurius' aesthetics do not deal with copying or mimicking an eternal canon, a perfect measure or true proportions, he makes the original disappear amongst the copies, 'abolishing simultaneously' the world of truth and the world of appearances.

Another example of the idea of the simulacrum in Rome – as argued by Perniola – is the religious ritual of *evocatio*. The Romans believed that the deities of the cities they conquered were not enemies a priori; therefore, the dictator or Roman general would pronounce the so-called *evocatio* before a siege (see Scheid 2011: 75–8). This consisted of an 'invitation' to that city's tutelary deities to move to Rome, where they would be given a cult and dedicated temples. An indispensable condition for the success of an *evocatio* was that the city and its deities had to be indicated with their true names. In doing so, the Roman military attitude is welcoming: the otherness is not crushed; it is received because – developing Perniola's argument – an enemy does not remain as such forever: everything has a temporary nature and can turn into its opposite.

Perniola underlines a second key aspect of the *evocatio*. Macrobius writes that to avoid receiving an *evocatio* from a rival city, Rome kept its tutelary deities and the Latin name of the city itself a secret. As Pier Aldo Rovatti points out, commenting on Perniola's perspective on Roman ritualism: 'as if by keeping secret the god and the Latin name of the city itself and, therefore, not letting itself to be identified, they preserved themselves from the most threatening capture: the symbolic capture' (1981: 43). The *Urbe* entered a 'logic of seduction': a seducer who empties themselves; who becomes vacant, free from all identity and ready to welcome the specificity of each occasion (this essential aspect of seduction – namely the lack of an identity – will be developed in the fourth chapter, especially when focusing on the dandy, who is an exemplary model of desubjectivation).[2]

To sum up, by hiding its true name and tutelary deities, Rome belonged to a third dimension – one alien to the metaphysical polarity described above – and set its identity as a simulacrum from the very beginning. It is in this sense that Rome emerges as a simulacrum by posing itself as a copy of *itself*. No fraud or deception are to be found in this, only subtle motivations stemming from strategic, religious and political perspectives for the sake of Roman civilization's survival and continuation.

Guy Debord and fake news

Several questions may arise at this stage: how does Perniola link Christianity (specifically Jesuit Catholicism) to the notion of the simulacrum? Is it not true that God belongs to the series of metaphysical and Platonic ideas that entail the criticized distinction between a true and contingent world? And how can the sixteenth and seventeenth centuries' Catholic Baroque tradition be linked to today's world?

Perniola's starting point is the role and value of images within the context of the growing post-Second World War mass media and information society. He claims that to understand contemporary approaches to and perspectives of images, it is useful to compare and contrast them with the image theories of other eras. Specifically, he goes back to the eighth and ninth centuries' religious debate between 'iconoclasts' and 'iconophiles' that took place in the Byzantine Empire. The fervent 'battle' between these opposing sides can be summed up in the following interrogatives: what is the relation between the image of Jesus and Jesus himself? Can Jesus and the saints be represented through images and icons? The iconoclasts (which literally means 'image breakers') believed that no visual artefacts could represent both the divine and human nature of Christ, and thus, these images should be banned or destroyed. In other words, they held that divine nature cannot be encompassed or represented within a painting or statue – or, to remain within the conceptual horizon of the simulacrum, an image of Christ is a degraded copy of his original substance. The iconophiles, on the other hand, claimed that God – both through the creation of the world and through the incarnation of Jesus – made visible matter worthy of worship. With the icons of Jesus and of the saints, therefore, the iconophiles believed they were venerating the very work of God. For the iconophiles, the 'original', Perniola claims, is not beyond the icon but is the icon itself: 'the image must not be considered a simple representation of the original, but an evocation, a "door" through which God enters in the sensible world.... For the iconophiles the original, the Platonic idea, is susceptible of sensible evidence. Theirs is a concrete metaphysics, a visual theology' (RT: 159). Perniola then investigates the 'modern' versions of both iconoclasm and iconophily, which echo the metaphysical premises of their religious predecessors.

The modern iconoclasts are – for Perniola – those individuals and groups (such as Situationist International) that condemn post-Second World War society as 'an immense accumulation of spectacles', as Guy Debord writes in his famous book *The Society of the Spectacle*: 'The spectacle is not a collection of images; it is a social relation between people that is mediated by images' (2005: 7). In these inflammatory assertions, the French revolutionary claims that images (from journalism to advertising, political propaganda and mass media in general) shape and influence our everyday lives in such a way that reality is debased into mere appearances. Most individuals would be passive spectators of a never-ending 'spectacle', one in which they are told how to live, what to desire, how to work and how to spend their free time. The modern iconoclasts believe that images do not represent reality and life but only appearances and mere survival. For the Situationists, for example, reality and authentic life imply having the ability to effectively act and directly experience the world, that is, to live in the first person. They believe that the images of the 'spectacle' produce a screen between individuals' lives and their actions, mediating and influencing people's desires, beliefs and choices. In his *Comments on the Society of the Spectacle*, which was first published in 1988, the French philosopher develops a third form of spectacle, the 'integrated spectacle' (1990: 8), which unites several features of the first two forms (the Russian 'concentrated' spectacle and the American 'diffuse' spectacle). One of the crucial aspects of the integrated spectacle is 'generalised secrecy' and the 'unanswerable false':

> Generalised secrecy stands behind the spectacle, as the decisive complement of all it displays and, in the last analysis, as its most vital operation. The simple fact of being unanswerable has given what is false an entirely new quality. At a stroke it is truth which has almost everywhere ceased to exist or, at best, has been reduced to the status of pure hypothesis.
>
> 1990: 12–13

As emerges from this passage, for Debord, on the one hand, stands the truth and, on the other, the spectacle that covers, falsifies and makes this very truth hidden and secret by mystifying it or making it disappear completely. What unites these attempts to shed light on knowledge and truth, on the one hand, and on ignorance and falsehood, on the other, is the contrast between nudity and secrecy. Truth, knowledge and the good would be pure and self-evident, naked in themselves, while falsity and ignorance would be what veil, cover and make something secret. By doing so, not only do iconoclasts move within the polarity already criticized by Nietzsche – and by numerous other thinkers – between the real world and apparent world, but above all, they become the victims of their own project. To clarify this claim, Perniola's theses may be useful. Society, Perniola writes by summarizing Debord's conception:

> was wrapped in a cloak that made it impenetrable and incomprehensible. If only this cloak were removed, truth would once again shine forth on its own, without requiring any great effort on the part of reason. What I find unsatisfactory and at bottom naive in Debord's argument and, by extension, in the entire notion of the secret, is precisely this conception of truth as something that at different times will just appear or disappear quite independently of thought.
>
> E: 4

Perniola compares the activity of those who seek the truth following this theory to those who carry out a police investigation. Once the supposed 'truth' is reached, in fact, the exercise and activity of thought could also cease, and it would be left only a 'cultural framework of neo-obscurantism and neo-barbarism' (E: 6), which is precisely the goal of iconoclasts to contribute to criticize. 'The granting of a vital role to the secret is part and parcel of the abdication of philosophical thinking' (E: 6). In other words, Debord's militantism has a dualistic and Manichean vision of reality, for which reality is made up of secrets that dissolve in their communication. There is the risk of being entangled in a logic that contrasts truth and lies – news that corresponds to reality or misinformation.

On the other hand, the modern iconophiles are those who praise the 'society of the spectacle' by claiming that there is a connection between the image and its original: 'a relation of strong affinity between the news published in the newspaper and the event to which it refers, the illustration provided by the advertisement and the advertised product, the televised image and its object' (RT: 161). The Platonic dichotomy between reality and appearances is maintained but here in a manner diametrically opposed to that of the iconoclasts: the images *are* reality itself; the copies *are* the original themselves. Therefore, for Perniola, both perspectives share the same underlying principle: 'the *metaphysical pretence* to establish a relation between image and original' (RT: 163). They both remain stuck within a metaphysical conception that ignores the dimension of the simulacrum in relation to contemporary images. The modern iconoclasts and iconophiles are the heirs of two traditional religious positions that are inadequate when it comes to understanding the significance of the simulacrum. Specifically, as suggested, these two traditions go back to the Byzantine quarrel of the eighth and ninth centuries and to the Protestant iconoclasm of the sixteenth century, which grew with the Lutheran Reformation. What does it mean, according to

Perniola, to understand mass media and images within contemporary society as simulacra? And why can these images provide the conditions for a 'full realization' (*piena realizzazione*) of the simulacra? Perniola provides an example:

> These [the mass-media] can supply an image which is greatly more complex and developed (*costruita*) than that offered by any other reality and which, this notwithstanding, does not acquire the character of prototype or of origin ... Television, for instance, can offer a variety of images of a given event, without comparison, greater than the individual himself could see if he were personally present in the location.
>
> RT: 169

This passage includes several statements that are useful for understanding Perniola's claims about the relationship between the simulacrum and mass media. Perniola does not claim that *every* image produced within a mass media society is a simulacrum. He employs the expression 'can supply', implying the idea that an image can be considered a simulacrum only if it possesses certain properties or qualities. In the above quotation, at least two of these qualities emerge: *artificiality* (image 'complex and developed') and *lack of an original* ('does not acquire the character of prototype or of origin'). Artificiality consists of the fact that – for instance – a given event can be limitlessly reproduced, reworked, post-produced, used for various purposes, transmitted through several media and so forth. Hence, it does not 'mirror reality'. Only a metaphysical approach, such as that of the modern iconophiles, would still consider mass media images as realistic representations, linking the realm of 'reality' to that of the 'copies' (also see Fabris 2000; Matos 2000). At the same time, these images – to meet the requirements of the simulacrum – should be 'independent', 'with no identity': namely, they should not refer to a supposed 'original' or 'prototype'. 'This depends on the fact that the choice is not, as in the metaphysical images, between truth and lie, but between an image that pretends to be a present or a future reality and an image that presents itself as image' (RT: 170). In other words, Perniola claims that understanding mass media images in oppositional terms (realism/falseness or original/copy) means remaining blind to the dimension that they can potentially open: the simulacrum.

The Jesuit-Baroque tradition and the Internet of Things

For these reasons, Perniola believes that the debate between iconoclasts and iconophiles cannot bring a new understanding to the issue of images. He investigates a third and alternative position, one that can disclose the significance of the simulacrum: the aesthetics of the Jesuit-Baroque tradition. Specifically, three sources are examined by Perniola: the treatises *De arte bene moriendi* and the *De controversiis christianae fidei* by Cardinal Roberto Bellarmino and the *Exercitia spiritualia* by Ignatius of Loyola, the founder of the Jesuit Order. The main object of Perniola's enquiry is the Jesuit approach towards images, which is closely connected to spiritual life and the art of living. As Else Marie Bukdahl writes in an essay on Perniola's interpretation of Baroque aesthetics: 'Bellarmino points out that the image has its own autonomy and its own specificity. The image has no relation to an original or a prototype, but has its concrete, intrinsic and *historical* character' (2017: 67). In other words, Perniola finds in Bellarmino a third and alternative perspective on the nature of devotional images. For Bellarmino, in fact, these images are neither a 'door' leading the soul to the original substance of God (iconophily), nor are they debased as mere copies of the invisible exemplar (iconoclasm) 'The image of Christ and of the Saints should be worshipped not only by accident, or inappropriately, but still *per se* and individually so that they themselves determine the worship so that they in themselves may be considered closely, not only as those carrying a replacement of the original' (Bellarmino 1837: 400); 'however, when the image is praised *per se* and individually, than the praise is indeed being restricted to that same image' (1837: 500). The third way elaborated within the Jesuit tradition, therefore, implies that the value of images is not grounded on the ideal world or the distinction between the original and copy but, rather, on the images themselves, here in their worldly and concrete aspects.

This does not mean that there is no relation at all between – for instance – the image of God and God Himself: 'in Bellarmino's text God is far away. The relation between image and God is, according to him, equally indirect and mediated, just as the relation that exists between the poor, to whom one gives alms, and Christ in whose honor we give alms' (RT: 165). If, for the iconophiles, there is a direct relationship between the image and Christ and, on the opposite side, if, for the iconoclasts, there is an irreconcilable difference and alterity, the Jesuits seem to have found a third way, one in which this very relationship is 'indirect' and 'mediated'.

Specifically, Perniola's interpretation takes into account two kinds of images within the Baroque tradition. On the one hand, there is the 'emblem', the image often used by the Jesuits to illustrate their works; on the other hand, there are the spiritual images emerging from Loyola's *Exercitia spiritualis*. Perniola's view of the emblem, as he recognizes (SS: 80), draws on Walter Benjamin's *The Origin of*

German Tragic Drama. 'The emblem is a pictorial code, an image, thought or a rebus' (Bukdahl 2017: 73–4) – in other words, an image accompanied by a sentence or a motto. According to Perniola, Baroque emblems can be considered simulacral images because they do not belong to a metaphysical opposition in that they are not considered inferior copies of a superior original, yet at the same time, they are not original. On the contrary, the emblems are linked to two central aspects of the simulacrum: 'repetition' and 'emptiness'. They are repetition because these emblems were made through printing: 'printing, does not allow the development of a fetishistic interest towards it, as in the case with single works, such as paintings' (RT: 168). The emblems are not downgraded versions of an original, nor do they represent the loss of the aura and the *hic et nunc* of the artwork after its potential unlimited reproducibility through mechanical means. From their very beginning, the emblems are thought and reproduced in the horizon of copy images, which, nonetheless, have their value.

Another aspect of the emblem investigated by Perniola is that of 'emptiness', which is linked to the idea that a single image is susceptible to multiple interpretations: 'the object is incapable of transmitting (*irradiare*) a meaning or a universal sense, namely, when it is removed from its own identity, "any thing whatever can signify any other"' (RT: 168). The emblem, in other words, does not express any univocal sense; rather, it can be the vessel for a variety of messages. Perniola does not provide any specific example of a Baroque emblem, which is a gap filled by Bukdahl's research. In developing Perniola's image theory, Bukdahl gives a concrete example of a Baroque emblem. Specifically, she discusses an emblem included in the *Imago Primi Saeculi Societatis Jesu* (1640), a publication intended to celebrate the centennial of the Jesuit Society. The selected emblem displays the two hemispheres of the globe, with Eros placed between them:

> The subscription underneath 'One world is not enough' refers to the Jesuit mission in South America. The Latin poem printed together with the emblem, informs us that Hercules and Alexander did not go far as the Society has done in their missionary work. . . . But the motto might also allude to the fact that our world is not enough – we should have our salvation in mind. The emblem is framed by twining and folding abstract decorations, which indicate that it is an independent whole, what Perniola calls an 'artificial construction', containing neither precise depictions of our world nor reflections of the divine. But it contains the conditions for a concrete understanding of the Jesuits' missionary work and religious aims.
>
> Bukdahl 2017: 74–5

Bukdahl underlines the 'independence' of the emblem, which does not fall under the traditional metaphysical scheme. In fact, not only is the 'artificial' image of the emblem susceptible to different interpretations, but it also refuses to assert itself – so to speak – as a new original, as a 'metahistorical entity universally valid' (RT: 169). Thus, the emblem can be considered an in-between image, neither entirely this-worldly nor entirely other-worldly; this raises issues that range from the practical organization of the society to the spiritual involvement of the Jesuits themselves.[3]

Linked to the consideration of images as simulacra is Perniola's perspective on *Exercitia spiritualia* by Ignatius de Loyola. Loyola's exercises are a series of meditations and contemplations on several themes that take several weeks to complete. Every week corresponds to a different phase, in which the practitioner's tasks change: the first week deals with sins and repentance; the second focuses on the life of Christ; the third with the Passion; and the last with the Resurrection. Specifically, Perniola examines Loyola's approach to images. Although Loyola's exercises would influence the Baroque visual arts (see Bukdahl 2017: 69–71), the images involved in the exercises are not concrete paintings or artefacts – they are instead connected with contemplation. To make the exercise a much more involving and effective spiritual experience, Loyola elaborates on a method in which images and imagination are bound together through a sensory experience. To put this another way, it is by engaging with the senses that the images contemplated (i.e. the temple where Jesus was) can provide spiritual progress. To give an example, in the Fifth Contemplation, Loyola writes the following:

> First Point. The first Point is to see the persons with the sight of the imagination, meditating and contemplating in particular the details about them and drawing some profit from the sight.
>
> Second Point. The second, to hear with the hearing what they are, or might be, talking about and, reflecting on oneself, to draw some profit from it.
>
> Third Point. The third, to smell and to taste with the smell and the taste the infinite fragrance and sweetness of the Divinity, of the soul, and of its virtues, and of all, according to the person who is being contemplated; reflecting on oneself and drawing profit from it.
>
> Fourth Point. The fourth, to touch with the touch, as for instance, to embrace and kiss the places where such persons put their feet and sit, always seeing to my drawing profit from it.
>
> Loyola 2017: Second Week

Thus, the contemplations depicted by Loyola are intended to evoke *vivid* images of the life of Christ, wherein all five senses are involved in a spiritual and yet embodied experience. The senses are not enemies of prayer – on the contrary, they are crucial to heighten the spiritual experience. Loyola himself claims, at the beginning of his manuscript, that 'For it is not knowing much, but realizing and relishing things interiorly, that contents and satisfies the soul' (2017: Annotations). In so doing he 'succeeds in evoking an image that is larger, more unexpected, and more sensual than that which our usual viewpoint is able to produce' (Bukdahl 2017: 69).

Nonetheless, at the same time, this 'application of the senses' (*applicazione dei sensi*, RT: 166) is accompanied by a seemingly incompatible and opposite stance: 'indifference'. Loyola states that it is necessary 'to make ourselves indifferent to all created things' (2017: First Week). The peculiarity of Loyola's approach (and with it, the Jesuit tradition in general) lies precisely in the acceptance and maintenance of oppositions. According to this view, one must be ready to give up everything while being willing to enjoy anything that is to be brought along by the future (including suffering and pain, such as those of Christ and the Apostles). It is not a regime of chastity, there is no personal resignation: 'The Jesuit's application of the senses is inseparable from indifference. The meaning of their paradoxical connection is in the *disposition* to accept, to elect, and to want whatever historical form, without attributing to it an absolute or definitive value' (RT: 167). Indifference is linked by Perniola to non-identity, desubjectivation and emptiness, a philosophy 'outside of the ego' (Di Rienzo 2020). In other words, the Jesuit-Baroque lifestyle does not share the metaphysical principle of identity upon which the dichotomy between original and copies is grounded. On the contrary, it means being open to the world and its prismatic manifestations precisely by silencing oneself and becoming indifferent to it. Perniola's continuous reference to the idea of the 'world' in his interpretation of Jesuit thought clarifies a relevant aspect of his overall standpoint. In fact, if the society of simulacra is opened by the indifference emerging after the death of God, the Jesuit thought, by contrast, presupposes a faith that this world is ultimately not God forsaken. For the Jesuits, one becomes indifferent for God's sake, *ad maiorem gloriam Dei* (for the greater glory of God); for Perniola, there is no place for mourning what once was but only to commit oneself to the theatre of the world, *ad maiorem gloriam simulacri* (Burch 2002). Thus, it is crucial to bear in mind that Perniola's understanding of Jesuit thought should be placed in a postmetaphysical horizon of thought.

Loyola's indifference is summarized by his famous statement, *Perinde ac cadaver!* ('Like a corpse!'). Living as if one is a corpse is the condition needed to reach consolation and joy (the ultimate goal of exercises): it is the very experience of 'indifference' that allows the 'difference' of the world to emerge. As Bottani claims in commenting on Perniola's view of the Baroque: 'Only from the small death of indifference (towards all the possibilities) does the election of the difference of the particular situation emerge, inasmuch as possibility elected among the others' (1983: 299). It is no coincidence that, Perniola continues, there is a strong connection – in the Baroque world – between history and death and between nothingness and works.

In his 'Variations on a Baroque Tomb' (1950), Aldous Huxley points out that from the late Renaissance and Baroque, a new aesthetic fashion began to hold great importance: that of the mortuary tastes. The 'remainders of mortality' (1950: 168) especially involved tombs adorned with skulls, skeletons and the personification of death (such as Bernini's tombs of Popes Urban VIII and Alexander VII in St. Peter's, Rome). Death is seen, on the one hand, as the inevitable event that awaits everybody at the end of our biological life, but, on the other, is the starting point of action in the world. Bellarmino devotes a treatise precisely to the idea that to live well, one must learn how to die while still living: 'it is necessary, in the first place, that we die to the world before we die in the body' (2016: Chapter One). For Bellarmino, not only must one live well to have a good death – the contrary is also true. Bellarmino claims that we can be *in* the world while not being *of* the world. A seemingly small change in prepositions hides a much more complex and subtle perspective, which implies the paradoxical attitude of living as if nothing that we do, possess or taste actually belongs to us, that is, of a general indifference accompanied by the application of the senses:[4] 'Only those who are already dead, that is, indifferent, can operate in history which is [in] constant flux, becoming, and dissolves certainties, all fixed points, all identities' (RT: 142). That which can be termed *becoming nothing* is the precondition of such openness. According to this interpretation of the Jesuit tradition, death is neither an end nor something other than life: it is the starting point of *living*. The simulated death, that is, a *desubjectivated* individual who participates in the world and yet is not of the world is an individual who loves his/her fate and says 'Yes' to history, or, to put it in other words: 'the simulacrum is linked to the wonder that, in a historical world where each authenticity and originality is dissolved and in which each truth, reality and absolute value is revealed in its mystifying and disguising essence, there is something instead of nothing and to the gratitude with respect to this artificial presence' (Bottani 1983: 301).

To sum up, both the religious rituals of Rome and the contemplative images of the Jesuits show how the simulacrum can be understood – for Perniola – as a non-metaphysical dimension rather than a synonym for lie and falsehood. The simulacrum can be defined as an image with no identity, or, to be more specific, as an artificial image that does not refer back to any prototype.

In addition to the Roman and Baroque-Jesuit traditions, as well as the debate at the turn of the 1970s and 1980s, what can *La società dei simulacri* still say today? René Capovin's standpoint on Perniola's idea of the simulacrum can be examined here. Although Capovin provides a very well-documented and in-depth picture of the notion of the simulacrum, he nevertheless traces Perniola's reflection mainly to the 1970s (the text being published in 1980). Capovin's conclusion is clear: 'The court of history seems to have pronounced itself clearly: acquitted because of insufficient effects' (2020: 25). Capovin argues that the society of simulacra outlined by Perniola proposes cultural strategies and operations that never actually took place. The figure of an 'obstetrician of the simulacrum' of which Perniola speaks is perhaps only traceable in Perniola himself, Capovin continues. However, in my opinion, Capovin seeks the effectiveness of the logic of the simulacrum in the wrong place, that is, not going beyond the intellectuals and academics of the time (all within the Italian context only). Perhaps, it took a few decades before this fully emerged, but with the most recent developments of interaction technologies and social media, the 'cultural operator' (*operatore culturale*) is fully present on the Italian and global scene. Perniola had guessed this in 2011; when reprinting the second edition of *La società dei simulacri*, he adds the following sentence in italics: 'For some time now, a new alternative figure has emerged with respect to that of the artist and advertiser, the art dealer and the capitalist: the cultural operator, *who, following the invention and spread of the internet, becomes a social network manager*' (SS: 91). What Perniola calls the social network manager can be understood as that figure who no longer has anything to do with the old academic and ideological structures and who moves within a highly simulacral society: from the Internet of Things to collective forms of intelligence, from augmented reality to big data, where there a new type of non-metaphysical but reticular and ecological knowledge can be expressed. This knowledge is also at odds with the logics of the mass media of the second half of the twentieth century; it is no longer based on the hierarchical and polarizing logic between actors and spectators and between subjects and objects. Through the creation of information systems in which both human beings and a whole series of nonhuman actors interact (plants, animals, minerals, lakes and roads), spaces, architecture and the very ways in which we inhabit in the world, from rural villages through to cities and metropolises, are dramatically changing. In an article first published in 1980, Perniola asserts that cultural operators have replaced the traditional figures of modern cultural and intellectual life, from artists and critics to academics and journalists. He even goes further by claiming that they form a global network guided by a shared principle: indeterminacy, a notion for which Perniola should be understood in terms of openness to the world and its manifestations, alongside its potentialities and challenges. The cultural operator could be considered, Perniola continues, as the herald of a new aesthetic culture: the 'indeterminate international' (*internazionale indeterminata*, cf. II).[5]

In these terms, *La società dei simulacri* contains pages that only now are actually able to resonate as real manifestos of contemporary feeling, acting and communicating.

To conclude, by exploring Roman and Jesuit thought, not only does Perniola give dignity to the concept of the simulacrum, but at the same time, he shows in what ways it is possible to transform one's own life through the power of the simulacrum, be it an 'aesthetic of seduction' or the 'election of the difference'. In so doing, the theory of the simulacrum should not be understood as a mere attempt to explain the postmodern condition of the mass media society. The simulacrum does not mean a deceptive or illusory hyper-reality; rather, it conveys the idea of a full present, one open to the heterogeneous experiences, events and perspectives that the world constantly pours forth, that is, openness to the richness and profundity of reality and its manifestations.

3

Action at the End of Action: Rituals without Myths

This chapter discusses Perniola's conception of 'ritual without myth' (*rito senza mito*). Perniola has devoted several studies to ritual theory, drawing from the fields of anthropology of religion and of philosophy (such as T: 35–8, 119–22, 198–204, SC: 63–76, PP: 35–44, RIE, SS: 66–70). A compilation entitled *Ritual Thinking. Sexuality, Death, World* has been published in English. This volume is a collection of essays originally published in *Transiti* and *La società dei simulacri*. In addition to containing significant reflections on the concept of 'simulacrum', which plays a crucial role in Perniola's philosophy as shown previously, it also (as the title suggests) confirms that ritual theory can provide both a synthesis and a hermeneutical key to better understand Perniola's overall philosophical path.

Against the anti-ritual tradition

Perniola explains (PP: 36) that his reflections depart from what he refers to as an 'anti-ritual tradition', which is observed in both the supporters of the ritual's dominance (especially in the works of William James and William Robertson Smith) and those in favour of myth (especially Mircea Eliade and Lévi-Strauss). The first tradition, Perniola suggests, is linked to the concept of primitiveness. According to it, the more primitive a religion is, the fewer myths and beliefs it endorses. The second one considers the ritual as a concretization of the myth; this element will be explored here, as it allows us to understand Perniola's perspective by also avoiding possible misunderstandings of his theory.

As Mircea Eliade explains, many archaic civilizations had a cyclic vision of time, and this can be considered as 'their rebellion against concrete, historic time, their nostalgia for a periodic return to the mythical time of the origins' (1975: 9). Eliade highlights that rituals were intended to imitate a primitive population's own mythical archetype, that is, an action accomplished at the beginning of times by a mythical figure. Every human action, starting from the most important, such as the foundation of a city, to the most ordinary, like hunting, made sense only when the author did not ignore the exemplary and mythical model within which it was rooted. Such abolition of historical and linear time in favour of what can be referred to as 'the times of the gods' meant that every action had an absolute beginning, as it tended to restore the initial moment of creation. Thus, the real acquired its proper 'reality' only by replicating an archetype. As Eliade writes, this can be defined as 'the mechanism of man's transformation into archetype through repetition' (1975: 58). Even though the notion of repetition plays a central role in Eliade's perspective, it should not be confused with Perniola's privileging of the role of repetition. Eliade's repetition has value only because it allows the concretization of an *archetype*. This means that what is important is not the repetition itself but what precisely is repeated insofar as it stems from an original. On the other hand, 'ritual thinking', as Perniola elaborates, shares a conceptual affinity with the notion of simulacrum. As shown earlier, the simulacrum implies no ontological priorities related to a supposed archetype. Instead, the original is dissolved and the copy gains not only a substantial distance from it but also becomes autonomous. Maintaining the same conceptual register, Perniola considers ritual without myth to be a 'simulacral' ceremony, as it is grounded on a rigorous repetition of the same formal performance:

> Nonetheless, this word [repetition], in this context, does not mean loyalty or conformity to an original which is recognized as valuable or re-actualisation of a primal action for which the ontological primacy is affirmed. On the contrary, it means distance and even irremediable extraneousness with the original, [it means] autonomy of the copy.
>
> PP: 22

Perniola argues that by avoiding the (metaphysical) distinction between original-archetype-authentic and copy-repetition-inauthentic, it is possible to enter an *in-between* conceptual dimension where the very notion of repetition is not debased. Repetition, in fact, for Perniola does not mean conformity, banality or familiarity and does not imply a stereotypical attitude. Moreover, Eliade's underlying anti-ritual position reflects a traditional prejudice that considers the ritual action to be oriented to express something beyond itself. In other words, the word, the content, the meaning (the myth) is preferred against the form, the *habitus*, the ceremony (the ritual):

> A repetitive action that does not find its supporting point in genealogical history, in an individual or a collective belief, is considered almost unanimously by Western philosophical tradition, from Neo-Platonists to Diderot, from Augustin to Lévi-Strauss, as an empty, stereotypical, superfluous, residual, pathological, maniacal, desperate behaviour that can, at most, be the object of aesthetic appreciation.
>
> PP: 37

Thus, this tradition contends that the ritual represents an impoverishment of the myth. The myth appears ontologically prior and superior to the ritual: the myth would possess contents, truths, meanings, while the ritual would merely comprise a surrogate, a weak sign, a mere repetition of an action. Perniola, by contrast, understands the ritual as the particular welcoming disposition towards the world, history and their enigmatic manifestations that presupposes a 'suspension' of one's own subjectivity to assert itself. To develop his perspective further, Perniola draws on traditions and schools of thought in the Western world other than that highlighted in this passage. In the following pages, I explore Perniola's elaboration of the notion of *epoché*.

Perniola's expanded *epoché*

Perniola states (EE: 162) that it can be useful to borrow phenomenological language to comprehend his particular conception of the ritual at a theoretical level. More specifically, he devoted an article (EE) to elaborate on the notion of 'expanded *epoché*', which can be understood as an enlargement of the phenomenological *epoché* to cover political and practical domains, as will be clear by the end of this sub-chapter (also see Contreras-Koterbay 2021).

The concept of *epoché* can be traced back to Greek scepticism. It literally means 'suspension (of judgement)', implying the attitude of doubting one's own beliefs and claims on reality. This concept was subsequently pursued by Descartes, who founded his epistemology on the so-called 'methodical doubt' to acquire the gnoseological truth of the *Cogito*: one can doubt everything, but at the very moment he/she doubts, he/she exists (it is from here that the famous assertion 'I think, therefore I am' originated). Edmund Husserl developed the concept of *epoché* as a philosophical attitude towards the world. Specifically, the phenomenologist should put reality into brackets by suspending all beliefs in objects of experience. The peculiar element of the phenomenological *epoché* is freeing oneself from the 'captivity of the unquestioned acceptance of the everyday world' (Cogan 2014: online source). Questioning the validity of everyday life as commonly understood effects change in the experiential configuration of the subject, and one is thus able to see the world from a new perspective. Indeed, through *epoché*, the world appears to the subject as a *phenomenon*, that is, in its heterogeneous manifestations deprived of their ideological background: 'In the "natural", preanalytic and prephenomenological attitude ... we generally believe that objects perceived are real; we believe that we live in a real world. This belief is "put out of action", suspended, we make no use of it. We are left with a world-as-phenomenon, a world which claims to be; but we refuse, for the time being, to pass on the validity of these claims' (Schmitt 1959: 239). The Husserlian *epoché*, therefore, entails distancing oneself from the experience of the world understood as a set of certainties taken for granted and previously accepted without reflection. It indicates a step back, a suspension of one's own commitment to the natural world so to speak, by developing a neutral and disinterested attitude.

Given this brief account of the notion of *epoché*, in what terms does Perniola speak of an expanded *epoché*? Towards what does the *epoché* expand? Perniola does not embrace phenomenology to elaborate a transcendental theory of the subject; his objective is 'expanding the notion of *epoché* to cover the activity of everyday life' (EE: 162). In other words, Perniola is not interested in dwelling on the constitution of transcendental ego but in the interaction between *epoché* and effectiveness (that is, the practical realisation of something). Expanding *epoché* means precisely embracing the social, historical and political domains without perceiving them with an ideologically oriented attitude.

If, for Husserl, the essential forms of knowledge were the *eide* – the Greek plural of *ideas* – Perniola asks what the essential forms of action are and further claims that the answer can be found in rituals (EE: 165). Perniola's goal is to elaborate a formal theory of action that does not end in sterile and empty formalism. To justify what he calls a 'transcendental theory of action' (EE: 165), Perniola investigates the *a priori* conditions of rituals, which must be explored independently from empirical, ideological and material elements (to maintain their very transcendental nature). Perniola defines the concept of ritual as a 'form of pure activity', that is, a non-empiric action oriented towards effectiveness.[1] The *a priori* structure of the ritual is then discovered, by Perniola, in the notions of *repetition*, *habit* and *form*, as clarified in the following pages.

To sum up, ritual without myth involves a phenomenological *epoché* through which familiar routines and pre-given conceptions of the world are 'suspended' or bracketed. With the *epoché*, Perniola continues his exploration of the notion of the simulacrum and its periphery. In fact, both the simulacrum and the *epoché* share a central theoretical aspect, the former being understood as an 'image without identity' and the latter intended as the suspension of one's own subjectivity. In other words, they are both grounded upon the idea of 'indifference' as openness to the heterogeneity of reality and its manifestations.

The ritual in ancient Roman religion

Beyond expanding *epoché*, that is, enlarging the horizon of the ritual sphere, Perniola also wishes to free rituals from their dependence on myths. He calls this process the emancipation of ritual from myth, or the *demythologization* of ritual. Demythologization can be understood by examining Perniola's remarks on ancient Roman religion and Jesuit thought. The demythologization characterizing Roman religious ritual is founded in Rome's peculiar polytheism. Roman religious policy proposed absorbing deities belonging to other civilizations. For instance, as suggested, the military ritual of the *evocatio* is an example of assimilation, as the deities of the city to be conquered were 'invited' to join the Roman pantheon where they would find new temples and cults. Incorporating and preserving religious heritages and traditions from other peoples were important means of maintaining social stability throughout Rome's domains. At the peak of its conquests, the Roman Empire's borders encompassed large swathes of North Africa, the Middle East, the Mediterranean basin, Northern Europe and Asia Minor. This resulted in a peculiar pantheon, including not only autochthonous deities but also international ones, from Greek to Egyptian, through solar deities such as Mithras and Sol Invictus, and mysterious imported religions.

Religion permeated all areas of society, from public ceremonies in temples and festivals to meetings of the Senate and prayers. Several scholars of Roman history (Beard et al., 1998; Rüpke 2007) noted that *religio*, for the Romans, did not correspond to an 'act of faith', as in Christian tradition, but to an 'act of knowing'. This act was facilitated by knowledge of the correct practice and execution of rituals, as they were the most important means of communicating with the gods and demonstrating this communication approach publicly through the very performance of the ritual itself (Rüpke 2007; Scheid 2011). All the formulations and recitations of the rituals were selected according to their specific purpose and occasion and were observed through the correct knowledge and scrupulous practice of the ritual. Indeed, the scholar Clifford Ando refers to

Roman religion as founded upon an 'empiricist epistemology', because the 'cult addressed problems in the real world, and the effectiveness of rituals – their tangible results – determined whether they were repeated, modified, or abandoned' (2008: 13). Therefore, a religious practitioner, in this view, would not follow faith, strong beliefs or dogmas but rather carefully express a religious body of rituals through their performance: 'These convictions [actualized in ritual], these beliefs, were never collected in the form of a doctrine for instruction, and above all they did not express a belief in the proper sense – because, for the ancients, belief was an inferior form of knowledge – but a knowing' (Linder and Scheid 1993: 54). Here lies the link between phenomenological *epoché* and the practical domain that Perniola elucidates: Roman religion enables a suspension of pre-conceived beliefs through effectively oriented rituals. This can be viewed as an example of ritual without myth, as the attention to and respect of ritual formalism, though independent from a myth (that is, an ideological and moral meaning), is never oblivious to the pragmatic element. It is therefore not a coincidence that the counterpart of religious attitude, for the Romans, was not neglect or denial of the gods but superstition (Beard et al., 1998: 217). Superstition is strictly connected to the formal element of ritual as, on the one hand, it indicates 'excessive forms of behaviour' and 'excessive commitment to the Gods' on the other. In this context, superstition involves 'doing or believing more than is necessary' (Rüpke 2007: 5). Religion thus becomes a matter of self-control, of desubjectivating oneself and not letting one's own desires and passions erupt violently. As Perniola presents, in this ritual typology, beliefs or inner experiences are not privileged: it is not the interiority that justifies the cult, it is the ceremony, that is, the extremely precise and scrupulous repetition of ritual acts that pave the way for a kind of non-sentimental and non-intimate sensibility (as an excessive commitment leads to superstition).

By allowing for corrections, transformations and modifications of ineffective rituals, Roman religion maintains that rigorous and scrupulous respect for codified actions can be preserved together with a plasticity towards reality:

> The indeterminacy of Roman religion, the tendency to let things drop, to keep quiet and to forget the identities and function of individual gods, and the mythical meaning of rituals, corresponds to a precise philosophical, cultural and political orientation of caution and extreme prudence toward emerging historical data, to a will for the relative, and to a fear of absolute dimensions ... Roman religion consists in the ability to listen carefully to the *fatum*.
>
> RT: 84

Perniola is attracted to the indeterminacy of Roman ritual structure, which can acquire new dimensions precisely because the mythological aspect is secondary. Beyond the ritual of *evocatio*, Perniola provides several other examples taken from the Roman pantheon (DA: 22). For instance, he explains in what terms the Roman deities *Venus* and *Ops* offer such a variety of aspects and dimensions. *Ops Consiva in Regia* is associated with diet, banquets and abstinence, while *Ops ad Forum* with enthusiastic consumption of food; moreover, *Venus* oscillates between chastity and protection of virginity (*Venus Verticordia*) and of libido and prostitution (*Venus Ericina*). For Perniola, it is significant that the Romans did not view these aspects as complementary harmonies nor as dialectic contradictions, but as possible outcomes and manifestations of the divine essence, which was not entirely on one side or another. This shows the Romans' flexible religious intuitions to the extent of absorbing and assimilating extraneous cults while conceiving a same divine entity susceptible to multiple cults and interpretations of it.[2]

The difference of the Catholic feeling

Besides Roman ritualism, Perniola analyses ritual without myth in Catholic religiosity. The peculiarity of what Perniola defines as 'Catholic feeling' (SC, CTC) corresponds to the attention paid by Catholic religious thought not so much on a dogma, belief, commandment or God as the utmost otherness, but rather on aesthetics and imagination as well as on history, the world and man's neighbouring things (also see Greeley 2000). This account describes Catholic feeling as a 'ritual feeling' (*sentire rituale*), centred on historical processes and on their enigmatic manifestations. More specifically, Perniola examines what he refers to as a thinker of 'mundane Catholicism': Ignatius of Loyola. Loyola's religious thought is central to Perniola's philosophy. The founder of the Jesuit Order appears in several of Perniola's works (cf. especially T, DH, SC, SPB) and has heavily influenced his overall perspective. I have already focused on Perniola's theoretical debt to Loyola while elaborating the notion of simulacrum. Here, I will continue to explore Loyola's influence on Perniola by discussing the notions of 'difference' and 'ritual without myth'. In fact, Perniola claims that Loyola should be understood as a 'thinker of the difference' (*pensatore della differenza*, SC: 97), and his exercises can be inscribed in the horizon of a ritual feeling (SC: 66).

A preliminary explanation is needed to shed light on Perniola's understanding of 'difference'. To this end, I will develop the main points elaborated in the article,

'La differenza italiana' (The Italian Difference), published in the journal *L'erba voglio* (DI: 10–5, also see DIP). The article is devoted to the themes of national identity and populism in the Italian context. The underlying issue explored in the article can be summed up in the following question: what does the specificity of Italian history and culture constitute? Perniola analyses two different possible answers. Both reformism and populism, for Perniola, 'do not seek the Italian *difference* or the difference *in Italy* but merely the Italian diversity or diversity in Italy, namely an *identity* to set against other identities' (DI: 10). In this passage, Perniola indicates a distinction between 'difference' (*differenza*) and 'diversity' (*diversità*). To diversify would mean being able to indicate and circumscribe something peculiar to a given phenomenon. Perniola argues that according to the populist standpoint, Italian specificity consists of the supposed identity of Italian people against their ruling class; however, for reformism, the specificity would be the Italian national identity in relation to other nations. I will not dwell on Perniola's definition and understanding of reformism and populism in Italy. My claim is that the argument he develops in this article is useful to understand his conception of difference: for Perniola, to diversify means to identify, to produce an identity. By distinguishing certain features and aspects of a given phenomenon – Italian culture in this case – both populism and reformism fail to grasp the 'Italian difference'. If diversity is equal to identity, how then should the notion of difference be understood? The difficulty of explaining this notion emerges from the fact that, according to Perniola, it is closer to an experience than to a concept (CA: 109–10).

Metaphysical 'concepts', such as the concept of 'identity' in Aristotelian logics, the '*a priori* judgement' of Kantian criticism and the 'contradiction' of Hegelian dialectics, share an essential theoretical framework grounded upon 'pure speculation'. 'Purity', in this context, means abstraction from reality and concrete, practical everyday life scenarios. On the contrary, the realm of experiences, Perniola continues, 'is precisely the impure one of feeling, of uncommon and uncanny experiences, irreducible to identity, ambivalent and excessive' (CA: 110). Between the 'purity' of concepts and the 'impurity' of experiences, Perniola claims that the latter is the starting point required to grasp the idea of difference. In fact, throughout his philosophy, he mainly focused on thinkers, traditions and phenomena that showed an affinity with the anti-metaphysical 'impure' realm of feeling (on Perniola's idea of feeling also see Moretti 2020). In so doing, I will lay out Perniola's understanding of the idea of difference and, at the same time, show how it can be related to the phenomenon of dandyism. Here, specifically, I explore the 'difference' in the Jesuit–Baroque religious aesthetics of St Ignatius of Loyola.[3]

Before turning to Loyola, however, another claim by Perniola can help clarify the notion of difference. Specifically, the metaphysical conception of 'value' in contrast to the idea of ritual without myth. Here, another essay written by Perniola can be referenced: his introduction to Nietzsche's *Antichrist*. This essay presents several statements that may help the reader understand Perniola's critique of the notion of 'value'. Perniola, influenced by a long tradition of thought that includes Nietzsche and Deleuze, considers metaphysics as a theoretical construction that debases reality as an inferior copy of the 'true' and 'ideal' world beyond the world. In terms of morality, the metaphysical key notion is that of 'value' (*valore*). The polemic target of Perniola's article is, specifically, the Kantian idea of morality. For Kant, Perniola argues:

> Value is what counts independently from the fact of being, from its historical reality; rather, its conceptual status is based on un-reality (*irrealtà*). The ideal is, by definition, something that is valid regardless of reality and the historical process: it opens up a sphere which is above effectuality and which allows us to express a judgment, an evaluation, a sentence upon it.
>
> I: 8

In this passage, Perniola highlights the opposition between reality and history on one side and metaphysics and value on the other. Metaphysical evaluations are seen as doomed-to-fail attempts to define what cannot be defined, limit what cannot be limited and circumscribe what cannot be circumscribed. In other words, the ideal dimension of how things ought to be is a benchmark to judge things on how they are: '[a] movement which established a super-reality (*super-realtà*) from which judging life, and in so doing restrain, destroy and condition it' (I: 8).

In contrast to this notion of value, Perniola expounds on the experience of ritual without myth. In fact, ritual without myth comes with several aspects that are at odds with a moral perspective grounded upon the metaphysical idea of value: first, the 'epochistic' suspension of belief towards reality; second, the focus on effectuality and practical issues; finally, demythologization. I have discussed these three features earlier in this chapter, and I will now focus on St Ignatius' *Exercitia spiritualis* to continue exploring Perniola's perspective.

Loyola's thought was developed in the first chapter of this book, where I investigated the notion of simulacrum. In the debate on devotional images between iconoclasts and iconophiles, which is based on the metaphysical distinction of the real world versus the world of appearances, Jesuit religious aesthetics present the possibility of a simulacral image. To sum up, the *Spiritual Exercises* elaborated by the founder of the Jesuit Order are understood by Perniola as a method of contemplation that keeps the realm of the senses *and* indifference both active at the same time. In other words, the practitioner is asked to become indifferent to the things of the world as well as be ready to abandon him/herself with all five senses to joy and consolation (the ultimate goals of the exercises). Perniola is not the only thinker who interpreted Loyola's work with an emphasis on the significance of 'feeling' and 'senses'. For instance, Giovanni Giudici, who translated the *Exercises* into Italian, underlines the sensory dimension of Loyola's prose as well:

> Where the mystical tradition is oriented to the 'light-in-darkness' of the divine Nothingness, in Ignacio there is a continuous call to materiality – visual, but also olfactory, auditory, tactile, gustatory – such that, under certain aspects, it can be said that the five senses are … the strenuous protagonists of the Exercises. How was this and how was that, whether the road was wide or narrow, the room small or large, what did Jesus and the disciples talk about during dinner, how much the wounds of the scourging and of the crucifixion hurt on the body of the 'meek Lord': the spectator is not only immersed at the centre of the scene; he is almost forced to make himself the feeling subject of a representation.
>
> 1998: 130

Pinard de la Boullaye also focused on the relevance of the dimension of 'feeling' in Loyola. His essay entitled '*Sentir, sentimiento, sentido* dans le style de saint Ignace' (1956: 416–30) is devoted specifically to Loyola's understanding of these aspects. Pinard de la Boullaye underlines the extreme frequency of feeling-related terminology in the exercises (1956: 417–22) and asserts that the realm of feelings can help the practitioner in making the episodes of the New Testament 'alive again' through the senses: 'Thus, in his Exercises, far from proposing only a reflection on abstract considerations, he [Loyola] focuses his attention on God in the flesh, who in some way makes infinite perfections accessible to the sensibility, through methods of contemplation and of application of the senses, simple and engaging at the same time, since they revive every evangelical scene as their past witnesses lived it' (1956: 417).

Therefore, Loyola's starting point, rather than being grounded on moral judgements or transcendental values, revolves around emotional facts and aesthetic experiences: 'Feeling and tasting the things of which Ignatius writes about are the exact opposite of the passive reception of a dogmatic truth' (SC: 102). The various exercises do not present dogmatic assertions on the nature of God, nor do they provide pre-given choices that the practitioner should blindly follow. For instance, the first week is devoted to the self-examination of the peculiar defect or sin one wishes to amend, alongside a general review of one's life. Loyola never specifies the 'defects' that the practitioner should tackle, nor does he underline which are the worst ones.⁴ He employs broader and vaguer connotation, such as 'particular defect', 'particular thing proposed' and 'bad thought', among others. Not only are the defects not clearly indicated, but the social condition of the practitioner is also left unclear. It is for this precise reason that Perniola understands Catholic religiosity as a 'cultural form of a universal religion', as the subtitle of *Del sentire cattolico* goes (cf. NSC). Pedro De Ribadeneira points out that the exercises can indeed be practiced and experienced profitably by heterogeneous individuals:

> And the fruit of these holy Exercises is not limited only to helping religion, but it embraces all people, of all states, professions, ages and lifestyles. As experience has shown, many princes, whether devout to the church or secular, excellent or less fortunate men, married or unmarried, consecrated to God, young or old, have profited from starting to practice the Exercises either to amend the bad habits or to improve the good ones they already possessed.
>
> 1583: 29–30

Loyola's very definition of the exercises can help in understanding his supposed vagueness: 'Spiritual Exercises to conquer oneself and regulate one's life without determining oneself through any tendency that is disordered' (2017: Presupposition). According to Perniola, this premise is of crucial significance. In fact, it shows how exactly Loyola believes that humans have a tendency towards disordered affections and passions, which obstruct their way to joy and consolation. The exercises would thus consist of a method that enables the practitioner to distinguish what brings joy and consolation from what brings desolation. The fact that Loyola does not provide specific assertions nor a hierarchy of values implies, according to Perniola, that his perspective is at odds with the transcendental morality specific to metaphysical judgements (also see RC).

Metaphysical judgement implies an absolute assertion about how things ought to be, that is, a claim that should be considered valid every time, regardless of history and contingency. Perniola is interested precisely in the historical features of Loyola's exercises. By not expressing specific or clearly identified flaws, Loyola implicitly claims that the exercises are relative to each practitioner and depend on their peculiar biography and history. Whereas moral values are linked to an ideal world beyond the world (as suggested earlier), the exercises are instead linked to the realm of feelings (joy and consolation as sensorial experiences) and that of reality and history: 'Faith is emancipated from each metaphysical ground and finds its anchor in the historical experience' (SC: 99).

A crucial question has not yet been answered: if Loyola's premise is that human beings have disordered affections that his spiritual exercises can help amend, on what terms does this happen? Even more importantly, how can joy and consolation be attained? Perniola, as I will clarify in the following paragraphs, based his interpretation of the *Spiritual Exercises* on the notion of 'difference'. The chapter of *Del sentire cattolico* devoted to St. Ignatius is entitled 'The Election of the Difference in Ignatius of Loyola' (SC: 97–134). Perniola links difference with history and, conversely, identity with metaphysics. A quotation from Loyola's work can be useful to understand this position: 'it is necessary to make ourselves indifferent to all created things ...; so that, on our part, we want not health rather than sickness, riches rather than poverty, honor rather than dishonor, long rather than short life, and so in all the rest' (2017: Three Manners of Humility). History teaches us that each situation, each condition and each phenomenon is subject to continuous change and transformation. An apparent initial victory can turn later into defeat; an initial loss might become a new acquisition. For instance, the life of Christ shows that poverty, misery, death and crucifixion can bring victory, salvation and resurrection all at the same time. In other words, each event that occurs in our daily life should not be judged as good or bad in itself, as the theory of transcendental value would claim.

The premise needed to imbibe this perspective lies in the experience of indifference. In fact, only a subject with no identity can surrender him/herself to the 'ballet' of history and related events. Identity, for Perniola, implies believing that there are specific needs that can fulfil our desires, specific ideologies that shape our will, specific values that orient our conduct, among other things. When our will, our conduct and our desires do not meet their goals, that is, when life does not go according to plans, disordered affections kick in. Anger, suffering, hatred, envy, rage and so forth may emerge. In brief, identity and values easily bring human beings to a path of unhappiness and desolation. On the contrary, understanding the very movement of history – which for Perniola is that of difference – means being open to every possibility that reality can offer to an individual.

> Ignatius, however, does not trace the difference in God, but in his manifest will, that is, in history, in what happens, in the life of men and peoples; not in the exceptional, in the numinous, in the extraordinary, but in the most current things, in business and in everyday conversations.
>
> SC: 114

Only if someone dissolves their identity can history emerge as the realm of difference; in other words, only if someone does not channel everything that happens in the orbital of their mere desires and interests can the experience of difference become available. Therefore, the paradoxical link between 'indifference' and 'difference' can be explained in terms of a welcoming disposition towards every manifestation of reality. Elaborating on this idea, Carsten Friberg writes, 'We must remain in a state of being open and attentive towards the world, a state of being sensible to the context and take the context as the primary source of action. This is opposite to the modern strategy of looking inward for subjectivity either in its confrontation with the absolute different: God or as the absolute source of knowledge as the philosophical subject of the Enlightenment and idealism' (2007: digital source). Indeed, as Perniola highlights, the fundamental precondition for entering into the experience of 'the difference' is the dissolution of one's own subjectivity and identity (SC: 103). Loyola's exercises should not be seen as an ascensional and mystical experience but as a necessary suspension (*epoché*), to enter a ritual without myth:

> The entrance into a ritual feeling implies first of all distancing from one's own subjectivity, which is an essential condition of 'feeling from the outside'. Knowing how to see oneself with an external eye, considering oneself as a 'world' rather than an 'I', witnessing what is born and takes place without pretending to immediately enclose it in a pre-established interpretation or a logic of personal interests, these are all aspects that come from classical antiquity and have been often handed down to Catholicism under the garb of humility, piety and devotion.
>
> SC: 66

Indifference, in this passage, is expressed through the idea of a 'feeling from outside' (*sentire dal di fuori*). It may seem contradictory to link feelings and indifference; however, these two seemingly incompatible phenomena are key to understand the peculiarity of the exercises: *indifference* (which Perniola characterises in terms of 'desubjectivation', 'non-identity', '*epoché*', 'death as simulacrum' and, as I will explain in another chapter, 'inorganic' and 'thing') and *feeling* (the five senses). A central question may thus be posited: How can one be indifferent yet at the same time feel? Perniola's answer is that Loyola's exercises allow the individual to keep these two apparently incompatible aspects together. One can be *in* the world without being *of* the world, as though all our possessions do not belong to us. Therefore, 'feeling from outside' does not imply an abolition of the senses but rather their cultivation within the dimension of indifference.

Indifference, as suggested, allows the individual to experience the difference of reality. Still, the question of why difference should be 'elected' has not yet been answered.

The difference of the world – that is, history – should not be tackled with the principle of identity but rather by imitating its constant movements and transformations, so to speak. Metaphorically, I would argue that the principle of identity can be compared to a heavy object thrown into sea, which, due to its density, sinks very quickly. In contrast, the experience of difference is similar to a life-preserver that floats on the surface of the water. Identity, for Perniola, means not being able to adapt to or imitate one's own surroundings, a failure that ultimately brings unhappiness and desolation. At odds with this perspective is the joy that emerges from 'electing' the dimension of difference, that is, by attuning oneself to the fluctuating and ever-changing dynamics of history. The election of the difference, understood as an affirmation of one's own present, is precisely the dandy's attitude towards their times.[5]

Perniola versus Heidegger and weak thought

The central issue at stake in the idea of ritual without myth is, therefore, that of action and effectuality and, broadly speaking, the relationship between knowledge and power.

In this regard, a commonly disregarded book published by Perniola in 1982 (reviewed by Marroni 1981 and Panella 1983, among others) can help us better understand his view. The book was titled *Dopo Heidegger. Filosofia e organizzazione della cultura* (After Heidegger. Philosophy and Organization of Culture). This text is, in my opinion, one of the most obscure and enigmatic pieces that Perniola has left us. Beyond the fact that it is devoid of notes and bibliographical references, if we exclude the names of Napoleon and Romulus and a single reference to Ignatian thought, it does not (explicitly) refer to any thinker, writer or intellectual. Heidegger himself appears only in the title, but there is no explicit trace of him within the text. Below the surface, however, the book is full of implicit references to Nietzsche, Gramsci, Hegel and Guicciardini (just to name a few), in addition to the aforementioned Heidegger and Saint Ignatius.

The book is divided into an introduction, five chapters and a conclusion, through which Perniola investigates the relationship between philosophy and the organization of culture and therefore, more generally, the relationship between knowledge and power within the Western tradition. Perniola intends to show how there has been a millennia-long relationship of mutual complicity, often implicit, between philosophy and the organization of culture. This relationship has been active throughout the very foundation of philosophy and can be traced until the advent of the so-called 'nihilistic-populist fulfilment' (*compimento nichilistico-populistico*) in the second half of the twentieth century. This populist-nihilism, Perniola claims, does not care about 'organizing culture' and has no aptitude for scientific and philosophical knowledge, recalling what Jean-Baptiste Coffinhal, Vice-President of the Revolutionary Tribunal, said against the chemist Antoine-Laurent Lavoisier, who was sentenced to death and executed in 1794: '*la Republique n'a pas besoin de savants*' ('the Republic has no need for scholars'). This 'nihilistic-populist fulfilment' is for Perniola an ideology that relegates culture to mere 'decoration' and reduces professions to 'gangs'. If the Western world is increasingly dominated by populism and nihilism, what can philosophy do? After developing his diagnosis, Perniola encounters Heidegger's thought on this very issue, albeit without naming him.

Before investigating this issue, it should be noted that Perniola, especially at the end of the 1970s and throughout the 1980s, constantly engaged with the German philosopher, from Heidegger's theory on the origins of the work of art to the critique of humanism (UAP), the idea of being-towards-death (RT: 129–57), truth and beauty (VB), the notion of *Gelassenheit* (CA: 116–21) and the relationship between reality and appearance (RT: 175–93). Several scholars have focused on these texts, emphasizing the ways in which Heidegger's thought was a constant reference point for Perniola (see, for instance, Marroni 1981, 1986; Burch 2002; Hevrøy 2013). Aldo Marroni, in particular, has shown how Perniola's reflections can also be considered to be evolving precisely *in opposition* to Heidegger's conceptual scheme (1986). Here, within this complex and sensitive discussion, I outline only one aspect of his understanding of Heidegger, which I believe is pivotal not only to distinguish Perniola's position from Heidegger's but also to elucidate the Italian philosopher's overall direction.

This aspect lies in Heidegger's post-*Kehre* return to 'Greek primordiality', which for Perniola represented a 'proto-logic', 'proto-historical' and 'proto-institutional' world view while the state of things actually requires one which is 'post-logical', 'post-historical' and 'post-institutional'. Here, Glenn Most's article on Heidegger's interpretation of the Greeks can help us to shed light on Perniola's critique of the German philosopher (although to my knowledge Perniola was not aware of Most's research). For Most, Heidegger believes that to have a 'view of everything that is wrong with the facticity of our lives in this modern, technological world, Freiburg must be saved from New York and Moscow, but by Athens, not by Jerusalem or Rome' (2002: 86). Heidegger's frequent denigration of Roman culture as mere mediation and betrayal of Greek philosophy places him in a well-established tradition of German philhellenism that idealizes Greek thought. Within Greek literature, he focuses not so much on full texts but rather on 'single, heavily charged substantives' (Most 2002: 89) to meditate on unspoken associations that set certain thinkers and poets (such as Homer, Pindar and Sophocles) as the representatives of an original and primordial thinking not yet ruined by Western metaphysics. This prompts an obvious question: what aspects of Greek thought are included? Then, what is excluded or left behind?

> Much of what is typically Greek Heidegger ignores or suppresses or explains away: there is no slavery in Heidegger's ancient Greece, no homosexuality, no heterosexuality, no athletics, no war, no wine, no song, no anger, no laughter, no fear, no superstition. Instead, Heidegger focuses on those elements of the ancient Greeks that anticipate the values he would like the Germans to adopt: reflectiveness, receptivity, love of nature, admiration for their great poets and thinkers, sensitivity to their language.
>
> Most 2002: 94

In so doing, Heidegger subtlety projects modern German concerns and values onto the archaic Greeks. Not only does he exclude all these areas and narrowly select what ideally suits his strategy, but in asserting the superiority of Greek thought, he also tacitly indulges in nostalgia for beginnings. In his rejection of traditional European humanism, the German philosopher tries to dislodge modernity by returning to an imagined origin, that is, towards presocratic Greek philosophy (especially Heraclitus and Parmenides). In contrast, Perniola, by exploring the notions of simulacrum and ritual without myth, draws the reader's attention away from the thought of 'origins' and nature and towards the thought of 'replicas' and artificiality:

> Not pre-classical Greece, but pre-classical Rome, which built the effectiveness of the ceremony, of the *ars* and of the *ius* on the ritual without myth; not the Protestant reform, but post-Renaissance Catholicism, which on the election of historical difference built the operation of consolation, the principle of greater glory and sovereign Baroque indifference; not the most genuine and secret Europe, but the most hybrid and most replicated one.
>
> DH: 79

Roman culture, for Perniola, shows that from what can be considered mere mediation, copy and betrayal can produce a whole new set of strategies, aesthetics and perspectives that inform not only philosophy but also religion, warfare, lifestyles and eroticism. This is, in my opinion, a fundamental passage that allows us not only to scrutinize the sources that animate Perniola's perspective within *Dopo Heidegger* but also, more generally, to unfold the key concepts of his philosophical trajectory that, from the early 1980s, go on to be fully deployed in the following decades.[6] For instance, the premise of *Del sentire cattolico*, published in 2001, should be traced back twenty years earlier, when Perniola in *Dopo Heidegger* configured his philosophy in opposition to Heidegger's. Meanwhile, the cultural strategy that Perniola calls 'neo-ancient' (*neo-antico*), developed in the early 1990s (see PNA, NVP and De Donato 1995), comprises precisely renewed attention to ancient cultural practices, such as Jesuit thought and Roman rituals, to create a bridge between them and contemporary phenomena and experiences.[7]

Perniola's interpretation of Heidegger also puts him at odds with what was happening in the Italian philosophical debate of the early 1980s, specifically Gianni Vattimo's theory of *weak thought*. It is worth saying a few words about it, not only to distinguish Vattimo's perspective from Perniola's but also because I believe that, to a certain extent, this *querelle* is still relevant to the issue of anti-intellectualism today. A collection edited by Vattimo and Pier Aldo Rovatti in 1983, titled *Weak Thought*, gathers several authors who explore and interpret the role and value of thinking in the contemporary Western world.

Vattimo tackles the issue of metaphysics and its relationship to nihilism, starting from an analysis of the works of Nietzsche, Heidegger and Gadamer. As Peter Carravetta puts it, Vattimo elaborates on the claim 'that philosophy has entered a final declining stage and, at least as we understood it during late modernity, that it cannot really answer, or not answer credibly, the questions which we put to it' (2012: 4). In what terms can thought be considered weak? Something is weak if there is something else which, by contrast, is considered stronger. Vattimo's position can be clarified through this quotation: 'There is no doubt that once the characteristics of being and truth are rethought in weak terms, philosophical thinking, or the thinking of being, can no longer vindicate the sovereignty that metaphysics attributed to it – mainly through ideological deception – in the sphere of politics and social praxis' (Vattimo 2012: 50). Vattimo claims that thinking should take a step back and withdraw its metaphysical and ideological claims over effectuality. He claims that the old metaphysical thought is 'strong', while post-metaphysical thought is 'weak'. Still, Perniola highlights that, if we follow Vattimo's claims to their end, we should not refer to metaphysical thought as 'strong' but as 'deceptive' or 'illusive', that is, as an ideology that has finally lost its grip on society and praxis. Therefore, the actual opposition lying at the core of Vattimo's weak thought, Perniola claims, is between the lesser or greater strength of philosophy and thinking. Perniola's concern moves in the opposite direction: not with the resignation of thought's hold over praxis, but with the attempt to identify the forms and relationships that still connect knowledge and power in a non-metaphysical way. Perniola claims that, ultimately, contemporary thought is not weaker than the ideological strength of metaphysics; rather, it is the latter that is weak and unable to re-establish the relationship between knowledge and power. We must therefore look for a new type of strength. Perniola here has in mind his ritual thinking theory as an exemplification of this strength:

> It is the strength of the Romans who never imposed their gods on the conquered populations but, on the contrary, created a temple and cult in Rome for the foreign gods; it is the strength of the Jesuit missions that respected the multiplicity of cults and cultures. Finally, it is the strength of those nations that are not afraid of losing their ancestral heritage in the improbable combinations operated by the mass media, because they know that their true heritage lies in the ability to transform such combinations into a syncretism endowed with their own intrinsic sociality and rationality.
>
> DH: 58

Perniola elaborates on Vattimo's weak thoughts on several occasions in articles and books, even publishing a philosophical letter addressed to Vattimo in the journal *Alfabeta*. An insightful conversation between the two, which to a certain extent develops their *querelle* on aesthetics, philosophy and weak thought, took place in 1990. Examining these sources, which span almost four decades, it appears clear that Perniola did not change his position on the topic.

Beyond this philosophical standpoint, a key aspect remains to be covered in this discussion. The theory of weak thought, Perniola claims, reveals the anti-intellectualism of Vattimo and the other authors who contributed to the volume. On this sensitive topic, Perniola's critique of Vattimo's theory is still relevant in today's global landscape. He argues that there is not a lot of difference between Vattimo's highly elaborated theory of weak thought and the populist hatred of knowledge. In other words, if the public and political are more and more devoid of critics, intellectuals and theorists today, it is also because theorists themselves stopped taking their work seriously and legitimized ignorance within politics. Through the idea of weak thought, Vattimo winks at political parties and frees them from the 'burden' of knowledge.

Ultimately, [Perniola writes,] weak thought was the real 'organic' book of the Italian intellectuals of the 1980s, not in the sense that it educated or advised the politicians of the time, but quite the contrary, because it started to free them from all conditioning ... making them realize that this was the general trend of society. Finally, a philosopher had come ... authorizing their inconsistency, their opportunism, their ignorance, which granted them the right to store Gramsci in the attic and let him gather dust ... And all this took place in the name of a new 'philosophy of history', according to which a new age defined as 'postmodern' was unfolding, when everything and its opposite could be said at the same time!

BR: 68

4

George Bryan Brummell: the Ritual Clothing

We now approach George Bryan Brummell, the first exemplar dandy I have selected to compare with Perniola's overall philosophy. Apart from serving the purpose of examining several core concepts of Perniola's thought, the previous three chapters were also meant to pave the way for the following pages devoted to Brummell. By reviewing Brummell's life and the anecdotes and sentences attributed to him, I will initially propose a definition of the phenomenon of dandyism, with the aim of demonstrating how the dandy lifestyle can be compared with the notions discussed so far in this book. Although often associated with foppery and a showy attitude, the dandies, I instead assert, actually cultivate a 'simulacral' and 'ritual' lifestyle that can be understood, by contrast, as an aesthetics of disappearance. There is no place for history, absoluteness and spontaneity in the framework of a dandy aesthetics; it is rather a life under the sign of irony, witticism, elegance and *storiette*.

Brummell's assault on fashion

Before identifying the connections between Perniola's philosophy and Brummell's lifestyle, a brief overview of the essential biographical information of the English dandy would be valuable. Therefore, the following pages will consist of a short introduction to the fundamental stages of Brummell's life to familiarize the reader with his historical context. Several biographies have been penned on Brummell (Barbey d'Aurevilly 1897; Jesse 1844; Kelly 2005; Comi 2008) and numerous volumes and chapters dedicated to his conception of dandyism (Moers 1960: 17–38; Coblence 1988: 33–168; Carassus 1971: 191–200; Natta 2011: 25–63). Given the large amount of information available on his life, only the most essential will be provided here; subsequently, the conceptual significance of his lifestyle will be my focal point.

George Bryan Brummell was born in London on 7 June 1778 and died in Caen on 30 March 1840. Ian Kelly, one of his most recent biographers, divides his life into three distinct periods. The first period ranges from his birth until 1799 and consists of Brummell's 'ascendancy'. The year 1799, when Brummell purchased his London house, marks the beginning of the period during which his fame and influence spread throughout the high society of the time. The last period (1816 onwards) sees Brummell, pursued by debts, fleeing to France. He first moved to Calais, where he remained for fourteen years, and then to Caen, where he spent the last ten years of his life, dying in 1840 in asylum.

Brummell's father, William Brummell, Private Secretary of the Prime Minister Lord North, was an influential civil servant who could afford his son's fees to attend the prestigious colleges of Eton (1786–93) and Oxford (1793–4). Brummell's reputation in the fashion and clothing industries soared precisely in these years, and he also caught the eye of the Prince of Wales and the future king of the United Kingdom, George IV. According to Moers (1960: 25), the heir to the throne noticed Brummell during one of his royal visits of inspection to Eton. Brummell never completed his education at either Eton or Oxford; leaving the latter aged sixteen. Soon after, he was commissioned in the Tenth Royal Hussars Regiment, a cavalry regiment of the British Army known as the Prince of Wales's Own Command. Initially a cornet, the third and lowest grade of the cavalry troops, Brummell became captain within three years. This rapid rise was not only attributed on the basis of his skills but also to his growing friendship with the Prince, who was colonel-in-chief. The depth of their bond can be evidenced, for instance, in Brummell's selection as the *chevalier d'honneur* at the Prince's wedding to Carolina of Brunswick in 1795. He also accompanied the royal couple on their honeymoon to Windsor.

The year 1799 marks Brummell's 'assault' – as Kelly defined it (2005: 157) – on London society. Significantly, by his coming-of-age, one-third of the family estate was released to him, with the other two-thirds being passed to his brother and his sister.[1] Owing to his inheritance and the Prince's support, he gained economic stability (additionally, being one of the Prince's favourites, no one dared to ask Brummell for his accounts). Moreover, the Prince introduced him to the most exclusive clubs and fashion events in London at the time. In those high society gatherings, his prestige became such that a word, a sign or even an absence from him was enough to mark somebody's reputation for years to come. The complicity and intimacy between Brummell and the Prince are further evidenced by the fact that the latter often attended the various dressing stages of his friend – which could take up to three hours – and then stayed on most occasions to lunch. The apex of the 'Brummellian' domination of high society lasted thirteen years, from 1798 until 1811. Between 1811 and 1816, the relationship between Brummell and the Prince deteriorated. Several stories account for this fissure: Brummell might have ordered the Prince to ring the bell during a dinner (a highly impudent request), or he had commented too often on the increasing corpulence of the Prince, or he might have aroused antagonisms between the Prince and his wife (Moers 1960: 26). In addition to such episodes, in 1811, the Prince became Regent. As a consequence of greater duties and responsibilities, many intimacies had to be abandoned. However, Brummell managed to transform this loss into triumph. His impertinence, in fact, became legendary and contributed to him becoming on a par with the Prince rather than a subordinate:

> The Prince came down the street one day in company with Lord A., and met Brummell and Lord B. strolling in the opposite direction. The Prince stopped to chat with Lord B., ignoring Brummell; the Beau [Brummell], who had taught a whole generation how to cut, turned to Lord A. and inquired loudly, 'Who's your fat friend?'
>
> The other impertinence was merely a phrase. 'I made him what he is,' Brummell would say of the Prince Regent, 'and I can unmake him'.
>
> Moers 1960: 27–8

However, by 1811, without the Prince's protection, Brummell had to endure increasingly pressing debts as well as the loss of his sources of entertainment and commercial credit. Forsaking the fashion-oriented clubs, he progressively became addicted to gambling until, on 16 May 1816, he was forced to flee to Calais in France. There, he received letters, visits and financial help from his closest English friends, making him 'one of the notable tourist attractions of the Continent' (Moers 1960: 29). Still, Brummell's scholars and biographers (Moers 1960; Comi 2008; Coblence 1988; Kelly 2005) agree to mark 1816 as the end of the dandy legend and the beginning of the dandy decline. In 1830, he moved to Caen, where he was appointed English Consul. Despite the move, his affairs and luck soon plummeted. In 1835, at the behest of some of his creditors, the police put him in prison. From there on, 'he lost, one by one, the qualities that had made him a dandy' (Moers 1960: 30). In his final years, Brummell suffered several strokes and became prematurely senile. He became increasingly incapacitated and was eventually looked after by the Sisters of Charity. He spent his final days in a sanatorium near Caen, where he died on the 30 March 1840. Kelly's volume (2005) offers a significant amount of detailed information on Brummell's last twenty-four years in France. For the purposes of this book, the following sub-chapters will explore especially the second period (1798–1811), that is, the one that witnessed Brummell's ascent in London's high society. Lord Byron, who was his acquaintance and one of his devotees, once said that he would have more liked to be Brummell than Napoleon (Barbey 1897: 28). By focusing on the high point of Brummell's parabola, this book will argue its significant affinity with Perniola's thought.

Sprezzatura, je ne sais quoi, subtlety

Why have writers, poets and politicians attributed their admiration, esteem and devotion to Brummell? What lies beyond the renewal of high society's fashion habits in the first decade of nineteenth-century London? To answer these questions, it is necessary to first elaborate on the concept of dandyism. Many interpreters have defined the concept, going back to its uncertain semantic and etymological origins (such as Coblence 1988: 14; Kelly 2005: 2–5). In this genealogical path, it emerged that the term 'dandy' was first used as an insult related to exaggerated affectation and foppery in clothing. Only later did the term acquire the trait of a phenomenon worthy of theoretical, literary and philosophical attention. One of the first essayists and writers to use it in a non-derogative manner was Jules-Amédée Barbey d'Aurevilly, who, in his essay *Du Dandysme et de G. Brummell* (written in 1845), develops the phenomenon of dandyism from literary and theoretical points of view, choosing Brummell as the archetypal and uncontested master of the phenomenon. It is necessary to set aside, Barbey argues, the commonplace perception that considers Brummell, and dandyism in general, as a sole matter of hygiene and exterior elegance. Brummell's clothes, in fact, were actually simple if not austere. He used to wear a white shirt with a finely arranged neckcloth of the only colour accepted in those years: *blanc d'innocence virginal* ('white of virginal innocence'). Over the shirt, he donned a pale or white waistcoat. Under the waistcoat, he also regularly used suspenders, which were not so common in the wardrobes of the previous generations of gentlemen. He wore tight pantaloons made of leather or soft stocking fabric in the morning and breeches fashioned out of black silk jersey in the evenings. A deep blue jacket and black Hessian boots completed the outfit. Brummell, to sum up, did not favour showy or colourful looks. His palette was sober, monochrome, 'revolutionary primarily in its simplicity' (Kelly 2005: 174) and everything was individually sewn, from buttons to loops to buttonholes. The 'chaotic history of male costume', as Max Beerbohm argues, came to a close 'when Mr. Brummell, at his mirror, conceived the notion of trousers and simple coats' (quoted in Moers 1960: 33). Brummell used to spend up to three hours each morning on his appearance, which also included cleaning himself and shaving carefully. It did not involve, however, the use of any salves or perfumes, as he proudly used to claim, 'no perfumes, but very fine linen, plenty of it, and country washing' (quoted in Jesse 1844: 16). Of course, the meticulous focus on the folds of the fabric, the perfectly knotted tie, the nuances produced by the combination of certain colours and so forth is an essential part of the dandy's character. However, as Barbey wrote, 'It is not a suit of clothes walking about by itself! On the contrary, it is the particular way of wearing these clothes which constitutes dandyism. One may be a dandy in creased clothes' (1897: 18). A shirt, for instance, should not necessarily be perfectly smooth and immaculate. In fact, Barbey quotes, as an example of the dandy attitude, those gentlemen who tore their clothes before wearing them, to make them lighter and closer to a 'cloud'.

The English dandy described by Barbey appears as a combination of the aesthetic lifestyle and simplicity in clothing. Brummell's subtlety could indeed be appreciated only by expert eyes, being too small and minute, if not insignificant, to most. The dandy's attitude is closely related to the Italian notion of *sprezzatura*, that is, a sort of nonchalance in making one's efforts disappear by exhibiting a relaxed outlook. Commitment, awareness and concerns about getting dressed should not be evident. Although Brummell, as Barbey notes, used to devote hours to his laborious toilette, he forgot all the time spent once he was dressed. In other words, no vanity in showing the efforts accomplished was visible in his attitude. He wanted to disguise as spontaneous and harmonious what was actually the result of a long and tremendously complex endeavour. Thus, Brummell applies this zeal to obtain, paradoxically, the presence of an absence. As Brummell's biographer Ivano Comi writes, 'His presence was felt through absence; he built himself erasing the traces of his own passage' (2008: 38–9). In other words, Brummell wanted his efforts to disappear because, for him, it was vulgar to strive for the observer's attention at all costs. His precept, quoted by Barbey, states it clearly, 'To be well dressed, you must not be noticed' (1897: 68). Brummell thus suppressed excesses in clothing and invested in the small details, in the *je ne sais quoi,* which lends a fold that is at first glance insignificant an ineffable and charming quality. His style prominently impacted the fashion-conscious London of those years. The Prince of Wales became one of the first devotes (and used to imitate Brummell's clothing). The Prince was followed by several other aristocratic families, such as the Bucks, the Beaux, the Pinks and so forth, and 'in this revival of London's fashion, Brummell was easily cast as a priest and prophet' (Kelly 2005: 176).

What stands out from these introductory remarks is the fact that Brummell's efforts were focused on his exteriority. Brummell's aesthetically oriented his life following the surfaces of his fabric, silk, linen and leather. Philosophically, his life revolved around the concept of 'form'. This notion needs to be clarified in order to understand which specific typology of form permeates the dandy attitude. The dandy form does not refer to the intelligible and super-sensible form (*eîdos* or, in Latin, *species*) or to the sensitive form (*morphé*; *forma* in Latin) but, as Perniola points out in relation to Roman rituality, to the form as *habitus*. According to Perniola, *habitus* holds an alternative and lateral meaning, avoiding falling under the dichotomy between an exclusively phenomenal form and a form that extends beyond the senses. The notion of *habitus* carries a broader semantic significance and 'refers us precisely to the idea of an external form ... attributed to attitudes, clothing, modes of behaviour, dance forms, government, lifestyle, rhetorical figures, and to grammatical, geometrical, astronomical forms' (CA: 44). In the previous section, Perniola's conception of ritual without myth was developed following Roman religiosity and the Jesuit-Baroque tradition. This concept implies a prioritization of the *formal* aspects of the ritual (with its orthopraxy and manners) over the *material* ones, that is, over the myth (orthodoxy and morals). Brummell occupies the same anti-metaphysical path traced by Perniola, as he discusses the concept of form: through his everyday *clothing ritual*, Brummell seeks neither an ideal form (*eîdos*) nor an earthly one (*morphé*). He does not try to imitate an eternal and harmonious idea of manly masculinity and, parallelly, he does not reduce clothing to merely a utility (namely, keeping the body warm and sheltered from the elements). Brummell thus deals precisely with the form as *habitus*, a form that does not go beyond exteriority – being grounded in appearances and manners – and which, however, does not end in an empty formalism (a mere shell capable of containing anything indifferently).

Neither aristocracy nor the bourgeoisie

This book has previously developed Perniola's conception of ritual without myth in the ancient Roman religion. To review it briefly, the Romans emphasized the ritual aspect of their cults over its mythology. In their practices, the myth was discarded while the performance had to be undertaken with formal accuracy. Additionally, the ritual had to be practiced with temperance and self-control. This happened for a central reason: if the ritual subject was invested too deeply in the ritual, their emotional outburst could have implied the possibility of performing the ritual in a hasty and inaccurate manner. The result would have been an excess of superstition and vital subjectivity. Two aspects of this ritual typology find a parallel in Brummell's lifestyle: the respect for a form without *belief* and the disappearance of subjectivity. This sub-chapter will deal with the first aspect, whereas the following one is dedicated to the second.

To understand the terms in which Brummell practiced a form without belief, that is, without ideologies or mythologies, a concise historical framework would be useful to situate him in the context of those decades (the last decade of the eighteenth century and the first decades of the nineteenth). The background in which Brummell was active is inseparable from the decline of aristocratic ideals and values. He was a part of that 'uneasy atmosphere of shifting values that followed the French Revolution' (Moers 1960: 17), which unsettled both the monarchy and the aristocracy. Brummell privileged neither the falling aristocracy nor the new bourgeois class. Though he took part in high society events and gatherings, his impertinent and individualistic behaviour set him apart from aristocrats. Aristocratic society implied roles that were challenged by his almost disruptive manners (as elaborated later). At the same time, it is true that he was against the bourgeoisie, and yet, as Kelly points out, his clothing was 'quiet, reasonable and beautiful: free from folly or affection, yet susceptible to exquisite ordering. It appeared post-revolutionary, neo-classical, ordered and enlightened and in this it did indeed seem democratic' (2005: 177–8). In other words, Brummell's clothing was not foppish or showy; it could instead suit a large variety of classes and occupations.

Productivity, progress, utility, work and egalitarianism were among the most important key ideas of the nascent bourgeoisie. Brummell was at odds with each of them: as Émilien Carassus writes, 'among the social integrations – or alienation – that of the work inspires an unparalleled horror. He [the dandy] rejects the curse that God did weigh on the descendants of Adam, imposing them to earn bread by the sweat of their brow' (1971: 75). Instead of a productive working day, Brummell's everyday life was permeated by its opposite: a rigorous and disciplined cult of futility. The myth that progress privileges a proteiform mass of individuals oriented towards productiveness and utility; contrarily, Brummell – if judged by the bourgeois mindset – was an unproductive and useless individual, for he spent most of his lifetime taking care of superfluity: namely, his appearance.

To sum up, Brummell did not express allegiance to any ideals of his era: neither nostalgia for the lost power of the aristocracy nor a receptivity towards the ideals of the rising bourgeoisie. He resorted neither to the fallen myths and symbols nor the newly conceived ones; furthermore, he did not follow any topicality, namely the trivialization of everyday life into its bourgeois stereotypes. Instead, Brummell grounded his existence on the ritual element, specifically the clothing ritual.

Romantic history vs dandy *storietta*

To highlight the peculiarity of Brummell's subjectivity, it is useful to differentiate his attitude from that of another figure that emerged in Europe during the first half of the nineteenth century, the Romantic. Both Brummell and the Romantics were part of the same historical European context and shared a resentment of the dominant conception of the world. However, the two differed in their conception of the absolute; for the Romantics, history and nature emerge as the absolute (Carassus 1990). Contrariwise, Brummell behaved as if there were no ultimate truths to be reached or any absolute to orient oneself towards; his attitude was not permeated by any Romantic concept such as *Sehnsucht* (translatable as 'longing'/'craving') or *Streben* ('to strive' [for the absolute]). The Romantics tried to compensate for the boredom and disenchantment they felt 'by exalting the self, by recurring to nature, by expanding to the forces of the universe with a certain confidence in the progressive march of humanity' (Carassus 1990: 32). Brummell, on the other hand, lived as if he was not at all interested in any absolute, be it nature or history.

The Romantic conception of history is marked by the notion of titanism, alluding to the mythic war between the Titans and the Olympic gods. The Romantic movement *Sturm und Drang* borrowed the term to express an attitude of spiritual and material rebellion against an overwhelming power (be it destiny, God or natural forces). Thus, history is perceived by the Romantics as the theatre in which all these uncontrollable, gigantic and irresistible forces occur. The Romantic individual, despite occupying a disadvantaged position, can still behave as a Titan by heroically challenging these forces.

However, Brummell does not conceive of history as the realm of heroic actions or events. His attitude is at odds with that of the Romantics: it is not the magnificent, the enormous or the sublime that interests him. He instead lingers over the infinitesimal details of the fabric and focuses his witty remarks on trivial occurrences. To provide some examples of ironic anecdotes, he was once asked by a lady if he had ever eaten vegetables. His answer was, 'Madam, I once ate a pea' (Moers 1960: 21). His jibe at another gentleman has also become famous: 'Do you call that *thing* a coat?' (emphasis in original). In many cases, Brummell did not even use words. It was enough for him to raise his eyebrows or to cast a certain glance. As William Hazlitt wrote, Brummell 'has arrived at the very *minimum* of wit, and reduced it, "by happiness or pains", to an almost invisible point' (quoted in Moers 1960: 20). The wit allowed Brummell to triumph in an elegant, cold and ironic way in ordinary situations. His witty anecdotes and aesthetical lifestyle, I claim, share a relevant affinity with Perniola's understanding of history as the realm of difference and with the *storiette* (TBA). As I established earlier, the *storiette* can be understood as short stories permeated by irony and aesthetic detachment. Coblence refers to this attitude, affirming that Brummell has no last chapter and no history, as for him, 'history is nothing but a tasteless novel, or even a pure nothing' (1988: 152). The non-substantiality of the self is here configured by adopting an indifferent perspective to the historical events of the world. Specifically, Brummell's detached attitude is attained by plunging into the neutral sphere of artificiality and clothing. From the daily clothing ritual to the impertinence of his ironic remarks, Brummell does not expose himself as a subject in the etymological sense of the term *sub-jectum* (literally, 'what it thrown under', 'what lies under'). Instead, he devotes his efforts to his appearances precisely because he believes that he does not need an identity, a subjectivity, a *ubi consistam*: only a subject who wants to emerge, who strives to fulfil their desires, needs an identity and, with it, a subjectivity. Brummell behaves as if his subjectivity lacks substantial content, that is, those features that make a subject recognizable in terms of identity, desires, pulses and beliefs. In this regard, it can be argued that his is an *epochistic subjectivity*, for Brummell puts into brackets, so to speak, both his identity and the objects of his experience through a neutral and ritualistic attitude.

> Notable is the tale of Brummell asking his valet Robinson about his [Brummell's] favourite lake:
> 'Robinson.'
> 'Sir.'
> 'Which of the lakes do I admire?'
> 'Windermere, sir', replied that distinguished individual.
> 'Ah, yes, –Windermere', repeated Brummell, 'so it is, – Windermere.'
> Jesse 1844: 118

As Coblence notes, not only does this anecdote denote an outright opposition to the Romantic spirit (it would be hilarious imagining, for instance, Wordsworth referring in this way to a natural landscape) but, in addition, it also reveals how the valet 'represents in a certain sense the guarantee of the permanence of the dandy's subject, the depositary of the information, choices or preferences to which the dandy might be obliged by his mundane life in spite of his fundamental apathy' (Coblence 1988: 154). Even more significantly, 'The valet allows Brummell to expose himself as an empty consciousness, without interiority: he is responsible, when the dandy deems it amusing or appropriate, to play the role of the other's consciousness, which is presented with the detached humour of the dandy, as if it were something placed next to him' (1988: 156). These occurrences show how the dandy behaved as if he did not have a consistent self, devoid of memory and consciousness, which was in turn 'guaranteed' by his valet's comments and remarks. Another telling anecdote is the following: 'A friend one day called upon him, and found him confined to his room from a lameness in one foot, upon which he expressed his concern at the accident. "I am sorry for it too," answered Brummell very gravely, "particularly as it's my favourite leg!"' (Hazlitt 1934: 152). The quip is suggestive, as if referring to a 'dissociated body' composed of fragments and parts held together by threads and fabrics that cover it but which, in any case, lacks subjective content. This attitude can also be linked to Perniola's ritual without the myth. In fact, as Robert R. Shane points out, 'It is significant that Perniola says these things and models of behaviour [i.e. the rituals] "asked to be worn, brought to life and repeated". In other words, they called for a witness, for someone to bear witness to them. One cannot witness for oneself' (2004: digital source). Indeed, Brummell cultivates a lifestyle in order to suspend his subjectivity, to make it disappear and to suspend his *human* side.

Dandyism and the simulacrum of death

In what way is Brummell close to the existential detachment typical of Stoic and Jesuit thought? In what sense is it possible to argue that Brummell abolishes death by living like a corpse, following the Ignatian motto *perinde ac cadaver*? Perniola argued that the Jesuit tradition has to be considered an alternative way of approaching death, which does not fall under metaphysics. Instead of denying death, this approach introduces it into everyday life via a practice of simulation. Perniola's research on the simulacrum of death meets dandyism precisely at this point. In fact, the exercise and the daily simulation of death correspond to Brummell's ritualistic dressing, considered in this book as a ritual in which subjectivity disappears in the artificial realm of clothes. Brummell's clothes are not a second skin or an envelope, containing a subjectivity or a body with its natural necessities. Clothes are neither an extension nor symbols indicative of

Brummell's personality. Contrarily, they situate Brummell in his constitutive *becoming thing*. In other words, Brummell invests his efforts into deconstructing himself, in vaporizing his own subjectivity and consciousness. Through the clothing ritual, he performs an epochistic reduction of his beliefs and starts functioning as an object or a mechanism. In this process, he approaches the Ignatian simulacrum of death by transforming himself into a corpse in front of his mirror. Perniola condensed the Ignatian *Spiritual Exercises* by considering them as 'the election of the difference'. Election implies acceptance and affirmation of one's own present but not through a vitalistic approach, that is to say, not oriented to the satisfaction of individual desires and impulses. In the same way, Brummell attempts to free himself from physical and natural laws, from desires and needs. He dehumanizes himself and assumes an inert character, emptied from any identity or interiority. As Coblence contends, he becomes a puppet:

> The superiority of the puppet comes from the simplicity of the mechanism moving it ... The puppet is only subjected to the law of heaviness – and yet it is infinitely lighter than a human being. It is not disturbed by any disorder of consciousness, by any movement of reflection.
>
> 1988: 153

Although 'puppet' and 'corpse' are two different entities, they share a crucial aspect, namely they imply an exchange between the inert and the vital, the organic and the inorganic. For if the puppet is an inanimate object that mimics the living and the characteristics of living beings (such as movement and verbal and non-verbal communication), Loyola's motto 'to live as a corpse' should be understood as a devitalization of one's own body and subjectivity. In this context, therefore, both the puppet and the corpse can be compared to the dandy's lifestyle because they carry a transient status between life and death. In this vaporization of subjectivity, only Brummell's simulacrum reflected in the mirror anchors the English dandy to his existence.[2] The concept of simulacrum implies 'something that imitates another'. Perniola, as I stated earlier, departs from those aesthetic traditions that consider this type of imitation negatively, namely as falsehood or deception and praises several alternative traditions (especially Roman religion and Jesuit thought) that positively adhere to the simulacrum. As outlined in the previous sections, Brummell follows this alternative approach by literally living in a simulacral dimension through his dandy lifestyle.

Perniola also argued that one of the primary aspects of ritual without myth is that the ritual subjects – to observe the performance with accuracy – should control themselves by suppressing their subjective drives and desires. According to Barbey, the 'detached' and 'cold' lifestyle of Brummell echoes a fundamental Machiavellian precept: 'the world belongs to the cool of head' (Barbey 1897: 50). Coldness is connected to the ability to control one's own passions and emotions. As for Machiavellian coldness, here emerges an extremely aesthetic aspect of Stoicism that is based on the Latin motto *nihil admirari* ('let nothing astonish you'). Strong passion, excessive admiration and uncontrolled wonder for something imply, for Brummell, an inconstant, imprecise, exalted and vulgar subjectivity. Evoking the ritual without myth of the Roman religion is useful at this stage since the risk linked to an outburst of individual subjectivity could transform the proper religious ritual into a superstition. The dandy then becomes the herald of this peculiar form of serenity in the midst of modern agitation. The hours spent on personal toilette and clothing also carried this goal, serving as rituals against productivity. Thus, in a historical context in which utility and accumulation of capital are pivotal, Brummell grounded his life on a clothing ritual. Through his daily performance, he therefore expressed a political position of rebellion against the status quo.

Exploring the dandy with a suspended subjectivity, we are also approaching another key conceptual figure elaborated by Perniola, namely the so-called 'thing that feels', emerging from his book *The Sex Appeal of the Inorganic*. Part Two of this volume mainly revolves around this seminal work by Perniola, which is defined by Max Ryynänen as 'one of the key books theorizing our drift from humanist body metaphysics' (2017: 192).

Part Two

5

What Is It Like to Be a Thing?

A first conclusion can be drawn from Part One of the this book: Perniola is fascinated by the paradoxical copresence of seemingly opposed activities and attitudes, such as indifference/sensitivity, detachment/interest, suspension/participation and *epoché*/effectiveness. Perniola's philosophical perspective can be understood as an effort to think through and explore the role and value of these oppositions. This chapter examines several of these, starting with the uncanny union of thingness and feeling in *The Sex Appeal of the Inorganic* – Perniola's most translated book and one of his most misunderstood.

The Sex Appeal of the Inorganic is written in a non-academic, almost pornographic prose that intertwines heterogeneous cultural phenomena and schools of thought. However, the title might also lead the reader astray. The connection between artificiality and sexual attraction is not presented to emphasize the seductive aspect of commodities in terms of reification and alienation. To clarify its meaning, it is valuable to provide the passage from which the book title was borrowed:

> Fashion stands in opposition to the organic. It couples the living body to the inorganic world. To the living, it defends the rights of the corpse. The fetishism that succumbs to the sex appeal of the inorganic is its vital nerve.
>
> Benjamin 2002: 8

This passage condenses at least three core ideas that not only resonate with the dandy lifestyle but that have influenced Perniola's standpoint: the privilege of fashion and artificiality against nature; the osmosis between what is organic and inorganic; and the link between a neutral theory of sexuality and perversions. I will explore these topics here and in the following chapters.

In his *Arcades Project,* Walter Benjamin elaborates on the idea of an alliance between body and clothing, which lies at the foundation of Perniola's book: 'the body experienced by neutral sexuality is not a machine, but clothing' (SAI: 11, also see BCN, QC, USS). Perniola develops the experiential territories opened up by bringing together of artificiality, sexuality, perversions (such as fetishism) and the realm of philosophy. On the one hand the book focuses on Benjamin, Descartes, Kant, Hegel, Heidegger and Wittgenstein and, on the other hand, on fetishism, masochism, vampirism, radical fashion, cybersex, performances and plastic landscapes. For Perniola, inorganic sexuality is first and foremost an experimental feeling that unites the abstraction typical of philosophy and excitement linked to sexuality. It can be understood as a broad erotic category in which human subjectivity is left behind to enter into the suspended realm of artificiality and thingness. Thus, it would be very simplistic to consider it merely as an epiphenomenon of the hegemonic role assumed by technology in our world. Although Perniola claims that this type of feeling is fully manifesting itself today, he traces its presence in different cultures and civilizations over time.

Our relationship with things[1]

At first, *The Sex Appeal of the Inorganic* might seem to be made up of heterogeneous material of the most disparate topics, but if we look closely at the structure of the table of contents, an initial understanding of Perniola's project emerges. Divided into twenty-seven short chapters, the book follows a sequential pattern in which the three main theoretical guidelines are alternated in the same order and which is repeated nine times: philosophy (chapters 1–4–7–10 and so on); sexuality (2–5–8–11 …); and contemporary phenomena (3–6–9–12 …). This structure displays a recurrent objective of Perniola's thinking, one apparent in the coexistence of opposites. For instance, Kant's thought, masochism and music are brought closer in the book precisely because Perniola's goal is to show the subterranean and intimate link between philosophy, perversion and the contemporary world. The idea of the sex appeal of the inorganic is pivotal to Perniola's entire philosophy because it involves a cluster of notions such as 'thingness', 'neutral', 'transit', 'queerness', 'specularism' and 'radiation', which are paramount to his thought.

Let us start with the notion of the 'thing'. The *Oxford Dictionary of English* defines the thing as 'an inanimate material object as distinct from a sentient being' (2010: digital source). According to this definition, tools, weapons, works of art and artefacts – for instance – all fall within the inanimate realm of things (as opposed to the biological realm of animals and plants). In addition, the dictionary uses the term 'object' as a synonym of 'thing'. Interestingly, the dictionary defines the object as a 'material thing that can be seen and touched'. Therefore, the two terms appear to be interchangeable. In our everyday lives, we indeed tend to use 'thing' and 'object' interchangeably. For example, we would not find it baffling to describe a hammer (or a ring, an amplifier, a television just to mention a few) either as a thing or object; at the same time, we would be at ease hearing someone say, 'I am not a thing/object, not a work of art to be cherished, I am a person'. In everyday life, not only are the words 'thing' and 'object' understood as interchangeable, but they are also 'debasing' terms. An individual designated as a 'thing' – as I suggested in the example – perceives this remark as an insult.

One of the most enduring claims about the nature of things and objects was elaborated on by René Descartes. His standpoint on the relationship between things and objects – as Paolo Bartoloni points out – has had a tremendous influence on both scientific and philosophical Western thought (2016: 41). According to Descartes, Bartoloni continues, 'The relation between subject and object institutes an active agency (the subject) and a passive receiver (the object), to the extent of rendering the notion of relation null by reducing relation to possession' (2016: 42). In other words, the world for Descartes can be divided into subjects and objects: subjects analyse, while objects are analysed; subjects produce, while objects are produced; and subjects possess, while objects are possessed. Ultimately, Descartes' position conveys the idea that the world of things is owned by humans for their aims. In so doing, the Cartesian position is fundamentally anthropocentric. Things and objects would merely be instrumental entities in the service of human beings: a knife is useful in so far as it serves its purpose of – for instance – cutting bread; an optical microscope is only helpful if it helps the scientist in seeing small objects invisible to the naked eye. Descartes' view does not account only for human relationships with inert entities. The essential condition of things and objects as tools and instruments can be extended to the ways in which humans today *use* forests, wild animals and minerals as pure means to their ends. Scholars such as Timothy Morton (2010, 2013), Bruno Latour (2005), Roger Callon (1986), Hiroshi Yoshioka (2019) and Massimo Di Felice (2017, 2020) have elaborated on new theoretical frameworks in which the interactions between humans and nonhuman entities are reshaped and rethought, here in opposition to the enduring Cartesian model. Throughout the twentieth century, several philosophers (such as Benjamin 2002; Heidegger 1967; Sartre 1978) who were dissatisfied with traditional Western approaches to the world of things provided their own peculiar perspectives on the issue of 'thingness'. More recently, other thinkers (specifically Brown 2001; Harman 2002, 2011; Meillassoux 2008) have rekindled attention on thing theory within the so-called object-oriented ontology (OOO) school of thought.

Drawing from Heidegger's dissatisfaction with the metaphysic understanding of things and objects as mere instrumental entities dependent upon humans, 'Object-oriented ontology invites us to consider a philosophical shift away from relation and correlation and fluxes and encounters. The effort should be directed instead to the thing as such and to the thing's "reality"' (Bartoloni 2016: 44). In other words, one of the main challenges of the OOO's theoretical framework consists of exploring and rethinking about the significance of things in and of themselves, in their autonomy and suchness.

Perniola has conducted a significant number of studies on thingness, which are disseminated in his books and articles (specifically DI, E: 22–58, DH: 75–7, SAI, SAIC, T: 217–28). Perniola, much like with the OOO school (although writing in the late 1970s and early 1980s), starts from Heidegger's distinction between *das Ding* ('the thing') and *die Sache* ('the object') (T: 223–9). For Heidegger, *die Sache* corresponds to the 'represented object' or, to borrow Bartoloni's words, 'the result of a process of representational transformation of *das Ding*' (2016: 46). Therefore, *das Ding* would enter the conceptual realm of *die Sache* every time the symbolic spell of language is cast on it. On the one hand, the thing is as such (*das Ding*), and on the other hand, the thing is transformed into an object of representation (*die Sache*). Perniola, as Bartoloni points out in another essay (2011), maintains this distinction between things and objects. Bartoloni already provides a clue to this by entitling a section of his essay 'Things and Objects: Mario Perniola' (2011: 154), underlining that the two concepts should not be merged and taken as one. The object, in this usage, is the thing 'implacably transformed into an object of consumption' (Bartoloni 2011: 158). 'Objectification' is thus understood as a perversion of the thing which gets spectacularized 'in the context of a society of emotions' (2011: 158). In other words, objects not only fall under the category of usability and presence at hand (Heidegger's *Vorhandenheit*), but at the same time, they are symbolic representations (in this case, of the triumph of global consumerism and fetishism).

Perniola stresses that history shows that 'things' have not just been understood merely as commodities or instrumental entities. In other words, the individual has always had a mutual relationship with things, one that goes beyond fetishistic consumption or simple usability. Therefore, Perniola is at odds with the Marxist perspective, which inscribes things in the broader context of alienation and reification. Perniola does not propose a critique of what could be seen as an extreme stage of contemporary reification. For instance, his perspective departs from Debord's theory. The first thesis of Debord's celebrated book *The Society of the Spectacle*, written in 1967, states that 'In societies dominated by modern conditions of production, life is presented as an immense accumulation of *spectacles*. Everything that was directly lived has receded into a representation' (2005: 7). According to Debord, spectacle is the force that separates individuals by reducing them into social atoms – i.e. masses of isolated individuals – living a passive life. The means of mass communication, cinema, private property and the general world of consumerism are all factors that, for Debord, increase the isolation of the individual. The individual is, in fact, only left with the pseudo-freedoms of choosing *new things* to buy, to update and to get rid of.[2] For Debord, objects are the opposite of life. This appears to be the case for two main reasons: the spectacle isolates the individual by filling their life with a disproportional number of things, and these things transform 'what was once lived' (Debord here means lived actively, genuinely and in the first person) into an abstraction, namely a general passivity wherein actions are pseudo-actions because they are produced and controlled by the overwhelming system of the spectacle. In other words, if individuals act within the framework of the thing, their lives cannot but be alienated and dominated by a constant reification. Although aware of the Situationist critique of late capitalist society, Perniola does not share this perspective. What Debord considers as historical reification – or passive contemplation of one's own life by the means of consuming ever-outdated things – is actually the re-emergence of an ancient experience that has always been part of the human–world relationship and that would only be partially considered if the research categories taken into account were those of alienation, reification, and commodification. The Marxist critique, in other words, mystifies the thing. It remains anchored to metaphysical moralism, for which the human has a dignity superior to the thing. In so doing, the Marxist critique of alienation meets Cartesian anthropocentrism. Although these two traditions of thought depart from incompatible premises and reach divergent conclusions, they both share the assumption that subjects (humans) are superior to objects (nonhuman entities), and that objects are ultimately inferior.

Neutral dimensions, vibrating stones

In his autobiography, published posthumously, Perniola asserts that the idea of a neutral feeling, central to his theory of the inorganic, originated from an experience he had one day in Milan on a cold February day of 1990. He was in Piazza del Duomo with his partner and decided to take a photo of her near the cathedral: 'the day was splendid and everything was colored gold, also her fur, so that the cathedral, the fur and her were only one thing. All of this – and her eyes – were not inert, but vibrating of an extreme psychic energy, which created a sort of living mechanics incredibly more intense that natural life' (TCE: 283). Like Giorgio de Chirico, who had an experience of heightened sensitivity that shaped his following metaphysical paintings (but in Piazza Santa Croce in Florence), Perniola started to work on his *The Sex Appeal of the Inorganic* precisely after this event, for which things appeared to him in an unprecedented, enigmatic way.

For this reason, to better understand what the sex appeal of the inorganic is, it is useful to highlight a series of recurrent terms and notions that emerge from the book and from the literature Perniola published during those years: the neutral, the external, the uncanny and the transit.

The neutral is defined by Perniola as a 'process of reciprocal osmosis ... between man and things' (E: 44). That is, it is a process whereby things acquire qualities inherent to organisms (such as sensitivity and animation) and vice versa: human beings enter into an inorganic realm in which subjectivity disappears, leaving room for an impersonal feeling. The earliest evidence of the neutral experience is detected by Perniola in the Palaeolithic art sites in the Côa Valley in Portugal. These rock sites contain thousands of engravings – dated between 20,000 and 11,000 years BCE – depicting humans, animals including horses and cattle, abstract, zoomorphic and anthropomorphic figures. Apart from the rarity of these engravings, which were incised, carved or etched on rocks in the open – unlike most Palaeolithic engravings, which are usually found inside caves – Perniola's attention is drawn to some of the drawings' features. He tries to provide an alternative reading with respect to two major trends of rock art theory: the 'hunting magic' hypothesis (Heizer and Baumoff 1976; Breuil 1952) and the 'neuropsychological model' (Lewis-Williams 2006; Whitley 2007). According to the first theory, prehistoric drawings would have had a magical function, one where the painters would draw the art to ensure a good hunt; the second interprets rock art by linking petroglyphs and pictograms to the altered states of consciousness (ASC) of the shamans. The drawings would then be recordings of the visions and images perceived in the ASC. Perniola is not satisfied with these hypotheses because according to him, the interpreters did not manage to step out of a metaphysical approach. For Perniola, hunting magic falls under the category of spiritualistic naturalism and the neuropsychological model under shamanic spiritualism. In other words, by focusing on a transcendent or vitalistic explanation of the drawings, rock art theory scholars reproduce the Western metaphysical mindset into the hunter-gatherers' culture and everyday lives. Trying to disentangle rock art theory from these metaphysical conclusions,

Perniola claims that the incisions were possibly meant to show other concerns of prehistoric people: 'One of the most uncanny aspects of the remains of the Côa Valley is the animation of some figures carved in the rock, whose movements are represented in a synchronic manner. It is as if the stone itself became animated' (CV: 87). The prehistoric artists, according to Perniola, did not mean to evoke magical or natural forces, nor did they use the paintings as a means for a spiritual and mystic 'recording' of their own subjectivity and ASC. It seems to be the contrary: in the effort to reproduce movement on stones, they wanted to emancipate themselves from the constraints of life and subjectivity by animating what is in and of itself inanimate, here blurring the boundaries between the organic and inorganic. In other words, the engravings were possibly produced not for the purpose of subjectivation but for abstraction. Perniola underlines that by searching for movement and life through abstract and geometric figures, the incisions show a sort of suspended and artificial life, a 'living mechanics' (CV: 87) in which the limits of organic mobility are transgressed and 'energy is poured into the dead lines of the stone' (CV: 87). In addition, many engravings represent abstract anthropomorphic figures, which, Perniola argues, introduce other perspectives of the perception of the human body, felt more abstract, more material and closer to an enigmatic life infused by the 'stone that vibrates'. In 1990, Perniola first published his text *Enigmas* with the subtitle *The Egyptian Moment in Society and Art* before the paper was presented in Lisbon in 2009 regarding rock art theory. Possibly, if he had known of the carvings of the Côa Valley at the time, he would have subtitled it 'The Palaeolithic Moment in Society and Art' instead. In fact, the Egyptian and Palaeolithic effects share the same essential characteristics. In the text, he investigates Hegel's analysis of ancient Egyptian art. In Egyptian culture and religion, elements that would generally be considered inert or dead seem to possess a peculiar life form. For instance, deities' statues, bas-reliefs and monuments were thought of as being able to observe the visitors of the temples. On the other hand, Perniola does not dwell much on the transformation of the Egyptian man into a thing, affirming quite hastily that 'men, equally, without self-consciousness, are moved by a formidable objectifying impulse' (E: 45). According to Perniola's claims, these two sources (Palaeolithic and Egyptian) begin to shape the neutral experience. The first implication of Perniola's claims is that the outlined phenomena are not specific only to our time. The advent of artificial intelligences, robotic prostheses, prototype robots and cyborgs does not pose the perennial question of the exchange between organic and inorganic for the first time, but rather, it repeats this line of thinking between natural and artificial and between subjective and non-subjective feelings.

To explore and clarify the concept of the neutral, it is useful to investigate Rainer Maria Rilke's poetry. Perniola himself dedicated some brief remarks to Rilke and the concept of the thing in *Enigmas* (E: 46). In fact, both Rilke and Perniola share an attitude of 'anti-Prometheanism' towards the world. The pretentious arrogance of controlling the things of the world, to penetrate their essence, leads to a subjective pathos, which, for Perniola, is a key polemical target. Both for Perniola and Rilke, the subjective feeling appears to be driven by the individual's search for what they consider right or wrong, pleasant or unpleasant, desirable or undesirable and natural or unnatural. The subjects in this *personal* feeling never go out of themselves, and by doing so, they cannot but see themselves as reflected in the world. Alongside the Cartesian 'I think', Perniola criticizes its aesthetic counterpart of the 'I feel'. This Cartesian-aesthetic assumption debases reality by interpreting it solely from the individual's point of view. In Rilke's perspective, instead, 'The poet has no life of his or her own, but melts into the landscape, an animal, a tree, a mineral, does not mean diminish him or her in any way. They of course cease to be the centre of the world, but become larger than before' (E: 46). Turning oneself into a thing, therefore, is not a final jump into alienation and reification or a debasement of human dignity; on the contrary, it represents a privileged way to finally cast off the metaphysical approach towards reality and begin to enter the neutral dimension. It is no coincidence that Rilke wishes for someone to write a history of the landscape – here intended as an immense space full of things (Rilke 1955: 59); he argues that although historians have focused especially on individuals and their lives, specifically deeds and political actions, only very little has been written about the history of things. The landscape opens up a neutral dimension that allows an osmosis between the organic and inorganic and between heterogeneous life forms and things (for a discussion of the relationship between thingness, landscape and urban environments in Perniola's thought also see CLC, PD: 93–7, SAI: 81–8).³

In both its spiritualistic and vitalistic ramifications, metaphysics is considered by Perniola to be a theoretical construction through which the individual experiences reality by privileging what is far and transcended (God-spiritualism) or what is close but only insofar as it is organic (animal-vitalism). Metaphysics goes only upwards or downwards: what is organic remains separate from the inorganic. Perniola's perspective is instead lateral, marginal and moving *in-between*. The philosophy developed by Perniola can be understood only if classical polar oppositions and dualisms are left behind. Difference emerges if, within the same space – reality, human, thing, animal or plant – the process of reciprocal osmosis takes place. Perniola wishes to demonstrate how there has always existed, alongside the metaphysical dichotomies – organic/inorganic, life/death or exterior/interior – a less common way of thinking and acting, an alternative way of feeling and experiencing reality. By not focusing on only one of the two sides of the supposed polarity, the neutral dimension does not imply a neutralization of feeling. In fact, the metamorphosis of the human into a thing and of the thing into a feeling surface implies revitalization and devitalization; animation and inanimation; abstraction and concreteness; form and content; and, ultimately, life and death: 'becoming a thing . . . [means] venturing out in the open, having death behind one rather than before one, exiting from time as conceived as a straight line, little by little becoming space' (E: 46). The neutral dimension implies the awareness that polar oppositions are entangled within a logic of false conflicts: turning oneself into a thing means understanding how dichotomies are interpenetrating, constantly flowing into one another.[4]

Precisely because the 'thing that feels' redefines the relationship between matter, form, thought and speculation, it also implies a redefinition of the notion of *exteriority* that has been only hinted at and that represents an essential point to be developed.

Turning oneself into a mirror

To investigate the theme of exteriority, which is pivotal to understanding the concept of thing, it is useful to briefly review the notion of surface as developed by Perniola. In everyday language, what lies on the surface is considered superficial, generally understood in derogatory terms as lacking depth. Being superficial, from this perspective, means the inability to go beyond surfaces, forms and externalities, supposing that there is another side that is interior, distant, spiritually oriented and, therefore, superior. This interpretation is a spiritualistic legacy of Platonism, for which the things of the world are copies, ontologically inferior to their hyperuranic ideal matrix and origin. Against this, Perniola, echoing the Nietzschean critiques of metaphysics, states that the 'world beyond the world' debases reality by leaving unobserved or condemning the actual 'depth' of the surface. In fact, reality is a stratification of surfaces: a full, rich exteriority of layers to unfold, untangle and develop (Bianchi 2019). As a redefinition of the relationship between life and form and of organic and inorganic individuals and things, the neutral experience is essentially linked to the theme of exteriority and surface. In fact, whereas interiority is linked with identity, desires and subjectivity, exteriority is linked with forms, rituals and surfaces. To use Perniola's terminology, interiority is the 'feeling from inside' (*sentire dal di dentro*); exteriority is the 'feeling from outside' (*sentire dal di fuori*).

To begin with, Perniola focuses on the Zen everyday precept of harmonization between individuals and the world. To live in accordance with the laws of nature, Zen monks and practitioners try not to impose themselves on the surrounding environment and on the wider processes of nature. Instead of striving to adapt the world to their affections, they do the opposite: they attempt to dissolve their egos through a mimetic-oriented attitude. 'On entering the forest, the sage does not stir the grass, and on immersing himself in the water, he causes not a ripple' (E: 31). The sage applies a strategy of maximum exteriority because the sage acts not according to inner drives but *reflects exteriority* (in his case nature). For Perniola, this openness is a crucial aspect of Zen philosophy, which 'the mind of the sage as a mirror in which the entire universe is reflected' (E: 30). Precisely at this conceptual crossroads between exteriority, reflections, cosmic feelings and mimesis emerges a concept coined by Perniola in his book *Enigmas* and *Del sentire*: 'specularism' (*specularismo*).

Specularism derives from the Latin word *specularis*, literally meaning 'of the mirror'. To clarify this concept, a first misleading interpretation should be refuted. The mirror is commonly associated with the libidinal investment cast on the image of the subject that is being mirrored. In other words, the relationship between humans and mirrors can be connected with the phenomenon of narcissism. Within Greek and Latin mythology, mirroring oneself assumed a pathological meaning. The mirror is interpreted in several ways, none of which seems to have a positive connotation. In everyday language, the mirror is associated with vanity, egoism and superficiality; in psychoanalysis, it is linked to the initial stages of infant development; in sociology, it indicates the regression in a private self unable to communicate in a public and social sphere. Perniola intends to emancipate the mirror from this perspective by overturning its terms: becoming a mirror rather than mirroring oneself. As it was for the Zen monk, this is not a matter of mirroring oneself in the world but of practicing the opposite: allowing the world to be reflected within oneself. The individual becomes a mirroring surface where what is external finds a place to be. Thus, pathology emerges only when the image of the self is mirrored because it is linked to an always unreachable idealized image or to an antisocial regression within oneself. Specularism implies not only an exchange between the organic and inorganic – as the individual starts to enter into the neutral dimension of the thing-mirror – but a displacement of human feeling: it is not the individual who hears, touches, sees, tastes and so on. S/he does not say 'I feel'; rather, s/he becomes the intermediary of an impersonal feeling, one that is received and welcomed from the outside.

Alongside Zen tradition, Perniola examines Baroque aesthetics and then dwells – especially in his book *Del sentire* (Of Feeling) – on specularism within contemporary society. To introduce the theme of the mirror man in the Baroque period, Perniola recalls a tale written by Charles Perrault in 1661 titled *The Mirror or the Metamorphosis of Orante*, which he summarizes as follows:

> The story tells the tale of a man called Orante (from the Greek for 'seer') who specialized in creating portraits of the body and the spirit that reproduced the originals to perfection: he had no memory and was unable to hide anything. He was at ease in the worldly environment of the salons and was a great success with women. Yet it was a woman who occasioned his death. Orante was in love with Calliste (from the Greek for 'the most beautiful') and reproduced her beauties to her great satisfaction. As ill luck would have it, however, she was struck down by a serious illness, which left her facially disfigured. Whereas anyone else hid the grim truth from the young woman, Orante was unable to prevent himself from reproducing her new features exactly as they were. Calliste, in a fit of fury, stabbed him with a large pin, killing him. The god Love, a friend of Orante, arriving too late on the scene, was unable to prevent the murder, but managed to save the body of Orante from decaying in such a way that it retained its mirroring properties. Orante was turned into a Venetian mirror.
>
> E: 32–3

Perrault's tale contains several philosophical insights that are examined by Perniola. First, becoming a mirror is not intended as a mimetic strategy of effectuality and harmony (as it is for the Zen monk) but as the condition of the possibility of experiencing affection and love. This shows that Perniola's critique of vitalism, together with the perspective of a hedonistic subjectivity, is not a critique of feelings *tout court*. On the contrary, although it is aimed at the feelings through which the individual uses the personal pronoun 'I', it praises those feelings emerging from the impersonal 'it'. Paradoxically, Perniola argues, the 'I feel' is a narrow and partial aesthetic experience; only from the osmosis between 'I' and 'the world' is it possible to say 'it is felt' without perceiving it in derogatory terms. In addition, Perrault's tale provides an example of the difference between narcissism and specularism. As Perniola notes, of Orante's and Calliste's loves, only the first manages to last. Although Calliste's love turns into hatred when her narcissistic expectations are disappointed, the love of Orante continues, despite the tragic change of her beloved. Orante – the mirror man – embodies the idea of love as enduring acceptance and appreciation of the other (despite the constant decay to which human bodies are subjected). To feel and appreciate anything with even greater involvement, Orante's tale seems to suggest that it is more advantageous to turn oneself into a thing – such as a reflecting surface – that accepts and says 'Yes' to everything: 'a loving readiness to receive, to welcome and to entertain the external' (E: 33, also see EAI). The way in which Eros, the god of love, rewards Orante is also singular: in fact, he is not elevated through spiritual exaltation but, paradoxically, through the metamorphosis into a thing, or, to use Perniola's words, 'it entailed metamorphosis into a thing and a transit towards the inorganic world of matter' (E: 33). Significantly, Perniola also dwells on Jacques Rigaut's aphorisms and thoughts on the mirror, which defines him as an 'ultra-dandy' (E: 37). Here, a line is drawn between the radical dispossession of the self, involved in the idea of becoming a mirror and the exercise of adhesion to what is external: 'The meaning of this mode of being, which could be defined as ultra-dandy, is a challenge issued by Rigaut to the world to transform any thing and any event into beauty' (E: 37). This brief remark contains a key aspect at the heart of what we are exploring in this book, which will be further developed in the chapter devoted to Baudelaire: first and foremost, dandyism implies an aesthetic challenge towards the world, one carried out through a welcoming disposition where there is no place for the personal dimension and for identity.

In what way is the mirroring of the world on the individual – or the individual becoming a mirror – considered by Perniola as the condition of the contemporary, post-Second World War individual? Why, in other words, are we living in an age of permanent exteriorization? According to Perniola, the all-pervasive thingly dimension characterizes present-day society in 'alternative' experiences (such as drugs, perversions and artistic performances) as much as in the more commonplace occurrences of everyday life. According to Perniola, there is a strong connection between specularism and contemporary lifestyles. He links specularism with terms such as 'video culture' and 'telematic', which might be developed fruitfully if replaced with other terms that are more apt in describing the current situation (such as 'software society' instead of video culture and 'the Internet of Things' instead of telematic). However, despite this, Perniola's intuitions are still relevant today.

According to Massimo Di Felice, who has combined some aspects of Perniola's philosophy with the digital revolution, contemporary situations redefine the very categories of what is human and nonhuman. For Di Felice, Perniola's redefinition of the relationship between individuals and things corresponds to the 'intellectual challenge of our age' (2010: 283). In fact, the advent of collective forms of intelligence, the Internet of Things and biotechnological discoveries are all the consequences and expressions of a reticular knowledge in which the organic and inorganic develop and evolve reciprocally. From Wikipedia to social networks and to augmented reality apps, the subject can no longer be thought of in Cartesian terms namely, the subject can no longer be thought anthropocentrically. Digital networking systems redefine space, architecture and media; they transform the ways we inhabit rural villages, cities and metropolises; and they challenge our broader environmental perceptions and conceptions. Specifically, Di Felice claims that by drawing on Perniola's thought, informative ecosystems work in a trans-organic way. For example, when a geographic area (made up of human beings and nonhuman organisms and artificial objects) is described through biotechnologies in terms of information codes, flows of communication and big data, an interchange between the organic and inorganic takes place. 'The innovative element,' Di Felice argues, 'added in recent times ... has been the advent of another communicative era, the digital one, which, with the introduction of informational ecosystems and virtual worlds, has not only begun to reproduce environments that can only be crossed through the mediation of technical forms of interaction but that has questioned the same meaning of space and of inhabiting' (2019: 16–17). In other words, matter can become informatic code – a hybrid between human, technical, mechanical and nonhuman elements. Exteriority and specularism emerge again at this stage: the individual moves away from an organic, subjective, inner feeling and lets the world – including the technological world – be reflected in them. For this reason, it would be misleading to refer to our age as the age of narcissism, where video technologies and virtual reality are only taken into account insofar as they offer unlimited possibilities to multiply images of oneself globally. It is true that a narcissistic drift is always at hand, given that the individual has never had the ability to invest in his/her own image to the degree possible today. At the same time, the critique of the software society as a narcissistic society does not grasp at the anthropological transformations happening and fails to consider the hybridization between things and men as another step into the realm of alienation and reification (on this topic, also see Manovich 2013, 2020).

Uncanny, radiating and intense things

After exploring the neutral and specularist dimensions, a key notion in understanding Perniola's theory of the inorganic is the phenomenon of 'radiation'. 'To radiate' is the translation of the Italian verb '*raggiare*' (translatable as 'to shine' or 'to radiate'), which is used by Perniola in reference to things (SAI: 123). A first definition of radiation is provided by Perniola in an unpublished lecture he delivered in Naples on 6 December 1994. In this lecture, Perniola states that things can radiate when the individual can perceive them under new and different aspects. For Perniola, the first authors who delved into this experience are Edgar Allan Poe, Charles Baudelaire, Ludwig Wittgenstein and Sigmund Freud, among others. For instance, in *A Tale of the Ragged Mountains,* Poe writes, 'enduing all the external world with an intensity of interest' (1982: digital source). He specifically refers to the effects of morphine, and it is no coincidence that Perniola argues that the experience of drug addiction is close to *The Sex Appeal of the Inorganic*. Baudelaire's 'surnaturalism' – which I develop later – is conceived of by Perniola as an attitude able to evoke an aesthetic interest upon the things of the world (CC). Perniola also suggests that in Wittgenstein's *Philosophical Investigations* and in *Remarks on the Philosophy of Psychology* emerges – though not clearly defined by Wittgenstein – a peculiar kind of experience showing 'hidden and substantial affinities', here specifically emerging with Wittgenstein's theory of the inorganic. Perniola names this experience 'the feeling of this thing' and claims it consists of 'seeing an entity that remains unchanged now as one thing and now as another' (SAI: 123). A basic example can be found in the famous drawing in which the observer may recognize a duck's head or a rabbit's head, depending on how one looks at the picture. The thing remains the same; it remains 'this thing', but at the same time, one sees it in a different, new and possibly surprising light. For Perniola, this experience can happen at any moment and within any field: from music to architecture, language, sexuality and maths. In fact, it is possible, for instance, to see a geometric figure 'now ... resting on its base, now hanging from its vertex' (SAI: 123); it is possible to hear the same melody and have different reactions to it each time; familiar words can be found odd and estranging; the bathroom might suddenly become abnormal or mysterious. By following Wittgenstein's remarks, Perniola underlines that in all the phenomena mentioned, things are susceptible to rapidly, unexpectedly opening up a new dimension of feeling or, to use Perniola's words: 'a new sensorial and emotional world' (SAI: 124). The experience of seeing something as something else is not always connected to pacific and conciliant objects – it can also be ambivalent or disturbing. In this sense, the radiation of things implies not only openness to wonder but also the uncanny. Freud provided psychoanalytic theory of the concept of uncanny in his essay *Das Unheimliche* (The Uncanny), written in 1919. Perniola engages with Freud and his sources (CA: 111–16) and highlights the relevance of Freud's *Unheimliche* in the very history of aesthetics. Perniola argues that Freud opened up the 'aesthetic of difference' with the concept of the uncanny. Before him, the field of aesthetics was mostly influenced by Kantian formalism or Hegelian dialectics, which both focused on 'positive states of mind such as the beautiful and the sublime' (CA: 114). Through the uncanny, Freud introduced ambivalent or negative states of mind into aesthetics, the marginal and concealed aspects of feeling that lead to new problematics and fertile research territories. Literally, *Unheimliche* means 'non (*un*) familiar (*Heimlich*)'. The adjective *Heimlich* comes from *Heim,* which means home, household, family and yet something secret, hidden or clandestine. Thus, the ambivalence of the phenomenon of the uncanny is already present in the etymology of the word: on the one hand, it conveys the idea of something known and familiar, and at the same time, it provides the opposite. The uncanny might then be characterized as 'all that should remain secret, hidden but, instead, rises to the surface' (CA: 115). Among the sources of the uncanny Freud quotes Jentsch's, who exemplified it with 'the doubt whether an apparently animate being is really alive and, conversely, whether a lifeless object might not be in fact animate' (Freud 1963: 20). For instance, an uncanny feeling may arise by discovering that which lies in front of someone is actually an automaton and not a human being and vice versa. Freud provided an example from literature. In the story *The Sandman*, the main character, Nathaniel, falls in love with Olimpia, whom he believes to be – at first – a beautiful young girl and who is actually a doll.

This experience of confusion, ambivalence and exchange between the animate and inanimate, the organic and inorganic, is also an essential trait of Perniola's theory of the thing. In fact, it allows one to avoid a potential misleading interpretation: the movement between organic and inorganic – for Perniola – does not lead to a dialectical overcoming of the two poles in which identity is restored. In other words, even though the organic and inorganic are intertwined in the concept of the 'thing that feels', this process does not end up in a final unity. On the contrary, the thing is intimately permeated by ambivalent – if not restless – feelings and experiences brought about by the phenomenon of the *Unheimliche*. The uncanny is something that undermines 'our trust in the identity of living beings' (CA: 115) because it presents the familiar as alien and, conversely, the unknown into something rooted in one's psychological past and childhood. This is the reason why the uncanny is not an extraneous experience: it is a phenomenon that distances what was believed to be close at hand and uniting it and making it familiar while changing what was believed to be distant.

The idea of the thing as radiant can help the reader better understand Perniola's scope and objective in refuting subjectivism, spiritualism and Marxism.

Perniola does not simply wish to provide an alternative conception or theoretical framework for things. He advocates for a reconceptualization of our very relationship with them while exploring the possibilities and the experiential territories opened up by such a relationship. It is not just about how we see things, but also how they see us and how these visualities intertwine with each other.

6

A Queering Agency: Perniola's *The Sex Appeal of the Inorganic*

Several unanswered questions arise at this stage: how does Perniola bridge the inorganic realm and the sexual field? How can a neutral dimension open up new experiential and sexual territories? What are the gender implications of neutral sexuality? What does Perniola's assertion that philosophy and contemporary phenomena, from drug addiction to cyberpunk and hardcore music, converge in the sex appeal of the inorganic mean? My aim in the following pages is to answer these key questions.

The sexual Big Bang and the limits of orgasm

The sex appeal of the inorganic can be summed up as an anti-hedonistic experience, against desire, not seeking orgasm, beyond gender, unconstrained from beauty, age and form, within sight of 'becoming a common universe in expansion' (LC: 12) with the partner. At first glance, one may wonder, freed from all of these aspects, how can one even call this experience *sexual*? How can two individuals meet, without the goal of an orgasm, devoid of their mutual physical attraction, in sexual intercourse not oriented towards pleasure?

Interestingly, Perniola initially thought of a different structure for his *The Sex Appeal of the Inorganic*. The version that never saw the light of day had the subtitle 'Knowledge and sexuality' (*Conoscenza e sessualità*) and was meant to be divided into three parts: 'Turning oneself into a neutral body', 'Turning oneself into a different body' and 'Turning oneself into a cosmic body' (SAIA). The first chapter of the first part, titled 'Libertines and comrades' (*Libertini e camerati*), was written but not included in the final version. It, however, helps us better understand Perniola's overall idea of a neutral sexuality. Going through the unpublished material and the actual book, it seems to me that Perniola uses 'knowledge', 'thinking' and 'philosophy' almost interchangeably. Therefore, the subtitle clarifies that the main aim of the book is to provide insights into the relationship between a broad understanding of the realm of knowledge and the sphere of sexuality.

To introduce his perspective, Perniola first distinguishes it from the figures of the libertine and the comrade. The libertine is understood by Perniola as a financial capitalist of bodies, who, seduced by the idea of living a rich sexual experience, becomes similar to an accountant, conceiving sex as a means to the reaffirm the power they hold and their subjectivity. The comrade, on the other hand, seeks somebody to trust, to share everyday domestic life with, to give and receive the same amount of respect and recognition, and so forth. In brief, the comrade wishes for a symmetrical partner, a doppelganger with whom they can achieve the 'democracy of the bed, the triumph of good home management' (LC: 2). Perniola criticizes both these attitudes: the libertine always begins the same race over and over so to speak, adding start after start; the comrade merely seeks the reassurance of the other. The libertine understands sexuality as accumulation and the comrade as familiarity. Perniola is dissatisfied with these two conceptions insofar as they both take for granted the habitual way of representing the sexual experience as a curve which, starting from zero, grows more or less slowly towards the apex of the orgasm, to then decrease immediately back to the starting level. Perniola describes this common way of understanding the sexual act with several metaphors and images: the mountain of pleasure followed by the valley of relaxation; a diagram that measures the excitement; an infant who strives for the maternal breast; a cannibal who wishes to increase their vital dominion by incorporating food. Despite this heterogeneity, these phenomena and figures share a core aspect, namely they are grounded upon the model of hunger: sexual intercourse is seen as a means to satisfy one's appetite, and sexuality 'ends up being thought of as a degraded substitute of eating' (LC: 12). Considered in these terms, the *homo eroticus*, the seducer and all the traditional figures linked to the *ars erotica* move within the same horizon of cannibals and rapists, precisely because they all share the same vitalist conception of sexuality linked to the most elementary and primal states of animal experience. In doing so, according to Perniola, this conception also reduces animals to beasts, enslaved by their supposed irrational nature and merely dominated by the immediate urge to satisfy their needs; it further ignores the plasticity of the sexual experience by transforming it into an instinctual hunger oriented towards a specific goal.

Perniola asserts that the main issue that impedes the individual from conceiving and exploring a new knowledge of sexuality should be located in the fact that sexual intercourse is mostly seen and structured in functional terms.

Sex has become a technical–practical activity aimed for the satisfaction of an objective (i.e. achieving the orgasm), thus working like any utilitarian project.[1] Precisely for this reason *The Sex Appeal of the Inorganic* can be understood as Perniola's effort to disentangle sexuality from functionalism (and also vitalism).

In the first (unpublished) chapter, Perniola begins by outlining his perspective through the image of the Big Bang: the focus should not be the climax of the orgasm but precisely the opposite, namely an initial, sexual Big Bang not oriented towards any pre-set goal. The initial moment of the sexual experience should not be seen as merely a lead up to the orgasm, i.e. as a means to an end of a project. On the contrary, it is from the very beginning that the individual should venture towards the heart of the sexual experience.

But what does Perniola have in mind when elaborating on such an experience? In her 2010 review of *The Sex Appeal of the Inorganic*, Patricia Marino objects that 'the mental image of two persons touching one another in intimate ways with no desire and no pleasure is an unhappy one' (2010: 182). This critique misses the key fact that happiness is not what Perniola had in mind when writing his book. Marino remains stuck with a hedonistic perspective according to which sexual intercourse is meant to produce beautiful images of peaceful unity: 'No Big Bang can ever take place if the individual preserves themselves in their boundaries, if they are enclosed in the prison of their identity' (LC: 10).

In the third chapter of the book, Perniola distinguishes his views from naturalism and spiritualism: neutral sexuality implies an experience neither ascending towards the divine nor descending towards the animal. In other words, it is neither an exaltation that brings us closer to a higher spiritual dimension, nor is it a passionate vitalism grounded upon instinctual liberation and erotic effusion.[2] In addition, Perniola claims that even if spiritualism represents a transcendent movement towards the altitudes of the spirit and naturalism a descent into life and its instinctual manifestations, they represent the two sides of the same coin; namely, they are the opposite poles of the same metaphysical attitude. The spiritualistic aspect emphasizes the transcendent, the divine or the interior and profound in a spiritual connotation; the naturalist aspect stresses subjectivity, identity, desires, inner feelings and compulsions. Even if reaching opposite conclusions, spiritualism and vitalism conceive reality in terms of dualisms and polar oppositions; what they both miss, for Perniola, are the continuous and uncanny dynamics of reality led by the notions of suspension and *epoché*.

Perniola's neutral sexuality does not move vertically but rather horizontally, towards the anti-divine and anti-natural inanimate realm of things. Precisely for this reason, Perniola casts out all those aspects that are normally connected to sexual intercourse, such as beauty, pleasure, desire and orgasm, from his theory: they still belong to the metaphysical polarity of the divine/bestial. His goal, through the theorization of the 'thing that feels' (*cosa che sente*), is to find an alternative, marginal way, which no longer sees sexuality only as a vertical line. Sexuality should be rethought, starting from the category of the thing and the neutral, for Perniola, through philosophy and perversions.

If organic sexuality sees in perversion a deviance from the traditional sexual act, which is oriented to pleasure and orgasm through conventional forms of sexual stimulation, neutral sexuality is, on the contrary, influenced by a different conception of perversions offered by philosophical inquiry. For Perniola, philosophy allows us to produce new meanings and conceptions of the ideas at stake. The role of philosophy would therefore be to theorize and frame the dimension of sexuality beyond pleasure and desire, beyond vitalism and spiritualism.

Perniola does not provide a clear definition of what he means by the term 'philosophy' in *The Sex Appeal of the Inorganic*, nor does he ascribe his understanding to a specific tradition or school of thought. Rather, he does the opposite: he outlines a common philosophical thread that intertwines heterogeneous figures and thinkers. Perniola characterizes philosophy in the following ways: 'speculative extremism' (SAI: 1), a 'cold lens' (SAI: 12) and 'speculative suspension' (SAI: 13). To shed light on this terminology, Perniola's notion of the *expanded epoché*, previously investigated, can be taken as a cue that exemplifies his understanding of the philosophical attitude at the meeting point of neutral sexuality. Perniola explores the idea of philosophy as an inhibitory activity that can interrupt, bracket and suspend vital and natural drives by enabling the impersonal experience of the thing that feels.[3]

An example of the paradoxical neutral sensibility, which marks a shift from a natural and organically oriented sexuality to an artificial and inorganic one, can be found in the literature and in the experience of drug addiction. First, the addictive experience, according to Perniola, is characterized 'by feeling one's own body as a thing by making the body extraneous like clothing' (SAI: 15). Perniola suggests that these altered states of consciousness allow individuals to distance themselves from their bodies and thus experience them as things among other things, without a will, subjectivity or identity – just as an extension of textures, surfaces and patterns, similar to a piece of fabric. In this sense, it is a process through which the body is felt not as personal but as impersonal; not one's own but autonomous; not as close but distant. Addiction, Perniola underlines, devitalizes bodies by removing them from the natural cycle of tension, discharging and reloading and putting them into a state of permanent excitement.

Excitement is a crucial notion within Perniola's idea of inorganic sexuality. Perniola understands excitement not as a strong feeling of elevation, close to ecstasy, nor as a vitalistic descent into the realm of sexual libido, in which enjoyment and pleasure play an essential role. On the contrary, according to Perniola, excitement *accompanies* all those experiences related to the feeling from outside, that is, the experiences where the exterior and the interior transmute into one another. In an article, he maintains, 'Excitement arises and is maintained when the boundaries between one's own and the extraneous, between self and non-self fall: while pleasure keeps the ego closed in itself, in its intimate tact, in a feeling from the inside' (EC: 92). Because the ego is suspended, the *epochistic reduction* as a suspension not only of judgement towards reality but as a suspension of personal pleasure emerges. Yet, neutral, inorganic, epochistic sexuality does not mean the neutralization of feelings but an entrance into another realm, that of excitement: a feeling from outside that flows uninterruptedly because it frees sexuality from the crescendo ending in the climax of coitus.

According to Perniola, the addictive experience is paradigmatic for contemporary feeling. He even claims that drug addiction – or at least its main features – has shifted from a pathology to the physiology of modern society (SAI: 16). Perniola connects the experience of drugs to the feeling from outside, that is, to a type of feeling at the centre of which there is no first-person subject, but the feeling is displaced outside, giving itself in an impersonal Mannerism. One of the thinkers that rekindled Perniola's interest in this issue in the twentieth century is Edward Bullough, who in his article 'Psychic Distance as a Factor in Art, and an Aesthetic Principle', states: 'Distance . . . is obtained by separating the object and its appeal from one's own self, by putting it out of gear with practical needs and ends' (1912: 91). Also inspired and influenced by such statements, Perniola elaborated on the possibility of placing one's self in a state of abeyance and suspension.[4]

From Thomas de Quincey to Samuel Taylor Coleridge, Ernst Jünger, Aldous Huxley, Charles Baudelaire and Walter Benjamin, several *topoi* of *The Sex Appeal of the Inorganic* emerge, namely the dimension of neutrality, exteriority and the radiation of things. These writers and poets often linked inspiration to drug use, especially insofar as addiction allows for an impersonal and suspended feeling, sensitive to the poetic process. Philosophy and drug addiction, for Perniola, share the habit of suspension and detachment:

> The union of philosophy with sexuality in the neutral experience of giving oneself as a thing that feels, creates a state similar to that created by drugs, because

one is heedless of everything that is not one's own infinite continuation and repetition. Neutral sexuality sets up an infinite dependency because it is removed from biological rhythms and cycles. It is constituted by the radical movement of philosophy and is nourished by its excessive and uncompromising thrust.

SAI: 16

In other words, philosophical *epoché*, or suspension and abstraction, precisely implies a detached attitude similar to that caused by certain drugs. Thus, Perniola reaffirms that philosophy and drugs have both assumed a paradigmatic, exemplary status, as they can be considered the model of a radical contemporary feeling.[5]

Perniola's goal as an interpreter of contemporary feeling is to challenge established *clichés* and prejudices on sexuality. From the book, our daily and traditional perception of sexuality emerges as an heir to Platonic spiritualism, which has only ever considered sexuality through partial binaries, such as ascent/fall, tension/relaxation, beauty/ugliness, male/female, youth/senescence and abled/disabled. This division represents and reproduces the metaphysical discourse within the sexual field. The essential link between erotic attraction and its object's bodily beauty, for instance, which is usually taken for granted, was first established in Western society by Platonic tradition. Plato himself, in *Phaedrus*, asserted the essential unity between sexuality, attraction and love on the one hand and beauty on the other. Consequently, in his theory of ideas, love sparks upon seeing a body that reminds the subject of the ideal beauty contemplated by the soul beyond heaven (before being born and falling into the actual body). In this frame, sensual beauty is appreciated as a moment, a step in the ascent towards a transcendental and metaphysical spiritual beauty.

Perniola sets about refuting this argument, which he even describes as 'the racism of beauty', by claiming its partiality and one-sidedness. By investigating Egyptian art, Rilke's poetry, Zen philosophy and contemorary experiences, Perniola shows that the process of turning oneself into a thing has always been part of individuals' daily experiences. In other words, he points out the continuity between subterranean and alternative forms of feeling from outside across different geographical areas, contexts and ages.

Post-rock, suspended entities, perversions

Informed by the ideas of 'impersonal feeling', 'neutral sexuality' and 'thing that feels', in *The Sex Appeal of the Inorganic*, Perniola also explores the phenomena of music, post-human culture and perversions. Let's turn our attention to these three fundamental topics with which Perniola frequently engages in his book.

First, a distinction should be made to fully grasp Perniola's perspective on music and its relationship with the inorganic dimension. I find both the title chosen for the fifteenth chapter, 'Hardcore Sonority', and the several passages it contains misleading. Historically speaking, hardcore music stemmed from the punk environment of the late 1970s and early 1980s, particularly in Los Angeles, San Francisco and Washington, DC (cf. Blush 2001); it involves distorted guitars, fast drumming, short songs and a vocalist shouting. The beginning of the 1990s saw the emergence of many genres inspired by fusion and experimentation with hardcore music, such as post-hardcore, techno hardcore, metalcore, grindcore, rapcore, deathcore, screamo, mathcore and emo. Some of these genres have been influenced by the speed and rhythmic intensity of hardcore, others by the lyrics, which ranged from socio-political issues to relentless anger, disillusion or even a poetic desperation touched by personal feelings. The raw emotions brought on the stage by hardcore music and its subgenres are at odds with the neutral dimension that Perniola develops in his book; he writes that the posthuman sonority 'does not consist in the delirious performance of shout' (SAI: 67). In addition, the reader may remain puzzled when realizing that the musicians included in the chapter do not belong to the hardcore genre but to others. Perniola names Frank Zappa, Brian Eno and Klaus Schulze, especially referring to 'progressive music' and broadly speaking to 'rock'. If these musicians and genres were labelled as hardcore by Perniola, he probably did not know what hardcore actually was and used it as a vague notion just to describe other music as hardcore. To me, Perniola seems to be looking for a sonority that displays a *hard core*, not a hardcore sonority. In other words, he elaborates on another type of intensity: not that of raw emotions but exactly the contrary, a devolution of personal feeling into the neutral dimension of sound. The link between music and the inorganic dimension is drawn by Perniola in the experience of

> transferring feeling from man to things. This does not mean that man does not feel at all, in fact, this neutral and impersonal feeling is extremely intense but it does not belong to him anymore. A type of devolution, transference, passing of feeling takes place from the subject to something completely external that can appear now as cosmos, now as technological apparatus, now as culture, now as market.
>
> SAI: 67

From this passage, a neutral sensibility that does not share any affinity with hardcore music emerges. Other than the musicians he briefly mentions in the chapter, I wonder what Perniola would have thought about more recent genres such as post-rock, post-black, shoegaze and drone music, including heterogenous bands such as God Is an Astronaut, Godspeed You! Black Emperor, Explosions in the Sky, Deafheaven, Sun O))) and My Bloody Valentine (also see Cox and Warner 2004). To employ the Situationist conceptual tool kit these genres can be considered as an exemplification of the *détournement*: they have kept the traditional rock instrumentation (guitar, bass, drums, vocals and electronics) but have hijacked it by dismantling and reworking the canonical verse-chorus form, which is typical of rock music. In fact, through the heavy use of effects pedals (especially feedback, distortion, delay, reverb and chorus), mixtures of obscure and ethereal vocals, electronics and through the repetition of motifs and stretched and looped ambient patterns, these bands have produced diverse soundscapes and atmospheres that share affinities with the 'impersonal feeling' explored by Perniola: they do not express anger or resentment, and they do not wish to convey the personal feelings of the vocalists or of the band (most of the songs do not even have lyrics). Instead, they offer an artificial, filtered, often non-sentimental experience where music ceases to be the servant of meanings, spiritualism and vitalism.

After the ambiguity of 'Hardcore Sonority', a second one can be highlighted in the chapter titled 'Philosophical Cybersex', which may mislead the reader into believing that Perniola includes his theory of inorganic sexuality within the broad realms of advanced science and technology, appreciable in the post-human re-evaluation of sci-fi literature and generally non-human cybernetic entities. Within these realms, Perniola carefully distinguishes figures and phenomena which, so to speak, pass the test of a neutral sensitivity from those who do not. As is well known, sci-fi literature and culture is constellated by non-human, liminal figures such as cyborgs, replicants, androids and robots. These figures have been brought to the attention of the public since the early twentieth century, both through films and TV shows such as *Metropolis*, *Blade Runner*, *Tetsuo: the Iron Man*, *Ghost in the Shell*, *Westworld* and *Ex Machina*, video games like Metal Gear Solid, System Shock, Cyberpunk 2077 and Death Stranding, and by writers such as Philip K. Dick, Tsumotu Nihei and Isaac Asimov, to name a very few. According to Perniola, most of the characters involved in these stories do not fall within the realm of the inorganic due to their dependence on human/natural elements. For instance, both replicants (bioengineered beings not fully human) and cyborgs (man-machine systems) are enhanced, ameliorated versions of the human being. On the contrary, neutral sexuality does not imply the implementation of human faculties, capacities or senses but rather their suspension. It is disappointing to realize that in *Blade Runner* replicants are not seeking an alternative and artificial feeling but rather are tending towards a 'human normality', which humans fail to recognize in them. Although the figure of the cyborg allows Perniola to clarify and sharpen his perspective, it appears to be a restricted view that takes into account the literature and the popular culture on the area only narrowly.

The experience of neutral sexuality, for Perniola, cannot be associated with another fundamental category of the sci-fi imagery, namely xenomorphs, aliens and mutants. In fact, all these figures, rather than exemplifying an impersonal humanity, are inhuman:

> neutral sexuality is not inhumane or inhuman, it is, perhaps, posthuman in the sense that it finds its starting point in man, in his drive toward the artificial that constituted him as such by separating him from the animal, in his will to make the greatest virtuality coincide with the greatest actuality (as in money), in his irreducible tendency toward an excessive experience.
>
> SAI: 30

As the passage shows, Perniola wishes to underline not only the distinction between a suspended and an enhanced humanity but also that between simulation and virtuality. Simulation refers to an imitation of some aspects of reality or of human beings (as in the case of cyborgs and replicants) that fail to enter the dimension of the inorganic simply because they remain stuck within human-oriented issues and problematics. In contrast, virtuality is closer to *The Sex Appeal of the Inorganic*, but only if we do not view it as the dissolution and spiritualization of reality in the immaterial realm of data and information. To Perniola, the apologists of the virtual appear as metaphysicians who, like those who create a world behind the world or an otherworldly realm, flee from a reality that they often perceive as narrow and distressing into disembodied worlds and mere systems of representation of that very reality. In contrast with this approach, Perniola understands virtuality not as a digital space of representation but as a space of availability: 'virtual things are constantly at our disposal. All is offered and this offer constitutes, precisely, its virtuality' (SAI: 31). The idea of the inorganic, I claim, is thus much closer to today's online Clouds, storage systems and streaming services than to combinations of living organisms and machines. While the latter are imitations of humans, projected into futuristic cities and civilizations, the former, by making information and diverse media always available and accessible, imply the emergence of a non-metaphysical sensitivity at odds with traditional dualisms, such as present/past and original/copy.

Beyond post-humanism and sci-fi literature, a significant aspect of *The Sex Appeal of the Inorganic* is its theory of perversions. Perniola devotes four chapters to four different perversions and links them to his idea of neutral sexuality. The issue of perversions has a long history in the psychoanalytic and psychiatric domains (see, for instance, Morgenthaler 1980; Benvenuto 2016). The uses and perceptions of the word 'perversion' have varied greatly over the last two centuries, according to different customs and traditions. There has also been varying acceptance of certain sexual behaviours. To examine Perniola's understanding of perversions, it is useful to start from this quotation regarding neutral sexuality and performances: 'In the sexological sense, it is perverse because it derives excitement from inadequate – in fact, greatly inadequate – stimuli, such as concepts, numbers, sounds, spaces, objects, writings – all things that normal people keep immersed in a functional-utilitarian boredom, or in an aesthetic-formal tedium' (SAI: 137). This passage clarifies his view on perversions. First, he links them to a plethora of realms that are normally excluded from sexual interest; second, he underlines their deviation from the standard norms and normativity. In this sense, Perniola's perversions may also be referred to as *paraphilia*, a term coined by S.F. Krauss in 1903, which means 'coveting the wrong objects'. Still, Perniola would not consider the sexualization of these objects as wrong, implying a moral judgement, but more like a minoritarian behaviour that can upset the existing order, an order that is relative to the ever-changing orthodox and unorthodox ethical paradigms of a culture.[6]

Sergio Benvenuto explores the ways in which Freud debunked homosexuality, perversions and pathologies by showing the ways in which sexual intercourse is actually 'a successful *bricolage* of perversions' (2016: XXIX). Drawing from Freud's psychoanalysis and Lévi-Strauss' anthropology, Benvenuto uses the term *bricolage* in the sense of diverse elements which, combined, form a new whole from pre-existing material. For example, several disconnected chords arranged to form a symphony or a heterogeneous array of things (such as a chair, a bicycle and a hammer) that may construct a figure. The perverse is in turn one who is fixed on a single piece of the bricolage, in a sort of specialization of desire. Perniola's understanding of perversion is close to this idea of bricolage, for which, by the union of philosophy and sexuality, an 'inadequate stimulus' (that is, an object not normally endowed with sexual interest) can become a source of endless excitement.

Regardless, Perniola does not propose a philosophical justification of the perversions he explores (sadism, masochism, fetishism and vampirism/necrophilia). On the contrary, he engages with them, highlighting his dissatisfaction with how they are often understood and investigating alternative meanings and perspectives. He chooses the four perversions mentioned specifically because he wants to provide a broader picture that runs from the most distant perversion with respect to neutral sexuality (sadism) up to the closest (vampirism).

The bridge between perversions and the idea of neutral sexuality seems to be borrowed by Perniola from Benjamin's *Arcades Project*. Benjamin, discussing Baudelaire's *Spleen II*, states, 'Sadism and fetishism intertwine in those imaginations that seek to annexe all organic life to the sphere of the inorganic' (2002: 354). Benjamin sees both the animation of inert entities into a 'living matter' and the 'assimilation' of the living to the dead, which lies precisely at the core of Perniola's *The Sex Appeal of the Inorganic*, in Baudelaire's poetry.

However, Perniola does not provide clear definitions of the perversions he examines; mostly, he hints at them in brief remarks. For instance, he considers sadism as 'the appointment of a strong, autonomous, independent subject, master of himself who asserts himself and triumphs in a practice of appalling negation and destruction' (SAI: 23). In psychoanalytic theory, the sadist is paradoxically both an aggressive and violent subject, who seeks revenge against those who made them suffer, and at the same time a 'moralist' believing their enraged retaliation to be just. The sadist desires to 'purify' their victims by acting against them and making them feel pain (Benvenuto 2016: 84). Although the sadist can act in a perfectly serene and apathic manner, with no animosity or anger, a strong resentment still drives their desire. Understood in this way, sadism lacks the very premises of the neutral feeling; in fact, it is not concerned with suspension but with a reinforcement of one's psychological history and subjectivity, which ends up in the sadist's 'unlimited sovereignty' (SAI: 24). The absolute will of the individual is guided by a destructive resentment. Although both consensual sadism and the sex appeal of the inorganic imply giving oneself to the partner with no hesitation or reservations, the former is oriented to a consolidation of sovereignty and subjectivity, while the latter fosters an impersonal and suspended experience.

After considering sadism, Perniola asks whether masochism can be considered closer to neutral sexuality. Perniola sees masochism as that type of relationship established – even at a contractual level – between partners who turn sacrifice, beatings and humiliations into pleasure. Here as well, as Benvenuto notes, it is not the pain itself that is enjoyed but the fact that it is associated with punishment and sufferance, turning it into a moral sign (Benvenuto 2016: 59). Thus, the other one, the one who beats and humiliates, is actually only a means, an actor who is staging the play directed by the masochist themselves: 'When, for example, the masochist declares himself to be the "slave" of his "mistress", his pleasure stems from his own feeling of being her slave, not from having satisfied the woman's desire to be a mistress of slaves' (Benvenuto 2016: 59). The other's feelings, therefore, are just instrumental for the hedonist purposes of the masochist. Thus, the relationship between master and slave is basically overturned: the partner who humiliates is merely a puppet in the hand of the humiliated.

Masochism, like sadism, shares with neutral sexuality the giving and offering of oneself to an external agent. The sex appeal of the inorganic as well as in masochism imply the acceptance of the horizon that opens up when one says 'do with me what you wish' (SAI: 27). However, a crucial difference lies in the fact that the masochist, like the sadist, remains entangled in the vertical axis between splendour and worthlessness, between degradation and elevation, between humiliation and celebration, which are all practices and activities oriented to pleasure and display a general moral undertone. In contrast, neutral sexuality is at odds with this constellation of subjective feelings and moves, so to speak, horizontally, towards the suspension and excitement of making oneself available as a thing that feels. When someone gives themselves to their partner according to the phrase 'do with me what you wish', this does not involve – for the experience of neutral sexuality – the expression of the energy that animates the subjects, but on the contrary, it invites them to 'be transported by an irresistible excitement in assisting the transformation of the person who burns and throbs in your arms into an inert and opaque entity which, nonetheless, is utterly receptive and sensitive to feeling the most tenuous caress, the most imperceptible kiss, the slightest touch' (SAI: 23).

The third perversion examined by Perniola is fetishism, which represents a step closer to the realm of the inorganic. Here again, Perniola seems to be heavily influenced by Benjamin's *Arcades Project*: 'In fetishism, sex does away with the boundaries separating the organic world from the inorganic. Clothing and jewellery are its allies. It is as much at home with what is dead as it is with living flesh' (Benjamin 2002: 69). Fetishism has been subjected to a long tradition of studies, research and challenges, ranging from anthropology to critical theory and psychoanalytic therapy. Perniola briefly reviews the fundamental stages of the theory of fetishism, starting from Charles De Brosses' theory, according to whom fetishism is the most primitive form of religion, and covering Kant, Marx, Freud and the works of Tanizaki and Klossowski (SAI: 53–62). In Perniola's opinion, the connection between sexuality and fetishism lies in the element of arbitrariness: 'anything can become a fetish: a rock, a lock of hair, a tone of voice, an odour, a word, or a colour' (SAI: 54). Perniola emphasizes the insubordination of the fetish from the function it is normally supposed to perform. A foot, shoe, high heels or any part of the body can become an allegory for sexual interest. However, despite their irreducibility, the anthropological, religious, Marxist and psychoanalytic standpoints see fetishes as substitutes, surrogates and degraded copies of a more essential original (such as God, human labour and childhood traumas).

Perniola's critique of fetishism seems strikingly similar to the idea of simulacrum, which is considered an entity that emancipates copies from their supposed models. In fact, just as the simulacrum represents an alternative dimension with respect to the dichotomy between copy and original for Perniola, the fetish is interesting not so much as a substitute and replacement but as a sexual strategy. Perniola expands fetishism to the whole cosmos through his theory of neutral sexuality, with the intention of freeing this notion from the constraints of psychoanalysis and the Western tradition of thought in general (on this idea, also see Margat 2003).

Perniola's elaboration on the notion of fetishism can be considered a sexualized version of Baudelaire's surnaturalism. In an essay from the late 1990s, Perniola claims that the excitement caused by neutral sexuality is accompanied by 'a cosmic experience that involves the entire planet: the earth's crust is sexualized; the mountains and the seas, the protuberances and the hollows, the reliefs and the ravines acquire a sexuality which belongs par excellence to the sex appeal of the inorganic, of the mineral, of the non-vital' (PS: 16). This experience also appears closer to Gilles Deleuze's rhizomatic relatedness than to classical psychoanalysis. In fact, as presented in the following pages, I believe that although Perniola constantly focused on Freud's theory, his whole perspective is much closer to that of Deleuze and Guattari.

However, as a matter of clarification, the 'sexual cosmic experience' should not be understood as a pantheism or as a confusion between the human, animal and mineral realms. We have to remember that in Perniola's philosophy, we are always within a heterophenomenology, that is, in a dimension where personal feeling is displaced outside of us, over anything which for a philosophical eye can evoke interest and excitement. Discussing Georges Bataille's *Story of the Eye* and *The Solar Anus*, Perniola focuses on several passages to exemplify his idea of heterophenomenology, understood as a sensorial experience that is paradoxically detached from human subjectivity. For instance, in *Story of the Eye*, one of the main characters, Simone, gouges out the right eye of the priest Don Aminado and inserts it into her vagina: the eye, almost as if animated by an enigmatic life of its own, continues to observe the narrator from its new place. In this extreme episode, Perniola underlines the idea of an autonomous movement, no longer organic or dependent on the consciousness of relatedness to organs. He elaborates a feeling that is no longer linked to organic functionality, which unties organs and bodies, similar to Deleuze and Guattari's Body without Organs (I will explore this connection in the following pages).

Finally, Perniola includes vampirism in his analysis of perversions. In the seventeenth chapter of his book, Perniola explores the sensitive horizon of the literary and cinematographic figure of the vampire. Although, in the collective imaginary, the vampire is connected to Romantic themes such as horror, the sublime, and the nocturnal, Perniola – drawing from the stories of Edgar Allan Poe – is interested above all in what comes *after* these feelings: 'what counts is the after-fear, the after-suffering' (SAI: 76). The vampire is a peculiar being who has survived death and belongs thus to an in-between realm that nonetheless is not transcendental or heavenly. The vampire is a being halfway between life and death, an intermediate entity beyond the naturalistic cycle of life and death who presents a lethargic, suspended feeling, a feeling of standstill. The vampire literally lives like a corpse and, in doing so, represents another figure ascribable to the detached dimension inhabited by the Stoics, the Jesuits and the dandies.[7]

Ultimately, neutral sexuality is perverse not because it can be assimilated to the psychoanalytic understanding of perversion but because it allows individuals to free their organs from their functions and to expand this attitude towards the cosmos. It could be called cosmic sexuality without nature, which transcends regimenting forms such as the difference of the sexes.

The transit or how to endlessly multiply genders and sexes

To explore Perniola's view of gender theory and sexual difference, it is useful to take a momentary step back from *The Sex Appeal of the Inorganic* and outline a relevant concept within Perniola's thought: the 'transit' (*transito*).

The word 'transit' comes from the Latin *transitus*, namely 'passage', 'transfer' or 'transition', which also refers to the verb *transeo*, 'to go across', 'to pass through' and 'to transform'. Different uses of this term have been arrived at from its Latin etymology: in its daily usage, 'transit' can mean carrying people from one place to another or passing through a place; philosophically speaking, different conceptual declinations are involved. Frequently, the idea of transit refers to certain specific literature based on the transience of life – that is, on the precariousness and the shortness of our earthly passage. A telling example of such literature is the novel *Ukiyo Monogatari* (Tales of the Floating World) by Asai Ryōi, written in 1661:

> Living only for the moment, savouring the moon, the snow, the cherry blossoms, and the maple leaves, singing songs, drinking *sake*, and diverting oneself just in floating, unconcerned by the prospect of imminent poverty, buoyant and carefree, like a gourd carried along with the river current: this is what we call *ukiyo*.
>
> quoted in Hickman 1978: 6

Perniola's philosophy takes a different direction on the concept of transit – this topic is elaborated in a volume tellingly titled *Transiti. Come si va dallo stesso allo stesso* (Transits. According to Perniola, the first to dwell on the nature of transit in Western tradition was Heraclitus, for whom the things of the world share the essential characteristic of the so-called *enantiodromia* – the coincidence of opposites. This implies considering every reality as always becoming, as everything being susceptible to turn into its opposite. For instance, the famous aphorism 'You can't step in the same river twice' implies that while one may apparently be immersing oneself into those same waters, in reality, the river flows on and thus changes unceasingly 'at once a process of passing from same to same and a persistence of what is in itself different' (E: 17).

Enantiodromia and transit share a fundamental feature – namely, they imply the *atopic* character of every reality. The adjective *atopic*, from Greek *atopos*, means both 'a-topos' ('devoid of a place', 'placelessness') and 'singular', 'unusual' or 'unclassifiable'. The very history of philosophy, for Perniola, can be understood through this concept. Why have so many philosophers, from Thales to Socrates, Boethius, Giordano Bruno and Heidegger, been denigrated, hated or persecuted? Because of the 'atopic nature of philosophy' itself: 'the hatred of philosophy has deep roots, unmentionable motivations, surprising manifestations: what actually animates it is the philosopher's avoidance of a definitive collocation, his/her staying in transit' (T: II). The philosopher, according to this view, does not follow any *utopia* or *topicality* but is oriented towards the *atopia*. These three terms share the same Greek etymological origin, namely the word *topos* ('place'). However, where utopia means 'no-place' and topical means 'actual' in the sense of a 'deposit of stereotypes' (T: II), only *atopia*, according to Perniola, has a privileged relationship of affinity with reality. Utopia is considered by Perniola to be a non-existing representation that revolves around an ideal community or society only imagined, without a proper consistence and significance: a 'motionless and perfect republic of the spirit' (T: 7). The topical, on the other hand, is that particular, ordinary dimension of thinking which dissolves reality into ephemeral actuality. In contrast with these two concepts, Perniola sees philosophy as that particular and unique thought that can account for reality, being understood as multi-layered and enigmatic. Even if, at first glance, the subtitle of *Transiti* ('How to go from same to same') seems to imply a sterile movement terminating with the state of a certain thing or phenomenon remaining unchanged, the actual meaning is the opposite, namely the flourishing of differences within each reality:

> To think of the richness of changes implicit in the same phenomenon, at the same time, in the same reality. Not to claim that A is equal to B, C, D ... and ultimately, that one thing is as any other – but indeed to show that B, C, D ... can be derived from A through minimal distinctions, subtle slips, imperceptible declinations.
>
> T: I

Perniola develops the transit as a wide-ranging and multifaceted notion: from an 'erotic transit' (T: 69–83) to a 'transit ritual' (T: 189–203) and from a 'telematic transit' (T: 217–29) to an 'artistic transit' (AMN).[8] Specifically, in *The Sex Appeal of the Inorganic* Perniola explores the relationship between transit, sexuality and gender. What happens when the theory of transit meets the inorganic sexuality? What are the implications of rethinking the idea of gender through the notions of transit within the framework of the sex appeal of the inorganic? I contend that the combination of these theories allows Perniola to elaborate a queer philosophy (although he never used this term himself).

Perniola's philosophy can be considered as quintessentially queer, starting from his first novel, entitled *Tiresia*, written when he was twenty-four years old and published in 1968.[9] Tiresias appears in several Greek and Roman myths and stories, from Hesiod to Homer, Sophocles and Ovid (not to mention more recent authors, such as Guillaume Apollinaire, T.S. Eliot and Pier Paolo Pasolini). One of the most famous versions of the myth claims that while Tiresias was walking on Mount Kyllini, he came across two snakes that were mating, he killed the female and, for causing trouble, was immediately turned into a woman. She spent seven years in this condition and had to have sex as a woman. At the end of this period, she found herself confronted by the very same scene with the snakes. This time, she killed the male serpent and was instantly transformed back into a man.

One day, the story continues, Zeus and Hera were split over whether the man or the woman felt more pleasure in love. Since Zeus said it was the woman and

Hera claimed it was the man, they failed to reach an agreement. They decided to call upon Tiresias, who due to his experiences was thought to be the only one who could resolve the issue. When asked by the gods, he replied that pleasure is made up of ten parts: the man feels one and the woman nine; therefore, a woman feels nine times the pleasure of a man. The goddess Hera, outraged that Tiresias had divulged such a secret, blinded him, but in compensation, Zeus granted him the gift of longevity and the power to predict the future.

For the purpose of this book, the crucial point is that the myth of Tiresias revolves around queer and transgender issues. Tiresias is a queer figure par excellence: he transgresses not only the boundaries of the sexes but also the divine and temporal norms, creating bridges between the present, past and future with his divination.

It is not a coincidence that Perniola entitles his first novel *Tiresia*. Numerous themes typical of queer literature recur in this text, such as the reversal of gender roles, homoeroticism, critique of the biological family, contempt for the bourgeois and patriarchal mentality, and the search for alternative ways of experiencing one's sexuality, love and friendship. Perniola explains that *Tiresia* is essentially about a boy who suffers from ontological insecurity and shows homosexual tendencies, who seeks the company of other men 'to do subversive things' but is attacked by a nymphomaniac woman, whom he hates and loves at the same time, so much so that he literally becomes her.[10]

Throughout *Tiresia*, the narrator blurs gender by unceasingly changing pronouns and agreements: 'When I see *him* again he is so different that I am not quite sure [*sicura*, feminine] I see him; then I ask him why he is no longer bleached as before. *She* replies that I am wrong, that she is never bleached, that she always tells the truth, that I must believe her, that she begs me to believe her, that I am the first one [*il primo*, masculine], that those things she does with me, never before with anyone else' (TR: 15, emphasis added). I have tried to highlight the agreement changes through the comments in parentheses, as the English language makes it hard to convey all the genderqueer aspects emerging from this passage. However, as the passage makes quite apparent, sometimes the narrator seems to be a man or at least a hermaphrodite and, at other times, a woman. The novel displays a constant variation between masculine and feminine pronouns, and after a few pages, the gender of the characters becomes completely fluid. The queerness of *Tiresia* evokes the notion of transit precisely in this enigmatic and atopic movement that allows us to think about the richness of the changes occurring within the same entity. Perniola calls this phenomenon the 'non-identity, the difference of each reality with respect to itself, the blooming of its virtuality, of its becoming, of its metamorphosis' (T: I).

It is interesting to note how Perniola refers to himself in *Tiresia* as 'Mario androgynous', when the experience of gender fluidity that the narrator experiences is far from this sexual category. Androgyny refers to the ideal of completeness and unity provided by the coexistence of the masculine and the feminine. As Jack Halberstam argues, 'Ultimately, androgyny always returns us to this humanist vision of the balanced binary in which maleness and femaleness are in complete accord' (1998: 215). Perniola's philosophy, as suggested, moves instead in the frame of a co-existence of oppositions, which nonetheless do not merge into a final unity. The queer experience that Perniola presents in *Tiresia* in fact is not deployed as a harmonizing experience in which genders are balanced. On the contrary, an enigmatic and uncanny feeling approaches the reader, who at first identifies the narrator with a male figure, then realizes that the narrator's identity suddenly changes into female and vice versa for the whole length of the novel. In doing so, Perniola sets in motion a queering agency that destabilizes the standard of heteronormative desire and its heterosexual matrix. To echo Judith Butler's thought, in *Tiresia*, the narrator displays a queer performativity that goes beyond and redefines the boundaries of social, cultural and political recognition of the status quo. Thus, we are not simply talking about a homosexual individual who fits into existing society but a much more complex and subversive entity.

In *The Sex Appeal of the Inorganic*, the queering agency of Perniola's perspective moves a step forward. It is the very notion of gender that is put into question, given what can be described as a *sexuality beyond gender*, namely a type of sexuality which is not informed by the division of masculine and feminine but is oriented towards a neutral dimension where genders and sexes are multiplied. Inorganic sexuality is neutral because it goes beyond the masculine and the feminine. It is the result of experiences that do not belong specifically to one sex, but into which one can enter by freeing oneself from the prison of biographical identity. In a chapter titled 'Division and the Sex Appeal of the Inorganic', Perniola investigates the precise relationship between gender and neutral sexuality. This discussion of the difference between the sexes appears only very late on in his book, that is, in chapter 23 of 27. He begins this chapter by wondering how a book on sexuality can fail to take into consideration masculinity and femininity and the broader framework of gender issues. Despite considering this a legitimate point, Perniola stresses that his perspective is not based on the premise that there are two sexes (SAI: 111). His first aim is to refute harmonic and dualistic perspectives on sexuality. The first of these views sexuality as a desire for union with the other, which sees masculine and feminine as two sides of the same coin, always striving to reach a final unity (as in the myth of the androgyne presented in Plato's *Symposium*). The second perspective sees something essential and ineliminable in sexual difference. Here, Perniola is thinking of Sigmund Freud and Jacques Lacan, for whom the male–female opposition is readable through terms such as phallic/castrated, as well as Luce Irigaray's claim that the difference of femininity is inaccessible to the logics of dialectics. Perniola is dissatisfied with these two perspectives as he believes they take for granted the dualistic standpoint anchored to two principles (masculine and feminine) and their unity or asymmetry. His theory, in contrast, dwells on the possibility of an infinite division within genders, related to the abstraction that links philosophy and mathematics:

> The sex appeal of the inorganic does not stop at the dichotomy between masculine and feminine but continues the division to infinity according to a procedure which is similar to that of infinitesimal mathematics. Inorganic sexuality is unable to understand why there should be two sexes, and not as many sexes as there are numbers, that is, infinite sexes.
>
> SAI: 113

Thus, Perniola claims that philosophy and mathematics, in their capacity to abstract and make something indeterminate, excessive and infinite, are able to free sexuality from its dependence on the organic and from the dichotomy between masculine and feminine. The very etymology of the term sex is taken by Perniola as a cue: sex derives from the Latin *sexus*, which in turn comes from the Proto-Italic and Proto-Indo-European *seksus* meaning 'to divide' or 'to cut', reflecting the distinction between two genders. Perniola's position is that the idea of division implicit in the etymology of the word sex should not be understood in terms of the lack and absence (as in the case of androgyny) but should instead be seen as the possibility of opening up new sexual and experiential horizons precisely through the endless continuation of this division. This experience does not arrest itself at the first stage – so to speak – of the division between two genders; it does not consider the male and the female as organic entities that strive to reunite through sexual intercourse, unceasingly missing each other. For Perniola, neutral sexuality emerges only if the sexual act is not perceived as 'filling a cavity and being filled by a protuberance' where 'everything is resolved in a division between empty and full, concave and convex' (SAI: 114). He is dissatisfied with this perspective precisely because, for him, it merely represents the beginning of the division process, which is still entangled in the view that the other is the missing piece of the puzzle through which one can become whole. Perceiving the partner as a complementary opposite of ourselves does not allow us to enter the dimension of the thing, which is in turn only possible insofar as philosophical and mathematical abstractions are put into play within the sexual field.[11]

The connection between the notion of transit and a queer perspective is also hinted at by Perniola himself:

> The two sexes are within each one of us, but what is important is not their amount, as in the theory of human bisexuality, but the fact that each one of these two sexes is still divisible into two others and so on to infinity, so that within us there are an infinite number of sexes, and one moves from one to the other through a transit, a passing from the same to the same, without rupture.
>
> SAI: 114

This division should not be understood in terms of separation: what can be divided and multiplied endlessly, also can be re-united and re-combined according to new perspectives and experiences. Inorganic sexuality is oriented towards establishing new bonds that are not based on the canonical understanding of sex and genders (from the search for beauty to the goal of orgasm and so forth). This experimental undertone, in turn, conveys the idea of unconventional social and sexual relations that leave behind the traditional war between the sexes and between men and women. To step out from the ideologies of biological sexes and of psychoanalysis, the very practice and category of sexuality should be rethought, for Perniola, in neutral terms (PSN).

Perniola's dissatisfaction with the above-mentioned psychoanalytic approach shows his affinity with Gilles Deleuze and Félix Guattari. There is an aspect of Freudian and Lacanian psychoanalytic theory that both Perniola – despite his great interest in Freud, especially his elaboration of the *Witz* and the *Unheimliche* – and Deleuze criticize, which can be summarized in the 'supposedly inescapable biological sex of male or female organized around the materiality of the penis' (Shildrick 2009: 120). According to this theory, both the acquisition and stabilization of the self-image and the infant–mother relationship are grounded upon a triangular narrative depending on the natural sexes.

To put it briefly, at least for Lacan, the desire for wholeness stems from an imaginary unity with our caretaker, namely the one that can meet all our needs during premature infancy. In its primary stages, the infant does not distinguish between its body and the caretaker's, experiencing an imaginary unity and feeling of wholeness. Little by little, the new-born becomes aware of its own body through what Lacanian psychoanalytic theory calls the 'mirror stage' and the subsequent 'castration'. Whether or not an actual mirror is involved, the mirror stage occurs when the infant begins to identify its body with an imaginary object, that is, it begins to imagine itself as a separate being, with its bodily functions, orifices and organs, and it starts to see itself associated with a 'name' that their parents repeat. In other words, it is during this stage that we begin to form our independent identity.

Castration, on the other hand, does not imply the actual emasculation of the infant's genitalia. Castration is instead connected to the psychic loss that the infant experiences when the individuation process begins, feeling itself to be a separated, incomplete and missing being. It is not the physical removal of the phallus, but the threat of being separated from something against our will that lies at the core of the idea of castration.

This separation does not occur only through the mirror stage but also through the intervention of the father (who, like the mother, is a symbolic figure and thus disjointed from biological sex). For Lacan, the father is crucial in interrupting the mother–infant relationship. This figure is understood basically as the prohibition on incest and, generally speaking, of limitless *jouissance* (enjoyment), and in doing so, it plays a central role in the development of the infant: 'the "NO" that demands we socialize (outward) and become individuals. Such a demand is expressed through language. With the introduction of the "No" the child must look elsewhere for unity' (Meyer 2019: 37). For Lacan, individuals might spend their entire lives in this (mistaken and futile) search for the possibility of unity and harmony: 'our relations of Desire *aim* at that goal of that impossible reunification' (Meyer 2019: 94). The idea of ourselves as a whole that lacks nothing is impossible to achieve because it was only by mistake that we believed we were a whole with our caretaker during the early stages of our development. On the contrary, we always needed an outside source to survive. Since the union with our caretaker was only imaginary, we often desire an impossible and unattainable union with the other with the belief that they can complete us and make us whole again.

The triangular narrative of the Oedipal family is precisely what Deleuze, Guattari and Perniola (although the latter less explicitly) criticize. For them, the unconscious cannot be entangled merely within a domestic bond wherein the new-born is continuously castrated and blamed for its desire. Ultimately, they believe that the psychoanalytic dogma of Oedipus reinforces patriarchy and capitalism, which subjugate human desire to the law of the Father. As Camille Dumoulié presents, 'The common man, entangled in the Oedipus complex and in the guilt which subsequently follows, grounds his desire upon it, particularly on the hatred of the father-God who feeds his sense of guilt, reinforces the prohibited and thus prevents desire from overcoming this zone of the fear of death. A zone contaminated with castration anxiety, which lingers upon everyone' (2002: 179–80). Whereas desire is driven by a lack, which comprises the implicit and impossible promise of completeness and unity with the mother for Freud and Lacan as inspired by Plato, Perniola, Deleuze and Guattari have moved on to a different terrain on the notion of desire. On the one hand, Deleuze and Guattari still use the term desire, but they completely strip it of its subjectivist matrix: for them, desire is a 'network of flows, energies and capacities that are always open to transformation' (Shildrick 2009: 121). Drawing on Spinoza's *conatus* and Nietzsche's will to power, Deleuze and Guattari do not see desire in terms of possession, associating it with a missing object; on the contrary, they understand it as a positive immanence, which is not determined by or oriented to any object in particular. It is not a coincidence that Deleuze and Guattari state in the *Anti-Oedipus*: 'Desire does not lack anything; it does not lack its object. It is, rather, the *subject* that is missing in desire, or desire that lacks a fixed subject' (2000: 26). On the other hand, Perniola believes that psychoanalysis, and generally speaking the Western tradition of thought, has compromised the very notion of desire by linking it to a constitutive lack of the subject. Thus, in *The Sex Appeal of the Inorganic*, he prefers to use, as previously suggested, the term excitement to indicate a state of sexual intensity and interest that does not depend on subjective categories.[12]

Contrary to psychoanalytic theory, which is mainly concerned with the natural sexes within the frame of the Oedipal drama, for Perniola and Deleuze, gender is produced in performative terms, that is, via continuously making and undoing the sexes, which should not be understood either in biological terms or in terms of identity and fixity. As Judith Butler points out: 'gender ought not to be conceived as a noun or a substantial thing or a static cultural maker, but rather as an incessant and repeated action' (1990: 112). This action is not performative only in human terms; on the contrary, it downsizes human-centredness by proposing alliances beyond the human. Perniola calls this an alliance between man and thing, in the cosmic horizon inaugurated by neutral sexuality; Deleuze and Guattari call it rhizomatic relatedness. In Deleuzian terms, Perniola's queering philosophy produces *becomings* that go beyond normative couplings to invent new connections that involve not only humans but also animals, plants and machines (also see Deleuze and Guattari 2013; Beckman 2013; Sholtz and Carr 2021).

As Margrit Schildrick argues, this may mistakenly appear at first glance to be a version of the polymorphic infantile perversity examined by Freud, whereby the infant would feel sexual interest not only in the erogenous zones of his own body but also in external objects (2009: 119–20). However, Freud also states that this trajectory will then be abandoned by the individual for socio-political reasons, and that the price of this abandonment will be neurosis and repression. Deleuze, Guattari and Perniola take different paths. For them, it is not a matter of seeing how the body responds to the impulses of the unconscious; the terms involved are no longer 'repression', 'prohibition', 'castration' and 'disavowal', nor are they substitute for psychic loss. Against this constellation of thought, the quintessential queer ideas of Perniola, Deleuze and Guattari emerge. Specifically, I refer to the Body without Organs (BwO) here, an expression taken from Artaud and introduced by Deleuze in *The Logic of Sense*, developed in *Anti-Oedipus* and further explored with Guattari in *A Thousand Plateaus* and to the thing that feels elaborated by Perniola.

BwO, as is known, does not literally mean a negation of corporeality, an organ-less body. Rather, it is a critique of the normative organization of the body. BwO refers to a body in which organs are no longer submitted to organizing principles that structure natural functions as organisms. Eugene W. Holland argues that it would be better understood if it were called the body without organization (2013: 96), as it implies a programme of depersonalization in contrast with that of psychoanalytic therapy. Deleuze's theory does not see the fundamental productive force that sustains desire in the Oedipal lack. On the contrary, it sees desire as a connective and continuous flow akin, I would claim, to Perniola's idea of excitement.

For both Perniola and Deleuze, a crucial issue lies in re-thinking desire as a flow of uninterrupted intensity that is not bound to subjectification or driven by a constitutive lack. Therefore, orgasmic pleasure, along with the implicit fall after the coitus, is seen as an obstacle to the articulation of desire. In *Dialogues II* Deleuze states that desire has two main enemies: 'a religious transcendence of lack and a hedonistic interruption which introduces pleasure as discharge. It is the immanent process of desire which fills itself up, the *continuum* of intensities, the combination of fluxes, which replace both the law-authority and the pleasure-interruption. The process of desire is called joy, not lack or demand … This is not something to do with Nature: on the contrary, it requires a great deal of artifice' (2007: 100). The BwO for Deleuze and Guattari, and the thing that feels for Perniola, should then be seen in their queering agency, which produces desire in every direction against heteronormativity.

Although Perniola did not draw the parallel I have just outlined, he discussed Deleuze's philosophy explicitly several times in his reflections. It was only during his later years, however, that he realized how their philosophies share key concepts. In his *Enigmas*, Perniola explored the idea of the 'fold',[13] introduced by Deleuze in his study on Leibniz and the Baroque, and he devoted an essay to Deleuze's understanding of masochism. His last conference was titled *Becoming Deleuzian?* and his autobiography *Tiresia contro Edipo* is strewn with Deleuzo-Guattarian terminology. In more than the book's eighty short chapters, Perniola makes abundant use of notions such as 'becoming' and 'assemblage', and the very title can be ascribed to the broader Deleuzian endeavour to destabilize psychoanalytic theory.

In his autobiography, Perniola not only reviews his past life in a hybrid in-between style that combines the essay, the diary and philosophical prose, he also elaborates on a key hypothesis: the conceptual figure that best represents the contemporary world is not (and, Perniola seems to imply, perhaps never was) Oedipus, but Tiresias. There are at least two reasons for this. On the one hand, Perniola emphasizes that Tiresias echoes the contemporary struggles for the redefinition of gender and for the recognition of the queer world more vividly. On the other, as suggested, he ascribes his theory to the destabilization of Freudian and Lacanian imaginaries. Perniola states that he was planning to write an essay on the figure of Tiresias, but that unfortunately, urged by his terminal illness, he succeeded in writing only the autobiography, in which the references to Oedipus are fragmented and evocative. However, as suggested, Perniola sees in Oedipus an opposite force with respect to Tiresias: the former limits his desire to the affections of his subjectivity, while the latter informs his desire through a queering agency; the former wishes to know more about who he is, while the latter unceasingly becomes somebody or something else.

7

Beauty is Like a Blade: Towards a Strategic Theory of Aesthetics

Perniola has extensively written on the discipline of aesthetics, especially focusing on the experience of feeling. At the same time, he also investigated the idea of beauty and that of an 'aesthetic horizon'. The present chapter develops Perniola's idea of a 'strategically oriented beauty', one that implies a close connection between the aesthetic element and political one, between beauty, on the one hand, and effectuality, on the other hand. The following one will situate Baudelaire within Perniola's notion of aesthetic horizon.

Perniola has always avoided defining his philosophy using a set formula, especially given that one of the fundamental characteristics of philosophy – according to him – lies in its *atopy* or 'placelessness'. Nonetheless, he writes, 'my work can be considered as a form of Baroque neo-Stoicism that went through the experience of literary and artistic avant-gardes of the twentieth century' (SPB: 9). This statement represents a unique passage that helps to better understand Perniola's overall reflections.

Stoicism or beauty as action[1]

Before exploring Perniola's interpretation, I will provide some brief philosophical coordinates of Stoicism. In this way, it will be easier to understand the terms in which Perniola has distanced himself from classical aesthetics and, to a certain extent, from Stoicism itself. In fact, Perniola elaborates on neo-Stoicism, which departs from the traditional position in several ways.

The first great assumption that differentiates Greek (and late Roman) Stoicism from Platonism is a monistic view of reality. Whereas Plato elaborates on a dualism between the earthly world and the ideal world, where the former is an imperfect copy of the latter, Zeno, the founding father of Stoicism, affirms that the whole world is permeated by *logos* (reason), so true good, harmony and beauty are traceable to the world itself (and not in the *hyperuranium*).² The ordering principle that governs reality (*logos*), therefore, is not something distant or detached from the world but is present everywhere, in everything. In other words, Stoic philosophy is founded on the *physical* universality of *logos* (not a *meta*-physical Platonic universality). Moreover, because *logos* is the best ruler, the things of the world happen the way they happen; that is, they are as they ought to be and cannot be otherwise. For the Stoics, there is a universal reason that directs the universal order of the cosmos.

Although the world is given to people as it should be, this does not mean that they are enslaved to destiny or that they do not possess freedom. On the contrary, for the Stoics, the ultimate goal is to live following virtue (Sherman 2007) by accepting *logos* and distinguishing what falls under the control of the sage from what does not pertain to him/her. Epictetus, one of the most influential representatives of Roman Late Stoicism (together with Seneca, Marcus Aurelius and Cicero) exemplifies this attitude in the following way:

> Some things are up to us and some are not up to us. Our opinions are up to us, and our impulses, desires, aversions – in short, whatever is our own doing. Our bodies are not up to us, nor are our possessions, our reputations, or our public offices, or that is, whatever is not our own doing ... And if it is about one of the things that is not up to us, be ready to say, 'You are nothing in relation to me'.
> Epictetus 1983: § 1

Epictetus suggests that we should be able to monitor our actions and thoughts by distinguishing what is 'up to us' from what is 'not up to us'. Despite our unknown and uncertain circumstances, what we are capable of doing is – for Epictetus – mastering our judgements on external things so as not to be affected by them.

It might seem contradictory to argue that our emotions, impulses and desires are under our control, but, as Nancy Sherman notes on her volume on Stoicism and the military mind, the 'Stoics hold that an ordinary emotion such as fear or distress is not primarily a sensation or feeling but rather an opinion or cognition that something bad is happening and a second opinion that a certain course of action is to be taken or avoided' (Sherman 2007: 9). Emotions are a matter of judgement and will and, thus, are under our power. The Stoic's suspicious attitude towards emotions is based on their belief that ordinary emotions involve false opinions or misguided applications of reason: 'emotions, then, are assents to a mistaken conception of what is good and evil' (2007: 81). In contrast, 'good emotions' (*eupatheiai*) result from the education and transformation of the true sage and consist of a different set of feelings grounded on – as will shortly be clarified – the acceptance of one's own destiny: the *amor fati* (love of fate). Hence, the first objective of Stoic practice is to identify the causes of human unhappiness. For the Stoics, human misery is caused by looking for goods that are difficult to obtain (or destined to disappear) or trying to avoid evil (which is often inevitable). The aim of Stoic philosophy, as Pierre Hadot argues, is to educate the individual to recognize the worthwhile good and avoidable evil. This education implies, first, reversing the common conception that 'humanizes' reality – that is, it means abandoning the human point of view with its values, judgements, and evaluations of things. Specifically, the critical mistake does not actually lie in evaluating things but in casting value on things that do not depend on us as being external to us. More precisely, what happens outside the individual's control is included by the Stoics under the umbrella concept of *indifferent things* (Hadot 1995: 86, 197; Sherman 2007: 3, 27, 32). The Stoics distinguish between external goods and internal ones, maintaining that because only the latter are our responsibility, we should treat the former as indifferent things – that is, things that are neither genuine goods nor evils. Interestingly, Hadot suggests (1995: 197) that being indifferent towards things does not imply disinterest. On the contrary, it implies 'not making a difference' between things and not imposing differences based on our judgements. In fact, because what does not depend on us is the result of a necessary concatenation that goes beyond ourselves, people must live according to a more *desubjectivated* disposition towards the events of the world (a concept close to the *neutral dimension* developed by Perniola).[3]

Here, we are in control of our desires, tendencies and assent to things (Hadot 1995: 193). Conversely, all that presupposes an external cause – with respect to oneself – such as honour, fame and wealth, but also health, other people in general, should be considered outside of our control and, ultimately, accepted in its becoming. The Stoic sage aims to discern between what is in their possession from what is not, what depends on them and what does not fall under their control and what is essential against what is accidental. In addition, it is not only a matter of accepting what is necessary but also of loving it. 'Why love? Because nature loves itself, and events are the result of the necessary concatenation of the causes which together constitute fate and destiny' (Hadot 1988: 143). Loving one's own fate echoes Perniola's considerations of the election of difference mentioned by Ignatius of Loyola. Like Loyola, Stoic exercises were oriented towards experiencing a joyful and comforting disposition through one's life's events. The Stoics, alongside other Greek schools of thought (such as the Epicureans and Sceptics), but also together with several exponents of Christian philosophy (such as Loyola and Gracián), develop theories on how to behave well in the world.

Stoic philosophy is not oblivious to aesthetics. The key term through which the Stoics designate beauty is πρέπον (*prepon*, in the Greek context) and *decorum* (in Roman culture). First, πρέπον means 'the appropriate'. For instance, according to classical rhetorical theory, a speech can be defined as πρέπον if it is appropriate for the context in which it is given, that is, if it conforms to both the occasion and public. Perniola provided this definition of the concept of πρέπον: 'that a particular type of beauty which adapts, which is convenient and is, therefore, opposed precisely in virtue of the relation with respect to that which constitutes it, to the absolute and universal conception of beauty, implicit in the canon' (T: 190). This quote contains some essential elements for understanding the influence of Stoicism on Perniola. First, by interpreting the concept of πρέπον as 'the beauty which adapts', Perniola emphasizes its difference from the ideal beauty found in objectivism. An ideal beauty does not adapt to reality but instead does the opposite. Perniola privileges the concept of beauty elaborated within Stoicism precisely because its main feature (the πρέπον) does not forget reality – that is, it does not forget its relationship to history and situations.

Beauty is also linked with the concept of 'opposition'. If beauty adapts itself – that is, it depends on several factors within contextual circumstances – then it is produced in *opposition* to something else because it is generated by an alterity through which it emerges. In this passage, we can begin to see the position of Perniola on beauty: the beautiful is not that which is in and of itself perfect and complete, but what, placed in front of reality and its manifestations, can adapt to it and have a pragmatic relationship of effectiveness with it.

Perniola's philosophy is influenced by the Stoic idea of beauty precisely because it abolishes the pseudo-opposition between a real/ideal world and an apparent/false one, focusing on reality and its presence. It is no coincidence that Perniola in *Transiti*, before dwelling on the ritual without myth in ancient Rome and role of the ceremony (T: 189–204), anchors his discussion on Cicero's notion of *decorum* (translatable as seemliness). The Roman *decorum* is, in fact, the transposition of the Greek πρέπον. *Decorum* emphasizes a unity between behaviour and effectiveness. It is associated with being 'seemly' towards deities or, for an orator like Cicero, towards audiences. It means to possess an exterior *habitus* made of gestures, words, rhetorical styles and rituals that are convenient, suitable and decorous regarding the particular circumstances and to one's various roles in life. The link between beauty and *decorum* is highlighted by Cicero himself: 'for just as the eye is aroused by the beauty of a body … so this seemliness [*decorum*], shining out in one's life, arouses the approval of one's fellows, because of the order and constancy and moderation of every word and action' (1991: I, 98).

What the Stoics define as *logos* is referred to by Perniola as difference. Both *logos* and difference imply a focus on the realm of history, events and the material world. Thus, the cornerstone is set on reality and its discontinuous, uncanny and unpredictable manifestations. Stoics believe that what is external is not up to us and, thus, should be considered 'indifferent'. It is a cliché to consider Stoicism only as a moralistic asceticism based on virtuous discipline. Instead, the *nihil admirari* (translatable as 'do not let yourself be astonished by anything') of the Stoics is a desubjectivation not to be confused with self-annihilation. The disappearance of oneself is pursued to act more effectively in the world. As Nancy Sherman writes:

> It is tempting to read Epictetus as urging complacency in his listeners or at least a retreat to a narrow circle of safety. But this is not the message. We are to continue to meet challenges, take risks, and stretch the limits of our mastery ... In this sense, the message is one of empowerment. But at the same time, we are to cultivate greater strength and equanimity in the face of what we truly can't change. We must learn where our mastery begins, but also where it ends.
>
> 2007: 3

Stoic philosophy has been practiced by emperors (such as Marcus Aurelius) and slaves (such as Epictetus), by politicians (such as Cicero) and by contemporary soldiers (such as Stockdale[4]). To downsize oneself is also a crucial point for Perniola. Specifically, his aim is to find a new way between spiritualism and vitalism by highlighting the neutral dimension.

In addition, the Stoic conception of beauty as πρέπον and *decorum* meets Perniola's notion of ritual without myth. As developed earlier, Perniola's idea of aesthetics is grounded on the observation of manners and behaviours that are pragmatically oriented. Roman religious rituals and Jesuit tradition were developed as pivotal experiences where a strategic conception of beauty emerged.

Nonetheless, Perniola's philosophy does not wish to entirely replicate Stoicism in the contemporary world. What Perniola leaves behind from traditional Stoicism is the focus on the moral element, on the one hand, and, on the other hand, the search for harmony between the individual and the world. As will be clear from the next chapter, which will focus on Baudelaire's dandyism, Perniola praises a 'polemological' attitude rather than a harmonic one. In other words, philosophy is the identification and exploration of conflicts and oppositions rather than philosophy as the theorization of a conciliated worldview. The theme of conflict is precisely what characterizes the second theoretical figure considered in this chapter: Baroque thought.

Making unlawful matches between things: Baltasar Gracián's Baroque

A key author belonging to Baroque Catholicism, one to whom Perniola often refers in his texts, is Baltasar Gracián. Gracián, born in Belmonte (Aragon) in 1601, entered the Jesuit Order as a young man. He spent his life within the ecclesiastical hierarchies, teaching Latin grammar, moral theology, and philosophy in various colleges between Lérida, Gandìa, Huesca, Zaragoza and Madrid. At the same time, he knew Madrid's court environments well, having been the confessor of the viceroy of Navarre. He published most of his writings, such as *The Art of Worldly Wisdom* (1647), *The Hero* (1637), *The Complete Gentleman* (1646), *The Critic* (1651) and *Wit and the Art of Inventiveness* (1648), under a pseudonym and, therefore, without the approval of his order. His proximity both to court circles and some politicians of the time, such as Don Vincenzo Giovanni of Lastanosa, caused him internal enemies within the Society of Jesus. Eventually, in 1651, Gracián lost the Chair of Sacred Scriptures in Zaragoza (the most coveted within ecclesiastical studies) and was transferred to Graus. Almost exiled, away from his supporters and friends, he died in Tarazona on 6 December 1658.

Perniola focuses mainly on two works by Loyola: *The Art of Worldly Wisdom* and *Wit and the Art of Inventiveness*. The first contains a 'biotechnique' (Tatarkiewicz 1974: 386), that is, the art of living well. The second is his most significant text he wrote on aesthetic theory.[5] Specifically, Perniola focuses on three main notions emerging from Gracián works: *agudeza* (literally 'acuteness', translatable as 'wit'), *ingenio* (translatable as 'inventiveness' and 'ingenuity') and *concepto* ('concept').

Agudeza is presented in a variety of attitudes – a subtle comment, a witty remark or a seductive silence, which is also exemplified by Brummell's dandyism. *Agudeza* has its roots in treatises on courtesy, such as *The Book of the Courtier* (published in 1528) by Baldassarre Castiglione and Giovanni Della Casa's *Galateo* (1558). With these late-Renaissance writers, Gracián shares the attention to subtlety, *sprezzatura*, *je ne sais quoi* – attitudes and behaviours not understood as empty forms but rather that rest at the crossroads between seduction, politics and art (on this topic, also see Silverman 2001 and Patella 2020).

Agudeza implies an aesthetic conception of existence in which 'what glitters and what succeeds, form and action, ornament and substance' (E: 113) are closely joined. Here, we can clearly see the connection between the conception of beauty of Gracián's literary Mannerism and the Greek πρέπον and Roman *decorum*. In

Gracián's works, beauty is not unfolded by a proportionate and harmonious object; it does not depend on an eternal canon or measure; it is not essentially spherical, soft, round and object of contemplation. On the contrary, beauty is the result of a *challenge* between manners and circumstances. I emphasize the word challenge precisely to stress the attention Perniola's interpretation pays to Gracián's works. Being witty means being acute, pungent, sharp or pointed (like a needle or sword), penetrating the things of the world: 'Wit, "acuteness", belong within a semantic field in which speech, gesture, and even silence, are understood as a weapon and the literate person as a combatant, a warrior, a hero' (E: 113). Thus, wit (*agudeza*) is that particular notion that holds together the dimensions of aesthetics and existence, beauty and effectiveness, art and strategy and opportunity and seduction (on Perniola and the warrior, see also Van Sevenant 2021).

Although the concept of beauty has always been present within the Western tradition, aesthetic principles began to be studied systematically with eighteenth-century thinkers like Baumgarten, Burke and Kant. In fact, these figures put aesthetics side by side with ethics and logics and researched the conditions of the possibility of beauty, taste and pleasure. A question might arise here: why does Perniola write frequently on aesthetics – devoting two monographs (CA, EIC) to contemporary aesthetics – but state that his influences should be traced within the Stoics, the Baroque thinkers or even Palaeolithic engravings and Egyptian and Roman societies? To put it differently, why does Perniola seem to be suspicious of aesthetics, paradoxically since the precise period it was founded?

First, it is not entirely true that Perniola is not influenced by any authors and aesthetic schools of thought belonging to the previous three centuries. However, looking at this closer, he can be seen to be influenced by philosophers, artists and thinkers who had, so to speak, a preaesthetic and antiaesthetic approach to aesthetics. At a first glance, this statement might seem contradictory. However, it becomes clearer when the difference between aesthetics prior to its philosophical foundation and after it is highlighted. The main difference lies in the fact that philosophical aesthetics is oriented towards dissecting the various notions and experiences belonging to the realm of sensitive knowledge. The main objective is to produce a new typology of knowledge around *aisthēsis*: the perceptions of the senses. In doing so, aesthetics became a distinct and particular discipline with its own rules and principles. The aesthetics of the eighteenth century onwards has produced, above all, treatises on sensitive knowledge, in which the main aim has been to systematize it, catalogue it and grasp its properties. Beauty ended up being separate, if not isolated, from everyday attitudes. On the contrary, by combining rock art, Egyptian architecture, Roman and post-Renaissance rituals and Stoicism and the Baroque, Perniola tries to underline precisely the idea of an aesthetic that includes a global vision of the individual. To put it briefly: aesthetics and action are two sides of the same coin. This is the reason why a notion like *agudeza*, Perniola suggests, does not 'speak' easily to the experience of the contemporary individual. *Agudeza* still belongs to the ideal of an individual in which will, attitudes and tastes are inseparable from one another. In any event, as will be clarified in the next chapter, Perniola still praises those figures who have devoted their lives and research to this way of conceiving aesthetics (such as Baudelaire, Nietzsche, Bataille, Klossowski and Debord).

The second notion explored by Gracián and discussed by Perniola is *ingenio*. The meanings with which Gracián characterizes ingenuity are far from those made of traditional aesthetics. In fact, *ingenio* is connected to the figure of the *genius*. According to Kant, the artist genius is so because he/she possesses an innate talent that predisposes him/her to art and artistic creation. On the other hand, ingenious does not relate to art and aesthetics, but rather to the practical realization of something, especially in the field of technology and mechanics. As Perniola points out, modern aesthetics 'on the one hand ties ingenuity to a practical and mechanical effectiveness, on the other isolates genius in a poetic and formal purity' (E: 116). The ingenuity conceived by Gracián, instead, far from being solely spiritual or merely functional, is closer to the conception that Francis Bacon has of the imagination (and which Perniola borrows to define the influence that the Baroque has had on his philosophy), which consists of making unlawful matches and divorces among things. Here, Giuseppe Patella points out that Perniola's is a 'philosophy of the *between*, the intermediate ... which precisely represents the mediation that separates but also the distance that unites' (2019: online source). In the *Diccionario de conceptos de Baltasar Gracián* (2005), Jorge M. Ayala suggests in fact that 'Gracián believes that the universe is composed of singular things and persons. Nonetheless they are not incommunicable monads ... The *ingenium* discovers the subtle network of relations that things have in themselves' (2005: 154). To clarify an ingenious attitude, Perniola highlights (E: 116) a series of aphorisms within Gracián's work. The variety of operations produced by ingenuity can be summarized in the ability to transform nature into culture and to make this transformation seem natural. The dandy shares this feature of Baroque ingenuity. Recall Brummell's hours spent in front of his mirror, carefully taking care of his appearance and, at the same time, never alluding in public to all these efforts. *Ingenium* can be produced by forming paradoxes, concealing criticism through praise, setting enigmas, alluding, discovering affinities between distant things, among others. In other words, it implies the ability to move, dislocate and transform with art the data given in their immediacy. The goal here is to transform a mere fact, event or encounter into a prism of surprising possibilities. Thus, *ingenium* is an act of subtle artifice concerned specifically with beauty: '*ingenium* cannot content itself only with truth, like judgement, but aspires to beauty' (Gracián 1969: 18). In addition: '[*ingenium*] is an act of understanding which expresses existing and present correspondence between objects' (Gracián 1969: 242). Gracián writes of the 'existing and present' relationships between objects to underline that with this 'metaphorical comparison', *ingenium* is not addressed to creativity but to the development of something already present.[6] In this context, the focus on presence and the present, one of the main features of both Stoicism and Perniola's notion of transit, can be found.

Finally, the third pivotal notion of Gracián's aesthetics is the *concepto*. The 'concept' is usually defined as an idea collecting the essential elements of a given reality or phenomenon. A concept 'grasps', 'grabs' or 'seizes' its objects. To explain Gracián's notion of *concepto*, Perniola leaves behind this interpretation and returns to the Latin etymology of the word concept, which is *conceptus*, here derived from *con-capio*. *Con-capio* means 'to take' in the sense of 'welcoming' or 'gathering in' something: 'to conceive (*concepire*) does not mean therefore to appropriate anything, but rather to make room for it' (E: 122). In other words, a concept would imply not so much an activity of the subject towards an object but rather a disposition of the subject and a willingness to receive what comes from the outside. Indeed, as Serna writes, commenting on the notion of *concepto* in Gracián:

> The Gracián concept is not demonstrative. The logic of the ingenious concept cannot be formal or rational. Its concepts cannot express logical relationships, but always only new, real relationships, which constitute the unique essence of things. Gracián attempts to show, not to demonstrate. Concepts therefore must be a re-representation of reality.
>
> 1980: 252

The 'ingenious concept' is a method for displaying and showing original correspondences between things, combining them in a new language outside rational and logical structures. Here, *ingenium* is considered by Serna and Perniola as a faculty capable of creating a 'conceptual attitude' by drawing out the relationships between images and objects.

In this context, another theme shared by the traditions explored returns: that of a benevolent and affirmative disposition towards the events, towards what is independent and cannot be controlled by the individual. This implies becoming nothing, downsizing oneself and remaining in a state of suspension that ultimately allows the individual to transform the things of the world. However, because *agudeza, ingenio* and *concepto* are not three separate moments but should instead be understood as a fundamental triad for the art of living well, gathering in what comes from outside does not mean passively receiving everything. On the contrary, this implies using ingenuity, discerning, having discretion and knowing how to move in concrete circumstances. This conception is what Perniola praises as 'strategic beauty', in which aesthetics and manners are never oblivious to the practical element.

To conclude, Gracián grounds his aesthetic theory on the notions of *agudeza, ingenio* and *concepto*. *Agudeza*, as suggested, has the characteristics of something pointed close to a needle or a sword. The dimensions of penetrating, piercing and 'becoming' sharp are essential. The Baroque wise man is close to an elegant warrior who uses words, gestures, silences and witty remarks as blades. Gracián places the element of conflict and challenge at the core of an aesthetic attitude, which does not necessarily result in final harmony. Indeed, it is precisely the disharmonic element, as Tatarkiewicz points out, that is crucial for Baroque theory:

> The most desirable themes possible for an artist or thinker are precisely disharmonies, disproportions, dissonances, paradoxes, inconsistencies, immeasurables, *disparidad*, difficulties, contradictions, mysteries, enigmas, hyperbole (*exageración*), fictions, equivocations, unclarities, etc. All these are ideal subjects for *agudeza* and the very essence of *mannerist aesthetics*.
>
> Tatarkiewicz 1974: 387

Agudeza is highlighted here as the ability that enables one to perceive the conflict that animates the relations between the things of the world without consequently bringing it back to a final unity or conciliation. Its peculiarity – and at the same time its paradoxicality – is that of being, on the one hand, close to Stoic discretion and prudence and, on the other hand, to a Heraclitean conception of life. In fact, Heraclitus can be considered an outsider among the aesthetics theorists explored so far. His philosophy cannot be traced back either to the objectivistic theory of beauty, to the subjectivist theory or to that of the Stoics. For Heraclitus, beauty emerges from *enantiodromia*, the tension between each thing and its opposite. The originality of this perspective lies in the fact that opposition is never overcome by greater harmony: the state of ambivalence that characterizes everything remains. It is precisely on these grounds – that is, on the link between conflict in the Baroque and in the aesthetic tradition more generally – that we can move on to the next chapter, where we will uncover the relationship between Perniola and one of the most influential spiritual fathers of the avant-garde movements: Charles Baudelaire and his philosophical dandyism.

8

Charles Baudelaire: Greatness without Convictions

The second exemplar dandy I discuss alongside Perniola's thought is Charles Baudelaire. Like Brummell, Baudelaire shares several main assumptions and attitudes that are typically dandy (such as the privilege accorded to artificiality, elegance and provocation as well as the critique of utilitarianism). However, whereas Brummell did not leave any writings or theorizations on dandyism or, broadly speaking, on his life, Baudelaire focused on dandyism in various essays and poetic writings, such as *The Salon of 1846*, *Flares* and *My Heart Laid Bare* (Baudelaire 2011). In addition, in a letter to his editor Poulet-Malassis (Natta 2011: 7), he announced the idea for a text entitled *Dandyism, or the Greatness Without Convictions*, which in the end could not be realized. *The Painter of Modern Life*, however, remains Baudelaire's most significant and detailed contribution to dandyism, and it is from this text that I commence my discussion of his conception of dandyism.

To each age its beauty

Baudelaire defines dandyism as a 'vague', 'ancient' and 'mysterious' institution 'beyond the laws', also stating that Caesar, Catiline and Alcibiades should be regarded as dandies (1964: 26). In the first chapter of *The Painter of Modern Life*, entitled 'Beauty, Fashion, and Happiness', Baudelaire claims that beauty can be characterized in two ways: eternal and relative. At first glance, this invocation of an eternal feature can suggest that he supports an essentialist and Platonic aesthetic theory, in which beauty exists at an objective if not absolute level. However, the French poet does not dwell on universal measures or eternal canons that make something objectively beautiful. On the contrary, he states that 'absolute and eternal beauty does not exist' (1996: 1097). By positing that beauty is also composed of an eternal element, Baudelaire means that aesthetic activities, attitudes and conducts are observed at every age and thus are a universal constant of human behaviour. From Palaeolithic paintings and engravings to contemporary video art, from ancient monumental statues and architecture to hyper-realistic portraits, humans have always displayed artistic and aesthetic habits or behaviours. To this timeless aspect of beauty, Baudelaire adds one which he believes is relative to each age: 'We may assert that since all centuries and all peoples have had their own form of beauty, so inevitably we have ours' (1996: 1096). For Baudelaire, the task of the dandy entails living according to elegance and distinction, regardless of the specific period in which they are living, on the one hand and, on the other, to find, extract and bring to light the peculiar beauty of their times. The lifestyle of the dandy is aesthetically oriented and always seeks beauty in what is modern. Here lies the reason that dandyism, for Baudelaire, is paradoxically an ancient institution and simultaneously an essentially modern one. The dandies of the past were *modern* in their times; that is, they developed and explored their aesthetic lifestyles in light of, or rather in reaction to, their era's newest trends.

In academia, modernity usually refers to a historical period (the modern era) between the Middle Ages and postmodernity. By contrast, Baudelaire considers modernity to be an attitude towards one's own present. For instance, he claims, 'Every old master has had his own modernity' (1964: 13). Baudelaire seems to go back to the etymological roots of the late Latin adjective *modernus*, which is derived from the adverb *modo*, meaning 'just now' as well as 'manner'. Thus, modernity, in his view, does not imply a specific century. Instead, it involves the ideas of contingency, precariousness and circumstances that make something beautiful only for a certain period. The dandy's attitude does not praise any idea of an *a priori* beauty; it focuses on the peculiar beauty belonging to each time. Herein lies the specularist behaviour of the dandy. The dandies become mirrors of their contemporaneity and thus appropriate and reflect an always-modern beauty.

To present an example, Baudelaire himself uses the metaphor of the mirror: 'the lover of universal life enters the crowd as though it were an immense reservoir of electrical energy. Or we might liken him to a mirror as vast as the crowd itself; or to a kaleidoscope gifted with consciousness, responding to each one of its movements and reproducing the multiplicity of life and the flickering grace of all the elements of life' (1964: 9). Baudelaire argues that the dandy is first and foremost someone who engages every day in the work of becoming a mirror, that is, a surface that reflects the surrounding world. The multifarious external stimuli to which s/he is exposed are in fact gathered in the same way that, metaphorically speaking, a mirror reflects the surroundings on its surface.

Nonetheless, this attitude does not imply that the dandy considers modernity beautiful in all its manifestations. A dandy's task, for Baudelaire, is to unfold the beauty unique to each modernity. I would argue that this belief links Baudelaire's conception of beauty to the Stoics' notion of the πρέπον and to Gracián's Baroque idea of *agudeza*. *Agudeza* refers to an idea of beauty that, as in Baudelaire, does not emerge within a harmonic discourse, grounded upon aesthetic objectivity and unity of parts. On the contrary, it is the consequence of movement, surprise and conflict or of an event that in other words, like lightning, bursts into everyday life, as in the case of the electric lights mentioned in the extract. The πρέπον, or the 'convenient', implies that beauty depends on occasions, circumstances and continually transitory combinations of elements that are relative to a given context. As Baudelaire put it: 'Woe to him who studies the antique for anything else but pure art, logic, and general method! By steeping himself too thoroughly on it, he will lose all memory of the present; he will renounce the rights and privileges offered by circumstance – for almost all our originality comes from the seal which Time imprints on our sensations' (1964: 14). Baudelaire highlights that the dandy's relationship with the past should not be that of imitation, which may end up as sterile mimicry, blind to what the present can offer. Referring only to the classics and what is ancient, according to Baudelaire, 'is clearly symptomatic of a great degree of laziness; for it is much easier to decide outright that everything about the garb of an age is absolutely ugly than to devote oneself to the task of distilling from it the mysterious element of beauty that it may contain, however slight or minimal that element may be' (1964: 13). The dandy should therefore cultivate the idea of beauty in their person and not at an abstract level by imitating previous trends and fashions, but by becoming the mirror of their own modernity, focusing on its fugitive, transitory elements and the continuous metamorphosis that characterizes beauty in a given epoch.

It is no accident that Perniola included Baudelaire's artistic production in the category of 'art as occasion' (external circumstances) rather than 'art as inspiration' (internal urging). 'For Baudelaire,' Perniola writes, 'the key aspect of occasional art is its *modernity*, with its ability to know how to perceive the present in its social, collective, civilized, worldly reality ... The poet, the artist, therefore, must not be a specialist of words or colours but, above all, a man of the world, *un homme du monde*' (RT: 215).

To sum up, the dandy should firstly have a welcoming attitude towards reality (as each time has its own beauty) and then extract the peculiar beauty of that reality. Thus, the acceptance of one's present does not mean an unconditional acceptance of everything that is at hand. The task of the dandy often implies a challenge or a conflict, if not a revolt, to find beauty in what is considered a vulgar and trivial world.[1]

Perniola's aesthetic horizon and Baudelaire's anti-aesthetics

In an article published in the journal *Ágalma*, entitled 'Prova di forza o prova di grandezza? Considerazioni sull'ágalma' (Test of strength or test of greatness? Considerations on the ágalma, PF: 62–79), Perniola focuses on several of the themes surrounding the relationship between aesthetics and economy and devotes two pages to a brief theorization of the phenomenon of dandyism (PF: 76–7). According to Perniola, the greatness of the dandy is based on three main characteristics: 'provocation', 'exteriorization' and 'detachment'. Provocation refers to a conflict against the emerging bourgeois mentality spreading in nineteenth-century Europe; it entails challenging daily life, which is called into question by the dandy's disorientating, witty and subversive attitudes. Exteriorization entails welcoming what comes from outside (i.e. the external world) through a specularist view. The dandy, in other words, becomes a mirror, a reflecting surface of modernity. Finally, the notion of detachment is linked to Baudelaire's re-evaluation of Stoicism and warrior codes. The French poet elaborates a neo-Stoicism grounded on the cultivation of cold spirit and self-confidence. The three notions are explored in the following pages.

The provocation of the dandy, according to Perniola, is primarily a revolt against the daily life of modernity, with its cult of work, money, progress, utility and traditional understandings of family, love, desire and pleasure. The dandy opposes the typical bourgeois mentality of the nineteenth century that conceives everyday life as a polarity between work and free time, fatigue and leisure, and production and relaxation. Perniola's remarks are based on Baudelaire's perspective. Baudelaire is interested in the 'heroism of modern life'. To be such a hero, in Baudelaire's view, has to do with cultivating a lifestyle that defies the standards of modernity. Baudelaire himself helps the reader to better understand the dandy's peculiar type of revolt. In fact, the dandy is often called into question as an opponent of certain traits and aspects of the eighteenth-century *Zeitgeist*. As Favardin and Bouëxière note, 'the dandy becomes a weapon. Baudelaire quotes the dandy whenever he wants to affirm an idea, a revolution …' (1988: 89). For instance, Baudelaire says that money is a 'crude passion' (1964: 27), which the dandy should not regard as essential. Money is abhorred by Baudelaire because it is the core of commerce, which he considers the lowest and most vile form of selfishness (Baudelaire 1996: 1444). In fact, in several passages, Baudelaire endorses, so to speak, the equation 'natural = squalid', where 'nature' covers a broad notion of self-interest (for instance, animals struggling for their survival and self-preservation). Furthermore, Baudelaire writes that the figure of the merchant is morally ambiguous (he even states that 'commerce is satanic' in 1996: 1444), because besides the element of natural self-interest, the merchant also seeks interests and earnings and converts his time and life into a profit machine.[2] Therefore, first, the dandy revolts against the passion for money, which is perceived as crude and vulgar, as it enslaves individuals and transforms them into nothing more than profit-oriented functionaries. In fact, Baudelaire goes further in his provocative standpoint: in a fragment of *My Heart Laid Bare*, he affirms that 'there exist but three respectable beings: the priest, the warrior, the poet. To know, to die and to create. The other men are tallieable and corvéable, made for the stable, that is, to exercise what one calls *professions*' (1996: 1423–4). He has an aversion not only to money but also to the concept of utility and function. According to him, being useful in doing something or being functional means being dependent, bound by duty or a job. The individual shaping their life according to their profession thus ultimately becomes a fragment, completely consumed in their peculiar specialization. I argue that Perniola's aesthetic theory and Baudelaire's words share the essential characteristic of being anti-specialism. The previous chapter showed that the notions of *agudeza*, *ingenio* and *concepto* belong to an anti-aesthetic world view (i.e. against traditional aesthetics, which is considered as a narrow specialization of sensory knowledge by Perniola). In the same way, Baudelaire's dandyism is against specialisms, or as Favardin and Bouëxière put it in *Le Dandysme*, 'the dandy has terror of each specialization' (1988: 85). Specifically, Baudelaire not only challenges the specialism of academic theorists, but he also turns against the concept of specialism itself.

In *Contro la comunicazione* (Against Communication), Perniola defines Baudelairean poetics with the expression 'anti-aesthetic over-interest' (*sovra-interessamento anti-estetico*, CC: 76). Perniola also elaborates on this notion because he considers Baudelaire to be a crucial figure who anticipated what he calls the 'expansion of the aesthetic horizon'. Since its foundation as a philosophy discipline, the 'aesthetic horizon' (*orizzonte estetico*) encompassed – for Perniola – four main aspects: beauty, art, philosophy and lifestyles (HE: 3; also see EFH, COA). Multifarious aesthetic issues have stemmed from each of these aspects throughout the centuries: beauty has been explored alongside notions such as the sublime, the gracious, the subtle and disinterest, just to name a few; art has been considered a cluster concept that includes heterogeneous fields from poetry to painting, sculpture, architecture, music, literature, dance, photography and cinema; philosophy, in its long history, has encompassed a variety of literary genres, from the dialogue to the treatise, the poem, the letter, the fragment, the oral tradition and so forth. Finally, aesthetically oriented lifestyles can be seen in an extremely variegated combination: the saint, the hero, the martyr, the dandy, the femme fatale and the poet (HE: 3). The aesthetic horizon should not be considered to have a harmonic balance but as a permanent dynamism where each element is continuously called into question through research, conflict and experimentation; in addition, these elements do not stand alone or independently from each other but are inherently interactive and mutually affect themselves: 'It is about open and fluid notions which assert and evolve themselves within the aesthetic horizon depending on circumstances and opportunities, weaving alternately alliances and antagonisms, correspondences and contrasts' (HE: 4). With respect to the aesthetic horizon briefly outlined, Perniola claims that Baudelaire anticipated a 'cultural turn' (*svolta culturale*) which has occurred in the aesthetic field only recently. A project such as the *Encyclopedia of Aesthetics*, edited and directed by Michael Kelly and published in 1998, 'foreshadows a cultural turn in aesthetics that intends to bridge the existing gap between aesthetic knowledge and contemporary society' (CTA: 39). In other words, for Perniola, a new sensitivity within the aesthetic realm emerged at the end of the twentieth century, which explores new territories previously excluded by canonical aesthetic knowledge (on this topic also see Collins 1998; Patella 2001; Saito 2010; Di Stefano 2018; Somhegyi and Ryynänen 2020). Specifically, Perniola singles out at least three key additional territories: first, alternative or traditionally marginal phenomena such as 'grotesque', 'obscenity', 'situationist aesthetics', 'iconoclasm', 'popular culture and music' and 'fashion', just to name a few.

Second, the cultural turn expands the aesthetic horizon by also including non-Western and non-European cultures (African, Caribbean, Chinese, Japanese, Indian, Islamic, Latin American, among many others). The prestigious and well-known International Congress of Aesthetics, held every three years in a different place around the world, is a fertile soil to witness and experience the precise cultural turn of aesthetics that Perniola investigates: the traditional figures and concepts of aesthetics (from Kant to Hume, Hegel, Kierkegaard, Nietzsche, Dewey, Adorno and so forth) appear to have become negligible compared to panels, round tables and conferences devoted, by contrast, to 'urban aesthetics', 'aesthetics and technology', 'aesthetics and post-media practice' and 'aesthetics of East Asia, South America, Africa'.

The third and final aspect for Perniola is the re-definition of the boundaries of the aesthetic horizon, with entries in Kelly's encyclopaedia revolving around 'outsider art', the 'art of the insane' and the general thresholds between insider and outsider art. Ultimately, the cultural turn of aesthetics indicates a widening of the aesthetic horizon in which numerous disciplines and cultural traditions meet, giving birth to complex and multifaceted issues.[3]

Nonetheless, Perniola claims that at a closer glance, a group of 'non-canonical' aesthetic figures, from the Romantics to Nietzsche, Freud, De Quincey, Stendhal, Poe and Baudelaire, anticipated this expansion. For all these authors, Perniola writes, 'important phenomena of modernity such as fashion, the city, material life, drugs, prostitution, conflict, and exoticism find a sharp and profound treatment that still constitutes today a fundamental theoretical reference point' (CTA: 43). Paradoxically, whereas the recent cultural turn is institutionalized and ascribable to aesthetics, academies and specializations, that from the eighteenth and nineteenth centuries manifested as anti-aesthetics, anti-academism and anti-specialization.

Among these perspectives and ideas, Perniola specifically explores Baudelaire's theory of 'surnaturalism' (*surnaturalisme*). First, Perniola claims, Baudelaire is at odds with the Kantian notion of aesthetic disinterest. Kant's theory is based on a formal conception of aesthetics. Focusing on the formal elements that structure our aesthetic judgements *per se*, Kant is not interested in all the sensible content towards which the same judgements are directed. In other words, Kant elaborates a theory that is able to explain how our aesthetic judgements work, independent of any empirical object contemplated by the subject. A key distinguishing feature of this theory is the notion of disinterest. Kantian judgements are disinterested, that is, the existence of the artistic object is irrelevant to our understanding of how our own aesthetic perception works. Kant does not deny that a given object can generate impressions and sensations for its viewer; however, he does not include these within his formal theory of aesthetics. Conversely, beauty, for Baudelaire – as well as for Perniola – is always understood in relation to reality and its relativity and thus in its concrete historical existence.

Baudelaire's theory of surnaturalism is in fact at odds with Kantian formalism. Whereas formalism is based on disinterest, surnaturalism emerges only if the individual is over-interested in the world. Baudelaire conceives his poetic attitude as the ability to translate exterior life (1996: 1289), that is, to use the faculties of imagination and creation to transform the existing world into a marvellous and beautiful one and to also be able to see beauty in what is normally excluded from it. The dandy, for Baudelaire, does not create arbitrary correspondences with the things of the world. On the contrary, s/he is guided precisely by that which is external. Specifically, Baudelaire's surnaturalism revolves around the emerging urban life of the metropolis. As Perniola wrote:

> The landscapes of the metropolis, the splendor of civil and military life, the alternation of seriousness and coquetry, the multiform images of equivocal beauty, the challenges of dandyism, the seductions of the artificial, the *charm* of horror are the precise elements of a new sensitivity, which is a thousand miles away from the disinterested contemplation of academic aesthetics. This type of sensitivity is accessed through a worldly asceticism that has its highest expression in the dandy.
>
> CC: 77

The concept of disinterest is taken as a polemical target insofar as it produces a hiatus – a gap between aesthetics and the world. Baudelaire's surnaturalist dandyism sews together beauty and reality. The dandy, in this sense, can be considered one of the 'painters of modern life' (as Baudelaire's essay is titled), meaning that they are able to depict, provide and re-establish an aesthetic dimension in the modern metropolis without praising bourgeois mindsets. In fact, the French dandy is interested in tracing the ideal type of individual, or the dandy, who encourages a kind of aristocracy of behaviours and manners against what he feels is the decadence of modern habits.

Beyond the keywords of bourgeois life, such as money, trade and specialization, commerce, Baudelaire is against subjectivism and naturalism. The critique of naturalism is linked to the privilege that the dandy ascribes to exterior and artificial elements; the critique of subjectivism lies in the daily efforts the dandy makes to form a detached attitude.

Dandies, mirrors, blackness

As mentioned earlier, externalization is seeded in the privilege given by Baudelaire to that which is external and artificial; detachment indicates a day-to-day attitude of worldly desubjectivation on the part of the dandy. The two polemical targets here are, respectively, nature and subjectivity.

Developing the concept of thing in Perniola's philosophy, this book has also looked at his studies on the theme of exteriorization. Specifically, I have explored the concept of specularism in reference to the daily practice of Zen monks and Baroque literary aesthetics.

The phenomenon of specularism within dandyism was also introduced in the previous section, which details the daily clothing ritual of Brummell. I underlined how the English dandy was constantly striving, in the meticulous care of his toilette, to disappear under the material element of clothing. The toilette ritual is also found in several passages of Baudelaire's work. For example, in a fragment of *My Heart Laid Bare*, he writes 'A chapter on The Toilette / Morality of the Toilet / The pleasures of the toilet' (1996: 1434). Although these remarks are sketchy, they do suggest Baudelaire's interest in the theme. Again, in *The Painter of Modern Life*, he states: 'his eyes [of the dandy], are in love with distinction above all things, the perfection of his toilet will consist of absolute simplicity, which is the best way, in fact, of achieving the desired quality' (1964: 27). Baudelaire, like Brummell and Barbey d'Aurevilly, was convinced that this distinction is a matter of elegance, which cannot be achieved through showy, impressive or expensive clothes owned by the dandy. Conversely, it emerges above all from their manner, that is, the *way* in which they wear their clothes. On closer inspection, simplicity in Baudelaire's dandyism appears to be even more rigorous – if not more extreme – than Brummell's. While the English dandy used to in fact wear a heterogeneous palette of colours that he considered suitable for his style, Baudelaire praised only one colour for his clothes: black. As Moers writes, 'What most impressed Baudelaire's friends in those years was his insistence on black – overwhelming, gleaming black from his lustrous high hat to his impeccable polished shoes' (1960: 272). Here lies a key difference between Brummell and Baudelaire, relayed by the fact that the former belonged to the high society of the time. As suggested, he was an *arbiter elegantiarum* within balls, social events, royal weddings. Conversely, Baudelaire was not close to any aristocracy. His ideal companions were the bohemian free spirits and the Parisian artists, who shared with him a creative sensitivity at odds with the was at odds with the bourgeois cult of efficiency and work. Nonetheless, Baudelaire distanced himself from them precisely because he did not possess any extravagant affectation and negligent disarray (typical of the bohemians), but an 'old-fashioned politeness of manners' (Moers 1960: 273), which made him an anomaly in those circles.

Moers claims that black conferred upon the poet a 'spiritual aloofness' and an attitude of detachment in an 'age of mourning' (1960: 274). Blackness, in Moers' view, reflects a melancholic sensitivity that can indeed be found in many of Baudelaire's poems and essays. From *The Flowers of Evil* to *Paris Spleen*, his verses are filled with disturbing images and experiences and depressing, melancholic attitudes. Baudelaire claims that beauty should be found precisely in these representations and events. Again, beauty for Baudelaire, and for Perniola, is not the result of any harmony or unity of the parts of a given object. Instead, it emerges from conflicting, uncanny experiences, which 'pierce' the individual in their daily life. This is clearly expressed by Baudelaire himself: 'I do not pretend that Joy cannot be associated with Beauty, but I say that Joy is one of its most vulgar ornaments: whereas Melancholy is, so to speak, the illustrious companion, to such an extent that I can hardly conceive ... of a type of beauty where there is no *Sadness*' (1996: 1396). Sadness and melancholy are both key features of Baudelaire's choice of all-black clothing. He provided an explanation of his colour preference in the last chapter of *The Salon of 1846*, entitled 'On the Heroism of Modern Life'. Despite the decadence of manners and arts, despite the Americanization of European society, Baudelaire stresses that there still are some figures who to him are heroic. The dandy is a pivotal figure of this heroic revolt, and the black suit, according to Baudelaire, is first and foremost 'the symbol of a perpetual mourning ... each of us celebrating a funeral' (1996: 1097). In other words, black, being the mourning colour par excellence, conveys Baudelaire's attitudes towards beauty and society better than other colours possibly could. In fact, for Baudelaire, the most heroic challenge is precisely to *be able* to paint only with black, that is, to extract beauty from any age, even one which praises money, profit, commerce, trade. Black is the acceptance of one's own time and world: 'Parisian life is rich in poetic and marvelous subjects. We are enveloped and steeped as though in an atmosphere of the marvelous; but we do not notice it' (1996: 1099).

Therefore, I am not convinced by Benjamin's interpretation of Baudelaire's notion of modernity. According to Benjamin, 'Modernity turns out to be his [Baudelaire's] doom. There are no provisions for him in it; it has no use for his type. It moors him fast in the secure harbour forever and abandons him to everlasting idleness' (Benjamin 2006: 124). Although the black suit indicates mourning, it does not imply doom. Baudelaire's strategy is paradoxical. He opposes his society by sympathizing with it. I use sympathy here in the etymological meaning of *sym* (together) and *pathein* (to feel) and thus meaning feeling in common. Perniola himself underlined this aspect of Baudelaire's attitude: 'Opposition [in Baudelaire] succeeds only through the identification with the point of view of the opponent ... The same weapon both wounds and heals' (CA: 76). In addition, the implications of Baudelaire's black suit are akin to the attitude of the Zen monk and share conceptual affinities with Orante's transformation into a mirror, as explored by Perniola. All three, in fact, comprise a mimicry in which the external is mirrored and the outer world is welcomed. Indeed, the metaphor of the mirror helps in a better understanding of Baudelaire's overall aesthetic position, as it implies not living according to the past, imitating it, or reproducing its main features, but leaving room for one's own contemporaneity, that is, being *modern*. A mirror cannot choose what to reflect; it simply 'collects' what is external on its surface and affirms it, making the present rich.

Becoming a mirror should not be confused with narcissism. A narcissist uses, so to speak, the world as a mirror to see themselves reflected all around. A specularist, like the dandy, transforms themselves into a mirror to reflect, or assimilate, what comes from outside, namely the world and its manifestations. Precisely for this reason, I believe that Sartre, in his volume on Baudelaire, misses a crucial point on dandyism, when he states, 'Dandyism was an episode in a venture in which Baudelaire was continually resorting to grief; he was Narcissus trying to mirror himself in his own waters and catch his reflections' (Sartre 1967: 135). Not only does Baudelaire turn himself into a reflecting surface, thereby avoiding narcissism, but also, even if a dandy spends hours in front of a mirror, he performs a clothing ritual in which ego, subjectivity and vanity are shed to open up a neutral dimension. Paradoxically, therefore, the mirror is a means through which the dandy ascertains that all their efforts to disappear are well executed – not, as Sartre suggests, a 'water' in which to catch their own reflection.

Getting rid of nature

The dandy does not pursue harmony with nature (as it is for the Zen sage). Nature in itself, according to Baudelaire, has nothing to make it worth contemplating. It is only the individual who finds 'correspondences' between the outer world, the senses, and the imagination. Baudelaire writes, 'Nature teaches us nothing, or practically nothing. I admit that she *compels* man to sleep, to eat, to drink, and to arm himself as well as he may against the inclemencies of the weather: but it is she too who incites man to murder his brother, to eat him, to lock him up and to torture him ... Crime ... is natural by origin. Virtue, on the other hand, is artificial, supernatural' (1964: 31–2). Here, Baudelaire investigates two different registers: one ethical and one aesthetic. At the ethical level, he contrasts nature and artifice. He claims that where nature is the voice of personal interest, artifice corresponds to human faculties. Self-interest, for Baudelaire, can easily lead to criminal outcomes because it is driven by survival instincts, which he considers blind to their consequences. On the other hand, human faculties can help individuals cultivate alternative and ethical lifestyles.

Baudelaire also makes this argument within the aesthetic field: 'the majority of errors in the fields of aesthetics springs from the eighteenth century's false premiss in the field of ethics' (1964: 31). In this passage, Baudelaire criticizes the eighteenth-century á la Rousseau aesthetic claim that nature is the archetype of goodness and beauty. Baudelaire's view is at odds with this: nature does not make any object beautiful, and beauty cannot be produced by mimicking nature.[4] Baudelaire did not see nature as the source of the absolute (as several Romantic representatives argued), nor as the unspoiled and genuine root of human freedom and spontaneity (see also Jouve 1980). To him, nature's main objective is to guide individuals in their struggle for survival and the continuation of life, and this means pushing aside imagination and other faculties.[5]

Baudelaire did not use a scientific lexicon to express his perspectives; he maintained a provocative and challenging register that often disturbs the reader with uncanny and dark images and representations. Nonetheless, he separates art and nature and categorizes the former under human productions and behaviours. Baudelaire's critique of a lifestyle oriented towards nature's goals (self-interest and survival) also appears clearly in his *In Praise of Cosmetics*: 'face-painting should not be used with the vulgar, unavowable object of imitating fair Nature and of entering in competition with youth' (1964: 35); 'maquillage ... is successfully designed to rid the complexion of those blemishes that Nature has outrageously strewn there, and thus to create an abstract unity in the colour and texture of the skin, a unity, which ... immediately approximates the human being to the statue' (1964: 33).

First, Baudelaire suggests that make-up should not be used with hopes of getting one's own beauty back, competing therefore with the passing of time, namely with the natural course of events. The objective of using make-up, for Baudelaire, is not to re-establish a previous natural state of things. On the contrary, its purpose is to delete traces of nature from the body's surface. Baudelaire despises natural skin and praises the artificial one, almost suspended from time, statue-like, close to a paradoxical inanimate and inorganic life. Perniola's conception of 'thing' can be related to this claim. As suggested earlier, the practice of becoming thing falls under several traditions of thought and human experience. Baudelaire's dandyism can be placed within this perspective. On the one hand, by defending the use of make-up and cosmetics, Baudelaire praises an inorganic-oriented individual, where vital and natural elements such as blood and skin imperfections are covered and deleted. On the other hand, his dandy type is described as a 'mirror', that is, close to a material reflecting surface, a thing, which welcomes what comes from outside and which, as a 'kaleidoscope', finds the endless combinations emerging from urban life aesthetically marvellous. The attitude of 'extracting' beauty from one's own modernity is linked not only to the acceptance of time and presence (*amor fati*) but also to the aesthetic concept of πρέπον, wherein beauty depends on circumstances.

The process of turning oneself into a thing implies getting closer to a neutral dimension, where subjectivity disappears and the natural drives and impulses are set aside. As Coblence noted, 'the experience is akin to that of hashish: in the crowd, like under the effect of drugs, personality disappears, objectivity develops itself atypically and allows one to contemplate exterior objects, forgetting one's own existence; the subject mixes itself with the contemplated things. The artist too slips among objects and individuals' (1988: 287). This statement needs to be further clarified by developing the relation between dandyism and 'detachment', the third and last essential characteristic of dandyism pointed out by Perniola.

The dandies between stoics and samurai

Baudelaire refers to Stoicism and the Jesuit-Baroque world in several passages. For example, 'dandyism borders upon the spiritual and the stoical' (1964: 28); 'The strictest rigorous monastic rule . . . which also imposes upon its humble and ambitious disciples . . . the terrible formula: *Perinde ac cadaver!*' (1964: 28). Scholars often disagree on Baudelaire's Stoicism. Natta argues that although Baudelaire states that dandyism 'borders' on Stoicism and despite the fact that even Barbey d'Aurevilly in several passages dwells on this affinity, 'the dandies do resemble only from a distance their ancient models' (2011: 111). For instance, in his *Of Dandyism and of George Brummell*, Barbey writes: 'These [the dandies] Stoics of the *boudoir*' (1897: 102). Moreover, Barbey frequently associates dandyism with an ancient attitude of calm and self-discipline – typical of Stoic *habitus* – within modern societies' agitation. Natta specifically argues that while the classic Stoic sage accepts civil society and nature as necessary outcomes of the supreme *logos*, the dandy is a key figure of opposition, against both the bourgeois mindset and nature. She continues, 'Stoic resignation is not a dandy virtue. The dandy does not resign – he is against, surely with detachment, isolating himself, but he is against. All his behaviour is a protest against society and nature, which the Stoics associate with reason' (Natta 2011: 113). This criticism does not fully grasp the dandies' re-evaluation of Stoicism. In fact, the dandies' purpose is not to *reproduce* ancient Stoic doctrine but to develop neo-Stoicism. To claim that Baudelaire's dandyism is an attempt to imitate the ancient set of philosophical assertions and propositions elaborated by the Stoics would imply a failure to understand his aesthetic standpoint. As Aurie Zeran pointed out in her dissertation *The Evolution of Indifference*, a dandy's neo-Stoicism is based on the concepts of *appropriation* and *parody*: 'Appropriation is the practice of reworking or imitating a style from another work to incite re-evaluation or critical challenge. Parody is the use of that imitation to produce satire by applying it to an unlikely subject' (2014: 6). If Baudelaire's purpose was only to reproduce Stoic philosophy, then Natta would have been right in pointing out that, for instance, nature is praised by Stoicism and despised by the dandies. Instead, as Zeran argues, the dandy's goal is to 'rework', 'challenge critically' and 'produce satire' by appropriating and parodying Stoicism within modernity.

The main characteristic shared by the dandy and the Stoic is 'coldness of spirit' or 'detachment'. Baudelaire frequently refers to this characteristic of the dandy in *The Painter of Modern Life* but also in *Flares* and in *My Heart Laid Bare*. For instance: 'the dandy aspires to insensitivity' (1964: 9); dandyism is 'the joy of astonishing others, and the proud satisfaction of never being astonished. A dandy may be *blasé*, he may even suffer; but in this case, he will smile like the Spartan boy under the fox's tooth' (1964: 28); 'his lightness of step, his social aplomb, the simplicity in his air of authority, his way of wearing a coat or riding a horse, his bodily attitudes which are always relaxed but betray an inner energy' (1964: 29); 'The distinguishing characteristic of the dandy's beauty consists above all in an air of coldness which comes from an unshakeable determination not to be moved; you might call it a latent fire which hints at itself, and which could, but chooses not to burst into flame' (1964: 29).

Two main considerations arise from these quotations. First, Baudelaire links the dandy attitude primarily with 'insensitivity'. This characteristic emerges from the dandy's lifestyle, based on simplicity, distinction, cold air and ability to surprise without being surprised. As suggested earlier in this chapter, the dandy praises an artificial, neutral, almost suspended life without a place for a natural burst of passions and desires. This does not imply that the dandy has no emotions. Rather, they have a 'latent fire', namely they control feelings and sensations within a regime of self-discipline. Second, Baudelaire uses metaphors taken from the military world and mindset, from the Spartan who relentlessly resists adversity (symbolized by the fox's bite) to the clothing ritual that both the dandy and the soldier share daily. Like the dandy, the soldier – to which Baudelaire devotes the chapter preceding that on dandyism – puts efforts into a clothing ritual every day, paying meticulous attention to the aesthetic folds of the garment while maintaining the simplicity imposed by his profession. The dandy, too, cultivates the idea of beauty, training every day to be immaculate with clothes, practicing the gymnastics of dressing and aesthetically oriented manners.

At the same time, 'accustomed to surprises, the soldier is unlikely to be astonished. The particular sign of beauty will therefore be, in this case, a martial disregard, a strange mixture of coldness and audacity; here beauty springs from the necessity of being ready to die in every moment' (Baudelaire 1996: 1300). Ivano Comi's *Breve riflessione sul dandy e sul samurai* (Short Reflection on the Dandy and on the Samurai) is useful in clarifying Baudelaire's position on the figure of the warrior. Specifically, in his essay, Comi outlines the common grounds between the phenomenon of dandyism and the figure of the Japanese warrior *par excellence*, the samurai. Comi focuses on, for instance, the samurai's defence of make-up. According to Yamamoto Tsunetomo's *Hagakure* (the book of the samurai), a warrior should be 'handsome' during battles and combats, because given the chance that they may die at any moment, they must not be found 'unprepared' by death, as if it were an ordinary day. Make-up is also meant to cover the vital and natural expressions of involvement in the battle: a perfect warrior does not show their fury, rage or anger. In this sense, cosmetics, both for the dandy and the samurai, transform one's face into something more neutral and inorganic, close to the impersonal surface of a handsome puppet.

Comi also highlights a strong connection between dandyism and the precepts of *bushidō* (the warrior ethic) by stressing this passage of the *Hagakure*: 'It cannot always be spring, or summer, and equally it cannot always be day; therefore, even if we wished to bring the world back to the spirit of the past century, this would not be possible. It is important to make the most of each generation' (Tsunetomo quoted in Comi 2014: 44). A feeling of melancholy may accompany the transience of beautiful seasons, days, the passing of time and, broadly speaking, the precariousness of earthly things. Nonetheless, a major precept for the warrior is to accept this unchangeable law and practice daily to become more skilled, both practically and spiritually. The experiences of detachment and simulation returns at this stage. As Stein Hevrøy pointed out, commenting on Perniola's idea of death in relation to the samurai ethics, one of the fundamental precept of the *Hagakure* is that the warrior is encouraged to live as if already dead. Specifically, 'As the samurai is a practitioner of martial arts, this must be understood in light of his practical effectiveness: it may be difficult to grasp or hold the thought of being dead already, but it is not hard to imagine that this thought may be fruitful in combat. The logic behind this is that one must annul oneself, be indifferent, in order to be able to perform as good as possible' (Hevrøy 2013: 90).

This welcoming attitude links not only Stoic principles and the warrior's code but also the military world and dandyism. The crucial difference here is that, where the samurai seeks to protect, for instance, his homeland, the dandy assimilates the external world and accepts it from an aesthetic point of view. Where the ancient Stoics devoted their lives to the universal *logos*, where the soldiers and samurai protect their country, families and lords, the dandies are mainly concerned with being subversive and in opposition through their aesthetic-oriented lifestyles. Perniola links this sensitivity to Baroque literature. Referring to Baudelaire's art of linking disparate experiences and attitudes together (such as seriousness and frivolity, vanity and death, clothing and eroticism), he states that 'it is interesting [in Baudelaire's dandyism] only what unites opposites and keeps them in their opposition' (CA: 124).

> Whether these men are nicknamed exquisites, *incroyables*, beaux, lions or dandies, they all spring from the same womb; they all partake of the same characteristic quality of opposition and revolt; they are all representatives of what is finest in human pride, of that compelling need, alas only too rare today, of combating and destroying triviality.
>
> Baudelaire 1964: 28

The dandy devotes their time and effort to creating and maintaining a lifestyle revolving around the notion of greatness. This greatness is grounded upon distinction, simplicity, beauty and manners, out of love for one's destiny, perpetually revolting not only against banality and triviality but also against normativity (I will develop the relationship between queerness and dandyism in the chapter devoted to Wilde) and utilitarianism.

Part Three

9

The Artistic Alienation and the Situationist International

Between 1966 and 1972, Perniola elaborates, primarily influenced by protest movements and groups such as the Situationists and Ludd,[1] a political and militant theory of art that he would revise and rework in its basic assumptions and ideas from the second half of the 1970s. The year 1972, with the last issue of the journal *Agaragar*, marks the beginning of a theoretical rearrangement of art theory. This chapter explores Perniola's early theorization of art and his overall perspective on the Situationist International.

Art must be killed

Perniola's initial interest in art concerns the latest expressions of the twentieth-century artistic avant-garde (particularly Dadaism, Surrealism and the Situationist International), and especially with the volume *L'alienazione artistica* (The Artistic Alienation), the relationship between art and society in the broader Western tradition. In the article 'Il Surrealismo oggi' (Surrealism Today) published in 1966 in the journal *Nuovi Argomenti*, Perniola echoes a fundamental Dadaist standpoint: the essential aspect of artistic activity does not lie in the production of an artistic object but in the revolutionary aim of its project, which functions on the possibility of undermining existing social and political conventions in the pursuit of new experiences of life. For example, discussing Surrealism, Perniola states: 'Surrealism does not owe its name to a hypothetical relationship with the divine or the diabolical realms but with the incessant contestation of reality' (SO: 69). Although Surrealism is known as the art of the 'marvellous', understood as an expression of the unconscious desires of human beings, according to Perniola, the movement must not merely emphasize and carry forward the knowledge of the mechanisms underlying the human psyche but should also develop new lifestyles that can serve as alternatives to the dominant ones. Therefore, he praises only a type of Surrealism intended to constantly challenge reality and which can introduce an effective change in our collective life. In the same article, Perniola harshly criticizes the late 1960s' Surrealism. Attending the Cerisy-la-Salle Surrealist colloquium (July 1966), Perniola, alongside two other politically and artistically engaged friends, wrote and disseminated a short manifesto lamenting the state of Surrealist art. They argued that Surrealism, from Cerisy-la-Salle onwards, became the study of philosophers, sociologists, theorists and, in general, professors and members of academies and galleries. In so doing, it mutated from a life-change oriented movement into a historical, philosophical and aesthetical object of study. In other words, the manifesto's authors reproached Surrealism for being 'dead' from a revolutionary point of view, as it was gradually integrating itself with popular culture, institutions and, broadly speaking, the diktats of the status quo. Written at the age of twenty-five, 'Il Surrealismo oggi' gathers several key assertions on art theory that Perniola would further develop in the following six years.

'Il Surrealismo oggi' dwells on the relationship between art and revolution, specifically the *identity* between the two, which would be a constant in Perniola's reflections from this period:

> The absolute identity between art and revolution, between art and life, implies, above all, the affirmation that what is essential of art is not the artwork but the living, the creative process, the artistic activity ... there is no substantial difference between the believer who sacrifices themselves for the afterlife, the bourgeois who saves money to increase their capital and the artist who creates works for posterity: all of them renounce living, and the less they live, the more merit, the more money, the more works of art they accumulate.
>
> AR: 72

From this brief quote, Perniola's perspective starts taking shape. For him, producing an artwork means, among other things, pursuing a theological attitude that corresponds to challenging one's own mortality with something that lasts beyond one's own existence. Works of art are the artist's answer to the fear of death and the unceasing transience of life. Art is thus seen as offering a possibility to turn what is temporary (a feeling, a person, a landscape) into an entity not affected by the passage of time. There are no substantial differences between the artistic, religious and mercantile mindsets. As Perniola points out, instead of allowing one to live new existential possibilities and experiences, they all *alienate* the individual and their desires into objects, capital or an ideal world. Therefore, a closer inspection of Perniola's praise for an identity between art and revolution reveals that he is underlining the possibility of living in an authentic way that enables an effective realization of one's own 'desire' without falling into any potential reification.

The focal point of the following pages is Perniola's book *L'alienazione artistica*. Published in 1971, the work also contains two essays published in *Rivista di Estetica* (OR, OS) and three in the journal *Agaragar* (SRM, CR, TP). Also, several concepts explored in the book appear in other texts written by Perniola those years as well (see SO, AI, AR). *L'alienazione artistica* thus represents a compendium of the theoretical efforts that Perniola made in his early reflections to understand the relationship between art and society.

A crucial assertion that Perniola makes in *L'alienazione artistica* is that art, within Western tradition, has always been an alienated manifestation of creativity (AA: 18–34). However, what conception of 'art' is Perniola proposing here? He does not contend with an essentialist or *a priori* perspective; on the contrary, he considers it a 'historic category' – that is, art as the complex network between society, history, institutions and class struggle on the one hand and artistic undertakings on the other. This definition implies taking into account the functions, uses and goals informing artistic production throughout the history of the Western world.[2] Nonetheless, Perniola understands art as a manifestation of human creativity. His goal in *L'alienazione artistica* is in fact to dwell on Western history in order to evaluate whether artistic activity promotes a genuine experience of creativity or only realizes a poorer or alienated manifestation of it. Together with this anti-essentialist basic assumption, this book should be read in the broader context of the protests of the time. Its style is indeed profoundly influenced by the notions elaborated by Guy Debord and the Situationist International.

L'alienazione artistica is divided into three parts. The first one (AA: 9–78) can be considered a preparatory part that sets out and defines several key notions of the text, such as 'art as a historical category', 'alienation', 'separation', 'situation' and 'revolution of everyday life'. The second part (79–166) is dedicated to the origins of the so-called 'artistic alienation' in ancient Greece and its continuation during the Italian Renaissance, which I will explain shortly. Finally, the third part (167–266) explores the 'critique and realization' of art both within modern philosophy (from Hegel to Adorno) and within the artistic avant-garde of the twentieth century. In spite of his youth, Perniola (who wrote the book between the ages of twenty-seven and thirty) elaborates an extremely wide-ranging theory of art, which encompasses thinkers such as Marx, Lukács and Debord and, at the same time, comments on aesthetic, anthropological, economic and sociological issues.[3]

It is therefore a text with a multifaceted structure which, nevertheless, possesses a specific common thread: identifying the reasons for which art has carried forward an 'alienated' experience of creativity while parallelly exploring the possibilities of a genuine and authentic realization of human creativity. The main assumption emerging from *L'alienazione artistica* is grounded in the idea of *revolution*, which implies a *total* transgression of the status quo.

Perniola explores the relationship between art and society in various eras, starting with ancient Greece. His initial focus is specifically on the Greek *genos*, a basic organizational group grounded in the power of noble lineage. In this type of society, only the *basileus*, the householder, had access to rituals and effective power, while the other members of the family did not participate and could only repeat myths or witness religious practices/events. This hierarchy, Perniola continues, was not limited to politics but also infested creativity. Specifically, the *epos* (and the following Homeric epic poems) is understood by Perniola (following Adorno and Horkheimer's analysis) as 'the first Illuminist enterprise of Western civilisation' (AA: 88). This can be attributed to two main factors: first, the poems merely 'tell' and 'represent' the realization of morally significant actions and myths, creating a hiatus between passively watching an action which takes place on the stage and actively being able to change one's own life; second, the *epos*, by narrating legendary actions, celebrates a culture oriented around the figure and role of the master or the patriarchal ruling power.[4] The overwhelming majority of the population, Perniola continues, is only involved in a pseudo-participation which, in reality, consists of repeating and justifying the mythical history of the actual ruling class, in turn accepting the status quo. For these reasons, Perniola argues that the poetry, literature and theatre of ancient Greece allow the artistic subjects (the *aedo* or the actor) to express themselves creatively only on the condition that they convey a pre-established ideological meaning. Poetry, according to Perniola, is therefore counter-revolutionary because it is inseparable from the manifestations of power. It is also a 'separate' dimension because the action endowed with 'meaning' (*significato*) is only reproduced on the scene and imitated through masks.[5] Nonetheless, for Perniola, in the Greek poetic world, the meaningful action is portrayed not as something that can happen but only as something that happened, which can be observed and of which one can be a spectator without playing any effectively active role. The creative action is thus actualized within the framework of a story, but it is also segregated on the stage; this occurs in a context that Perniola, influenced by Situationist terminology, considers 'spectacular' or 'separate' (AA: 111) and which does not constitute a real alternative to the state of things and does not produce any genuine community.

One of the predominant notions on which Perniola's theory of art is anchored is that of 'separation'. Debord, the founder and main representative of the Situationists, wrote, 'Separation is the alpha and the omega of the spectacle' (2005: 13). For Debord, the capitalist Western world is a realm of divisions and specialism furthered by the bourgeois mindset. For example, everyday life under capitalist systems can be polarized between working hours on the one hand and leisure or recreational moments on the other. Consequently, Debord argues, individuals cannot find any totality or unity in their life: the working environment pushes people to work to get a salary while, simultaneously, mass media colonizes their free time in order to empower consumerism. Thus, separation would be the constitutive condition of individuals within a spectacular system: isolated and fragmented, they fail to reassemble the pieces into which their existences are torn.

Another practice that attempts to instantiate a situation qualitatively different from the status quo is the so-called *détournement*. This term can be translated as 'rerouting', 'hijacking' or 'displacement' and pertains to the attribution of a new value to pre-existing elements. For example, images belonging to the capitalist world, such as advertisements, comics and posters, are no longer used only for the purpose for which they were produced; their original context is transformed with a revolutionary perspective. To give an example, the image of a smiling couple next to a refrigerator, which, according to the advertising logic of the market conveys an idea of happiness linked to consumption, was completely subverted by the Situationists. Instead of a bubble where the couple expressed their satisfaction with the purchase, the Situationists inserted statements such as 'My thoughts have been replaced by moving images' or 'I didn't go to work today; I don't think I'll go tomorrow. Let's take control of our lives and live for pleasure, not pain.' In short, the Situationists sought to reorganize the meaning of a certain object by transforming its context and purposes. In this sense, *détournement* is a critical weapon against spectacle. According to Perniola, *détournement* carries two main aspects: 'the loss of importance of the original meaning of each individual autonomous element and the organization of another significant group, which gives each element a new end' (AS: 47–8).[6]

A drawback emerging from this analysis is that, in his early works, Perniola considers only the identity between art and revolution to be capable of bringing to fruition an effectively realized creativity and a genuine community. Everything that is not inherently revolutionary, that is, everything that does not imply an upheaval of the status quo and of the hegemonic order, is dismissed as 'pseudo-community' or as 'halved-creativity'. Hence, Perniola judges the world of art only in terms of pure entertainment and is de facto indifferent to instances of participation in which artists were personally involved as well. Nonetheless, he contends that in ancient Greece, a poetic and literary *alienation* arose and, influenced by it, artistic activity started to assert itself in the Western world as a dimension in which creativity is expressed as incomplete and mystified.

Perniola subsequently investigates the relationship between art and society in the Middle Ages and in the Italian Renaissance (AA: 135–66). According to him, between these two historical periods, the very notion of art changed, which is exemplified in Leon Battista Alberti's work. Perniola devotes a section of the third chapter of *L'alienazione artistica* to Alberti, considered a crucial figure in the paradigm shift point in craft and art. This section is aptly titled 'The Painter as Bourgeois: L.B. Alberti'. According to Perniola, Alberti theorized a major aspect of Renaissance art. In *The Family in the Renaissance,* he 'formulates the theory of the acquisition and direction of the work of others' (CTP: 127), that is, the conceptualization of manufacturing capitalism.[7] Trade capitalism implies the idea of the merchant as a dealer of goods made independently by himself; instead, manufacturing capitalism conveys a conception of the merchant as a 'manufacturer of goods made under his control' (CTP: 127).[8] During the Middle Ages, paintings, sculptures and carvings were included in the broad field of artisanal handicraft. Perniola, borrowing Marxist terminology, states that the craftsman placed himself in the commodity–money–commodity horizon, thereby selling his work (for instance, a painting) to make money and eventually buy other goods (for instance, bread). He therefore lived off his private work by producing goods and owning the means of production. However, starting from the fourteenth century, with the development of Florentine financial holdings (of which Alberti's was one of the wealthiest), alongside new commercial trends and mechanisms, the figure of the merchant emerges.[9] Perniola outlines the figure of the artist/entrepreneur in Marxist terms, where the notions of commodity, money and profit are central. According to him, Alberti's work reveals the bourgeois mindset emerging during the Florentine Renaissance. The Renaissance artist/entrepreneur, anticipating the methods of the fully developed capitalist production of the following centuries, focused on exchange value or the economic surplus that could be attained by selling a given commodity. In doing so, the value of use (i.e. the time employed to produce something together with its specific utility) is dissolved. Renaissance proto-capitalism therefore aimed to increase the exchange value of a given object. Thus, the value of a work of art started depending not so much on the customer's request but on the anonymous 'market demand', that is, on 'an abstract form which dominates the craftsman' (AA: 142).

Perniola further argues that between the Middle Ages and the Renaissance, the notion of art underwent a shift that transformed the artisan's workshop into a capitalist enterprise. Perniola is not the first scholar to focus on the economic developments occurring in Florence during the Renaissance. His sources are Werner Sombart's *Modern Capitalism* (1925) and Armando Sapori's *Le merchande italien au moyen âge* (1952) (although quoted only once each) and Alberti's *The Family in Renaissance*. Sombart argued that capitalism was first and also thoroughly elaborated in Alberti's work. The economic principles developed by Alberti, for Sombart as well as for Perniola, would still be relevant for future capitalism. Specifically, both Sombart and Perniola quote several passages from the text to emphasize its main precepts. For instance, 'keep the word', namely honouring a contract (Sombart 1925), or 'economize'[10] namely to being thrifty and moderate with money, or 'invest' both in and outside the household:[11]

> The old doctrines of Alberti still hold sway. Never let your expenditure exceed your income, he urged his disciples. And calculate. Today this advice is faithfully obeyed by the modern bourgeois. Herein his mode of living differs from the seigniorial. The seignior scorns money.
>
> Sombart 2017: 91

The same 'economic virtues', Sombart argues, can also be found in Benjamin Franklin's books and thoughts: Alberti wrote 'a book second to none in its bourgeois sentiments, a book which already breathed the spirit of Benjamin Franklin' (Sombart 2017: 52). At stake here is the fact that art, as a unitary category distinguished from crafts, was elaborated precisely during the Renaissance. This in turn implies that for Perniola, the modern concept of art was born together with a new spirit of capitalism exemplified by Alberti's precepts and reflections. This consequently made the historical category of art inseparable from capitalism itself and thus counter-revolutionary.

As Stefano Taccone notes in a recent article dedicated to *L'alienazione artistica*, while the Renaissance is commonly known as a crucial moment for artists' autonomy and creativity, for Perniola, it marked instead a loss of the creative dimension (2017: 19). Perniola cites two factors to justify this claim. On the one hand is the proto-capitalist mindset, which introduced new typologies of commerce and trade alongside the figure of the entrepreneur, which in turn started re-shaping the artworld. On the other hand, is the widening division between crafts and arts, that is, between manual labour and works of art. As soon as art is placed in an autonomous dimension and prioritized over craftsmanship, creativity is excluded from manual operation, and therefore a whole series of activities are cut off as 'servile' and 'vulgar'. Perniola argues that this turning point excluded creativity in everyday life and confined it to the realm of a 'gifted few', higher spirits or geniuses. As a result, the artist's autonomy in the Renaissance is a 'miserable' triumph: 'The misery of this triumph is equal to the misery of the bourgeois concept of creativity, which is tailored to the size of commodities. Creativity does not simply mean producing a new and original object, but first and foremost refers to creating a vital situation that guarantees its author and all participants a real activity' (AA: 145). The notion of 'situation' returns in this quote, implying a renewal of everyday life. As Sansot points out, Perniola 'evokes with much eloquence the double misery of art and everyday life that are based on a divorce between reality and meaning' (Sansot 1977: 14–15); thus, he highlights the separation between creativity, confined to the supposed superiority of the artistic world, and usefulness, which is expected of artisanal and manual operations.

Moreover, during the Renaissance, especially thanks to the influence of Neoplatonic spiritualism, the artist slowly becomes understood in terms of the emblematic figures of the 'solitary', 'melancholic' and 'counter-current' individual. According to Perniola, the Neoplatonic doctrine, which involves a metaphysical idealism wherein notions such as the spirit, idea and soul are considered superior to matter, earth and bodies, further deepens the general separation between artists and reality. For example, he notes that in Michelangelo, the influence of Neoplatonism can be observed in his conception of artistic activity as 'giving a bodily form, reproduce[ing] within matter the metaphysical Idea' (AA: 158). Michelangelo's early Mannerism thus implied a spiritualistic shift of the artistic product, which continued to debase all the crafts and handiworks insofar as their origin was not the soul of the artist but an everyday commission grounded upon applied skills and practices.[12] In this sense, Perniola underlines that in Michelangelo, 'the artistic product is qualitatively different from artisanal or industrial goods precisely because it is the result of a spiritual torment' (AA: 159). He also states that 'withdrawal from the world, solitude, isolation, which seem to be essential characteristics of the exercise of creativity, are actually the price that artists must pay to the new social order: it is allowed to be active, provided that one is by definition extraneous to life' (AA: 161). According to him, the tormented artists, or whom Rudolf and Margot Wittkower call 'the saturnine artists' in their seminal volume (2006) on the subject, are not so because they are struggling to express their creative freedom. Contrarily, the torment derives precisely from the fact that these artists perceive their activity 'confined in the ghetto of the invention of forms without a significant relationship with the social organization of life' (AA: 162).

The figure of the melancholic artist, at war with the world or with themselves, should not evoke an essential connection between creativity and mental imbalance but should rather be indicative of the fact that the artist compares their condition with that of someone who is left with a merely spiritual and abstract idea of creativity and which has no appreciable effect on collective everyday life. The ruling class, with its apparatus of institutions (from the Greek *genos* to theatre, patrons, politicians, lords and clergy), permits a certain degree of freedom to artistic behaviours precisely because they are ultimately reduced to substantially harmless and extraneous-to-life activities. In this sense, Perniola claims that art is a peculiar dimension in which, although 'meaning' finds an expression (through the work of art), it is a meaning without 'reality'; that is, it is creativity without effectuality. The very title of the book should be understood in this light, and throughout Western history, art should be considered as 'alienated' or, in other words, as an alienated way of expressing creativity. Hugh Bredin, reviewing Perniola's *L'alienazione artistica*, highlights the dichotomy between art and economy that emerges from the book: 'Art is an attempt to invest everything with meaning, an attempt which in so far as it is successful deprives its object of reality. Economic activity, by contrast, is an attempt to reduce everything to a material reality divested of meaning' (1972: 88).

The panorama that has emerged so far on the relationship between art and society is ambiguous. According to Perniola, artistic activity allows a certain degree of individual creativity; however, the possibilities of its expression are 'halved', as Western manifestations of art are integrated with the ruling powers, the merchant classes and, broadly speaking, the economic realm. Therefore, the artworld becomes a place in which power is celebrated – and hence justified and left substantially unchanged – or in which an 'isolated' meaning finds expression. It is isolated because it does not carry the social goal of achieving a more authentic life for the entire community (the ultimate aim of art from Perniola's perspective). Art is therefore alienated because it expresses a kind of creativity that maintains the segregation between individuals and their lives. In these terms, Perniola states that 'art is the ghetto of activity' (AA: 146, also see AC); instead of becoming an activity that aids the free invention of life, it echoes and promotes the separation and alienation already present in societies where, in the Marxist terms borrowed by Perniola himself, economic struggles occur.

Since art as a historical category has asserted itself as an alienated activity, if there is no alienation, there is no art either. In other words, according to Perniola, art in the Western world is synonymous with alienation, as it has always manifested itself as ideological or separated. Therefore, any efforts towards eliminating this artistic alienation would also imply dissolving the historical category of art. Art, for Perniola, should be overcome in everyday life; that is, on the one side, it should be criticized as an alienated activity and, on the other, its creativity should be spread into the realm of collective everyday life: 'Art does not die but it is necessary to kill it so that creativity is realized in the revolution' (AI: 12).

Perniola's perspective is influenced by the Hegelian-Marxist tradition (also supported by the Situationists, especially Debord), specifically referring to the to the tripartite logical movement of the dialectic: thesis–antithesis–synthesis, which Hegel labels the abstract–negative–concrete. Applying this method to art theory, Perniola argues that art as a historical category has always remained within the first stage: its alienation in fact implies its separation and abstraction from authentic social life. Although the Renaissance's artistic process of production still suggests a number of social interactions, both within and outside the workshops, Perniola claims that Florentine proto-capitalism triggers the evolution of these very workshops towards the progressive alienation of workers from their products, which eventually culminates in the modern industrial system. Perniola's critique can then work as an example of a negative movement (the second stage), wherein the alienation is criticized in sight of the third stage, where artistic creativity can finally be realized in a more concrete, collective way. This dialectic movement describes the 'supersession' or 'overcoming' of art. In fact, upon closer inspection, Perniola's main claim in *L'alienazione artistica* does not entirely pertain to the realization of art as the authentic expression of human creativity in everyday life:

> Art is the only manifestation of the ideas of creativity and desire that survive in the bourgeois world: it is a degradation and a perpetuation of desire. It corrupts the original total structure of desire by spiritualizing it; on the other [hand], it preserves its alienated form, removing it from the risk of complete extinction. Strictly speaking, therefore, we should not talk of a realization of art but of a realization of authentic desire, of which art is an alienated historical expression.
> AI: 12

The text quoted above suggests that it is not a new concept or idea of art that should be advanced. Despite its contamination with the political manoeuvres of the ruling classes and their economic ideologies, art appears to be – metaphorically speaking – a treasure trove from which what is precious (i.e. creativity) should be drawn and developed elsewhere (i.e. within a revolutionary existence).

For these reasons, in the third part of *L'alienazione artistica*, Perniola dwells on Dadaism, considered an exceptional movement that tried to lay the groundwork for the suppression of art as an alienated category. According to Perniola, Dadaists understood that 'the purpose of art is not the work but the living, the creative process, the artistic activity' (AA: 200). As suggested earlier, privileging the artistic object means still possessing a theological mindset. By fearing death and the transience of things, artists delude themselves into thinking that their artistic productions/works, which can last longer than their own mortal existence, somehow lend them 'immortality' or 'eternity' as well. The artistic object is therefore understood by the Dadaists (and Perniola with them) as one of the predominant causes of artistic alienation. Trying to produce a 'permanent form' (a potentially everlasting artistic object) means in turn providing a visible and concrete expression of an alienated activity. Subjective creativity is understood by Perniola as infinite, not objectifiable, and confining it within the parameter of the product means simultaneously mummifying it. To express one's own desires through art does not mean realizing them but, contrarily, implies not living them practically and reifying them into a product detached from life, enclosed in its abstractness as an inert object. Precisely for this reason, Perniola argues, art and economy are two complementary sides of the same coin: art implies a creative freedom with no concrete effects on the collective and social world; economy is instead the realm of efficiency which does not express creativity. Perniola explains this complementary relationship with the adages 'art is meaning without reality' (*significato senza realtà*) and 'economy is reality without meaning' (*realtà senza significato*, AA: 48). As Bredin points out, for Perniola 'Only when art and economics cease to be cultivated as autonomous spheres of activity will the alienation of each from the other be overcome' (1972: 88). In a review of Pierre Cabanne's conversation with Marcel Duchamp, Perniola underlines that 'Dada is not a poetic but a total lifestyle' (PC: 129). Totality means earnestly adopting a revolutionary and creative lifestyle every hour and in every activity. Being creative just in specific moments or for certain purposes means, as suggested earlier, again reproducing the individual fragmentation that takes place in spectacular societies. Each restricted form of creativity is considered by Perniola as being, following Duchamp's perspective, simultaneously partial, fragmented and limited. Here lies the reason why Perniola understood the revolution only as *total*. In fact, if the notion of totality is not central, all the alienation and separations attributed to a bourgeois mindset return.

Perniola's perspective has been discussed by several thinkers and scholars (such as Bredin 1972; Orlandini 1972; Costa 1973; Berardi 1973, 1974; Sansot 1977). Berardi claims that the project of the 'realization of meaning', elaborated in *L'alienazione artistica*, implies various contradictions. As suggested, Perniola's radical critique of art's alienation is grounded upon the opposite but complementary realms of meaning (art) and material reality (economics). By advocating for the overcoming of art within everyday life, Perniola (according to Berardi) does not actually propose a revolutionary practice capable of ending the alienations of both art and economics. While for Perniola the material and economic world is understood as devoid of 'meaning', for Berardi, meaning is precisely the outcome of the struggles, conflicts and contradictions that take place in the very economic world. Therefore, art's alienation cannot be ended through the realization of an autonomous and total conception of artistic behaviour and creativity. For Berardi, the primary goal of the militant practice should not be to overcome the alienated dimension of art but to understand the struggles that occur in the economic realm and then to develop new meanings and possibilities. Berardi claims that 'the avant-garde of which Perniola speaks is the art of utopia which aims at realizing an identification between the aesthetic sphere and life' (1973: 165). Hence, Perniola's idea of the realization of meaning does not indicate changing the present order but, on the contrary, seeks to merely aestheticize it. Paradoxically, Perniola's radical critique would instead be an idealistically informed utopian justification of the status quo.

Nonetheless, I argue that Berardi's argument misses a key point. Perniola does not in fact understand art and economy as two ideological, eternal and necessary dimensions at odds with each other. Art's realm, in other words, is not an autonomous and metahistorical concept. It is rather a historical category that is alienated precisely because of the constitutive contradictions of capitalist society. Perniola's distinction between art and economy does not propose notions and practices in their respective isolation, autonomy and separation. On the contrary, his starting point is the refusal of this very separation precisely through the exploration of history and social reality.

I believe that the most significant critique of Perniola's perspective comes from Perniola himself. In the reflections following *L'alienazione artistica*, Perniola argues that a revolutionary viewpoint-oriented theory, guided by the dialectic principle of overcoming, fails to consider the 'negative' element to its very end by mystifying it into an ultimately conciliated vision (BN). Dialectic omits or sets aside what would unhinge its theoretical structure, namely the *opposition* which is articulated through its radical *difference, asymmetry* and *historicity*. No longer supporting the overcoming of art, Perniola would later develop his theory by focusing on and delving into the thinkers and schools of thought I have explored so far. His primary efforts would no longer be devoted to re-thinking the separation of life and art from a revolutionary and dialectic standpoint but would instead focus on it from the intersection of the spheres of feeling and form. This shift can be referred to as a passage from a *more-than-life* to a *more-than-form* aesthetic and political theory, where experiences and notions such as 'transit', 'simulacrum', 'ritual without myth', 'inorganic', 'enigma' and 'shadow' would emerge.

Guy Debord's dandyism

Perniola has often been associated with the Situationist movement and, generally speaking, with a critique of capitalist society. The previous sections also show and confirm his fascination with the counterculture of the 1960s, at least up until the early 1970s. Though his engagement with issues such as the role of art in contemporary society and the value and significance of artworks and artists continued into the next decades, Perniola's standpoint changed radically. I will now focus on his departure from the Situationist International (from now on SI) and, in the next chapter, will explore his overall perspective on art theory. After *L'alienazione artistica*, Perniola devoted a monograph on the Situationist movement in 1972 and then published several articles, interviews and essays on the topic throughout the decades (see, for instance, IS, SA, ASC, IMP, AGS). If it is true that Perniola was still investigating the SI up until 2017 (when he released his last interview on the subject), he nonetheless can be considered as the first killer – so to speak – of the SI or, rather, the first thinker who declared the failure of the movement and examined it as an object of historical study.

Let us briefly summarize the SI project. The SI was conceived in 1957 in Cosio d'Arroscia (Cuneo, Italy) from the union of the International Movement for an Imaginist Bauhaus, the London Psychogeographical Committee and the Lettrist International. These heterogenous and experimental groups merged their forces, keeping in sight a revolutionary overcoming of art alongside the reappropriation of everyday life in capitalist societies. Several perspectives were active at the advent of the SI's activities, including the abandonment of urban functionalism, the study of urban spaces and their effect on human psychology, industrial and experimental painting, anti-modernism, the radical critique of bourgeois society and contempt for institutions, cinema, academia and traditional politics. Above all, these aspects were explored with the aim of creating new and meaningful life 'situations' (from which the name of the movement originated) that would allow people to regain possession of their everyday life in the capitalist and spectacular universe.

Beyond these concerns, also inspired by those of the historical avant-gardes, the SI gradually shifted and relied heavily on social, political and revolutionary claims. In short, two trends can be detected in the movement: one which is more artistic, technical and scientific and which positively considered the developments of technique, especially in terms of human liberation from work, and thereby highlighted the possibility of expressing creative energies; and another one, led by Debord, links the liberation of the individual to proletarian social revolution configured as an anti-Leninist standpoint inspired by the workers' council movement that emerged in Russia at the end of the 1910s. The revolutionary tendency linked to the workers' action was also consolidated by the fact that across the world, the 1960s witnessed violent strikes in which workers demanded the reorganization of the entire production system in capitalist society. In this context, the Situationists believed themselves to represent the theoretical conscience of their time, particularly with respect to the malaise towards the bourgeois and capitalist society.

The movement reached its apex with the Parisian protests of May 1968, which is regarded by scholars, including Perniola, as the historical moment to which the SI contributed most in terms of theoretical endeavours. The Situationist programme featured the occupation of factories and the establishment of workers' councils according to a direct democracy model. These councils were intended to abolish classes, workers' exploitation and, roughly speaking, allow the people to live authentically instead of merely 'surviving'. Although the protests of 1968 were initially associated with students' vindications, the general strikes and occupations soon surpassed the university environment and sparked a social crisis of immense proportions. The Situationists, together with other groups of the time such as the Enragés (The Wild Ones), occupied factories, offices and public buildings and formed a Council for Maintaining the Occupations on 17 May. As Jappe notes in his volume on Debord, in the immediate aftermath of May '68, the SI's popularity grew considerably. In addition to welcoming new members, several national sections of the movement were set up (Italian, French, Scandinavian and American), with each publishing a Situationist journal. At the same time, the French state restored order in June, after less than a month of protests; the council organized by the SI soon ended, the revolutionary projects failed and the SI eventually dissolved in the spring of 1972. Both Perniola and Jappe attribute the demise of the movement to two key factors: the SI's constitutive sectarianism and the spread of the Situationist theories in the student environment rather than among the workers: 'formally, at any rate, the Situationists subscribed to the theory that only the proletariat, by virtue of its position in the production process, and of its historical tradition, had the capacity to bring down the system' (Jappe 1999: 103). History shows that their theories only occasionally penetrated the proletariat.

Perniola never became a member of the SI, not even the Italian group set up after the protests of 1968. Nonetheless, he corresponded with Debord between 1966 and 1969 and collaborated with other revolutionary groups of the time such as Ludd and with journals including *Errata*, *Il re nudo*, *L'erba voglio* and *Quindici*. Above all, in 1970, he founded his first journal, titled *Agaragar*.[13] The journal was heavily influenced by the Situationist terminology and contained three articles that were later included in *L'alienazione artistica*. Thus, it is no coincidence that it lasted only up until 1972, the year that marked the split of the SI. Additionally, Perniola devoted the last two issues of the journal to monographic research on the SI, which constituted the first critical history of the movement itself. This monograph seems to me to have been the final nail in the SI's coffin. The analogy can be justified first for a reason that is self-evident: the Situationists were against the very idea of history. To make the Situationist theory, which is so strongly oriented towards revolutionary practice and against every institution, the object of historical study is akin to a doctor dissecting a dead body.[14] By writing a history of the SI, Perniola was thus implicitly asserting that the movement had had its time and that its limits and greatness can be analysed, examined and discussed the same way as for any topic.

His monograph on the Situationists covers several key aspects of the movement, from the overcoming of art to the critical theory of society up to the practical realization of the theory. Here emerge the fundamental concepts studied by the members of the IS: the idea of 'spectacle', the *détournement*, the urban drift, psychogeography, the situation, radical subjectivity and workers' councils. I have already discussed some of these concepts previously, and my aim here is to dwell on Perniola's considerations on the SI after the end of the movement. The monograph on the Situationists, first published between 1971 and 1972 in *Agaragar*, was then re-published as a book in 1998 and 2013. The 2013 version includes a new chapter entitled 'Considerations on the Success of the Situationist Movement'. First, in this chapter Perniola argues that when discussing the SI, it is possible to distinguish at least three facets: the actual Situationist group established in 1957 and which ceased in 1972, which produced its own journal; the *situs*, that is, the sympathizers of the movement and those who were influenced by it and, finally, the figure of Guy Debord, who not only founded the movement but was also its heartbeat.

For Perniola, a crucial weakness of the Situationists can be detected in their extreme sectarianism. In the fifteen years of its activity, out of a total of seventy members, over forty-five were expelled for not being revolutionary enough or for not sharing several beliefs of the other members. This sectarianism contradicted the ideas that the group promoted, generally linked to the reappropriation of everyday life and the liberation of society from the totalitarian capitalist spectacle. One of the crucial factors driving the dissolution of the SI was its idiosyncratic nature. It asserted itself as an anti-institutional institution, two opposing aspects which did not last in the broader climate of spontaneity and triumphalist vitalism of the time. Perniola attributed the sectarianism to the SI's assertion of being an absolute totality, holder of the revolutionary subjectivity of the time (SA). The Situationists gave birth to a dogmatism of unity, whereby only one solution to each problem is given (the Situationist one) and which, in turn, made each member interchangeable. Perniola sums up the Situationist attitude in the following quotation: 'Each Situationist, immersing themselves in the authenticity of their own lived experience, will spontaneously find it, even independently of any agreement and any common research' (SA: 265).[15]

Alongside the Situationist group, Perniola considers the *situs*, who are sympathizers of the movement, who admire it and resonate the members' claims but, eventually, who play only a contemplative role instead of acting for the transformations they seek in society. Today, fans and followers who like, share and retweet posts and cultural products exemplify the figure of the *situs*. In this sense, the *situs* have never ceased to exist and are indeed functional to the logic of current capitalism.

Finally, Guy Debord. It is undeniable that Perniola considered Debord one of his two philosophical masters, alongside Pareyson, his tutor during his years at the University of Turin. Perniola was especially fascinated by the style of Debord, heir of the classical thought proposed in Ecclesiastes and by Thucydides, Dante, Machiavelli, Montaigne and others, which made him a refined strategic thinker. The first condition of style – Perniola writes in an article on Debord – is 'the detachment, the distance, the suspension of disordered affections, of immediate emotionality' (AGS: 156). This does not imply frigidity and inability to feel emotions; on the contrary, it presupposes them. Dominating passions implies that they exist. Debord's distance is thus first a distance from institutions (publishing, journalism, universities, cinema, political parties) and also from the variegated extra-parliamentary groups and realities that were active in the 1960s and 1970s. His aesthetic and polemological detachment is effectively summarized by this remark in his 1978 film *In girum imus nocte et consumimur igni*: 'To be in war with the entire world, but with a light heart'.

In these terms, Perniola has always praised and admired what can be seen as a significant dandy attitude in Debord, that of one who lives according to the 'grand style' informed by *habitus* and forms and which links detachment and distance with strategy, politics and effectiveness. In a self-interview which he never published, Perniola asks himself if there is anything relevant from the Situationist theory for today's society, answering, 'Very little in terms of content. Instead, a lot from a broader point of view: they [the Situationists] can be included in the tradition of the "free spirit"' (SSA: 5). Following this perspective, Perniola argues that Debord's seminal work *The Society of the Spectacle* should be regarded more as an artwork than as an innovative, radical critique of Western capitalism. He claims that most of the theses advanced by Debord were already developed by other authors of those years, such as Henri Lefebvre, György Lukács and the group managing the journal *Socialism ou Barbarie*. Nonetheless, the aspect of *The Society of the Spectacle* that most fascinated Perniola is its assemblage, which he considered similar to artistic and avant-garde collages. The text, in fact, presents itself as a set of *détournenement* of phrases by thinkers such as Hegel, Kojève, Marx, Lukács, Feuerbach, Melville, Virgil and numerous others. For instance, the opening theses of *The Society of the Spectacle* is a hijacking of Marx's opening line of *The Capital*, which emphasizes the shift from 'commodity' to 'spectacle':

> The wealth of societies in which the capitalist mode of production prevails appears as an 'immense collection of commodities'.
>
> Marx 1982: 125

> In societies dominated by modern conditions of production, life is presented as an immense accumulation of *spectacles*.
>
> Debord 2005: 7

Or also the beginning of Virgil's *Aeneid*, where the Roman poet writes 'Arms and the Man I sing' (2007: 3), echoed by Debord's 'The spectacle does not sing of men and their arms, but of commodities and their passions' (2005: 32–3). Debord reorganized the conceptual content of their theses in a revolutionary key, adopting the strategy of diversion. Perniola is very explicit on this point: '*The Society of the Spectacle* can be considered more a work of art than a treatise on political theory. Neither obsolete nor prophetic: it is a very refined assemblage, which deserves great admiration for the wisdom with which it was built' (ASC: 14).

In addition, Perniola has examined another aspect of Debord's relevance in today's cultural landscape. In 2009, Debord's work became a national treasure and was welcomed into the National Library of France as a token of recognition for what he meant and represented for the intellectual and artistic life of the twentieth century. A thinker against all institutions, who relentlessly fought for the destruction and the end of the state, was ultimately solemnized by the state itself. However, on closer inspection, this solemnization took place for a very specific reason. Yale University wanted to buy Debord's archives from his heir and the French state intervened to oppose this deal by transforming these archives into an untouchable national treasure (see Beuve-Mery 2009). Debord's 'intellectual merits' seem rather to be an instrumental pretext.

In addition to the 'solemnization' of Debord by the state, it is possible to appreciate how he was also re-discovered and recuperated in the academic (with courses, theses and conferences devoted to his figure) as well as in the culture industry realm. Several notions and ideas developed by Debord seem to have been fully incorporated by the spectacle: the inflammatory words written on walls in Paris have now become a perfectly integrated facet of the art world with urban art; the *détournement* now goes viral every day and is named 'meme'; the mottos *ne travaillez jamais* ('never work') and *vivre sans temps morts* (to live without dead times) have been finally realized by the general precariousness of working conditions and by the omnipresence of advertisements, leisure pseudo-activities and so forth. Even if one can speak of 'victory' for Debord, it nonetheless remains a bitter one since it comes from a world that he has always and consistently looked at with contempt.

Although Perniola was close to Debord and the Situationist theory from 1966 to 1972, he gradually distanced himself, elaborating his reflection through other conceptual figures (including Bataille, Freud, Nietzsche, St Ignatius, Baltasar Gracián and Heidegger). Still, his admiration towards the figure of Debord never ceased; he never stopped admiring a style so extremely close to dandyism oriented to a strategic beauty.

10

A Shadow and Its Art

From the early to the late 1970s, Perniola focused less on art theory and more on theoretical philosophy and psychoanalysis, interrogating Nietzsche (NO, I), Freud (WE, SSF) and especially Bataille (NP, IB, BN, BI, IEB). With *La società dei simulacri*, published in 1980, Perniola returns to the investigation of contemporary art. In this work, both his writing style and the crucial assumptions behind it diverge from those employed in *L'alienazione artistica*'s period. Perniola, in fact, no longer focuses on the historical avant-gardes, instead turning to the neo-avant-gardes from the 1960s onwards. If the historical avant-gardes were informed by the idea of transgression – that is, the critique and the overcoming of the status quo for a new, genuinely realized and collective creativity – the neo-avant-gardes now propose a pseudo-transgression, wherein subversive drives and motifs find an alliance with art institutions and the broader economic realm.

Art and psychosis

To understand Perniola's approach to artistic issues from the 1980s onwards, it is useful to look at the article 'Del arte como transgresión al arte como profesión' (From Art as Transgression to Art as Profession). In a passage from this article, Perniola highlights a fundamental shift that he believed to have occurred in the art world:

> The idea that the essence of contemporary art is transgression is derived from the historical avant-gardes, of which I think I am one of the last living witnesses, having participated at one of the last manifestations of Surrealism (the congress of Cerisy-La-Salle in July 1966) and having been involved in the activities of Situationist International from 1966 to 1969 ... Instead, contemporary art, starting from Pop Art in the early 1960s, having always been linked to institutions, has taken an opposite path to that promoted by the Situationists.
>
> ACT: 18

The Dadaists and the Situationists promoted – despite their different theoretical and militant standpoints – the idea of 'overcoming' of art that encourages creativity in the collective everyday life. These movements were dissatisfied with the status quo and therefore aimed for its 'transgression' to free individuals' desires and creativity in a non-alienated way. In this context, there was no dialogue between Dadaists and Situationists on the one hand and institutions (both artistic institutions and academia, the State and the market) on the other. In the countercultural atmosphere of the time, where artistic discourse was guided by the idea of a transgression, Perniola believed in the possibility of a genuine change that can help the individual in their search for a more authentic life. In other words, the possibility of freeing oneself from the *diktat* of the status quo (implying a standardized lifestyle based on commodity consumption) to a higher idea of life: from mere survival to more than life.

In the passage quoted above, Perniola argues that with the advent of Pop Art and the neo-avant-gardes, the situation changed radically. *La società dei simulacri* helps convey his account of this transformation – an entire chapter is devoted to the analysis of the neo-avant-gardes (SS: 63–90). First, neo-avant-gardes, according to Perniola, have led to the artistic solemnization of any possible image or object (even outside the art sphere). For example, with Pop Art comics, advertising images, and photography; with New Realism second-hand, ruined and consumed objects; with Land Art nature; with Minimal Art industrial and geometrical materials; and with Conceptual Art writing, graphics and information, among others (SS: 85). Perniola states that what seems to be an overcoming of the separation between art and life – since the art world opens its doors to objects that are normally considered extraneous to it – is actually the creation of an immense speculative bubble founded on the creation of a new artistic market: 'while before Pop Art, the artworks were born as such and only after became luxury goods, now they are already born as products of a market in which luxury goods circulate: commodification is their essence itself' (SS: 86). In other words, Perniola maintains that with the neo-avant-gardes, the works are conceived, created and promoted from the beginning to satisfy the market, and therefore, the artistic nature of anything, Perniola suggests, depends on the fact that the managers of the artistic institutions (merchants, gallery owners, critics) are interested in attributing an economic value to it. The neo-avant-garde involves the birth and development of a new type of art market, which has its new capital in New York, a shift from Paris. This market is presented not so much as the result of a creative activity by the artist but as a 'production' of a particular type of business.

In addition to the neo-avant-gardes, Perniola investigates the rise and development of posthuman art over the course of the 1990s. Among all the current trends of art theory, Perniola focuses on this one because, I believe, it resonates with his overall philosophical theory, especially the ideas elaborated in *The Sex Appeal of the Inorganic*. Exploring Perniola's reflections on that decade is pivotal for an exhaustive enquiry of his theory of art. It can be considered the most prolific and heterogeneous period in the path of the Italian philosopher: in addition to dozens of articles, several of the books he wrote in that decade have been translated in over twelve languages. The text I will mainly investigate here is *Art and Its Shadow*.

Published at the dawn of the third millennium, *Art and Its Shadow* is a collection of essays ranging from contemporary art to Warhol and the postmodern, from philosophical remarks on cinema to the elaboration of a 'third system of art'. Moreover, in this book, Perniola frequently refers to the other works mentioned above which were produced in those years. *Art and Its Shadow*, therefore, represents and assimilates Perniola's efforts at re-thinking the art world during the 1990s.

Perniola's theory in *Art and Its Shadow* presents several points of difference from his early writings and, to a certain extent, from *La società dei simulacri*. Specifically, he focuses on the diffusion of the concept of 'realism'. Echoing Hal Folster's *The Return of the Real*, Perniola notes that in the 1990s a sensibility spread around the so-called manifestations of a particular type of real, namely that in its harsh, repellent, crude, extreme, traumatic and shocking sides. The novelty of this realism is pointed out by Perniola in the following passage: 'It is not a question, as in the past, of the most naturalistic representation possible of this reality, but of a direct exposure of events, poor in symbolic mediation, that provokes dismay, repulsion, if not outright disgust and horror' (AIS: 4). It is not a matter of returning to reality in the sense of naturalism – that is, of objective reproduction of the external world – but of showing the most disturbing and extreme aspects of it without a theoretical-linguistic intervention, in their immediacy. Perniola provides two interpretations of these phenomena. One classifies them with the term 'idiocy' (*idiozia*) and the other with 'splendour' (*splendore*). I will develop the first characterization now and the second later.

The interpretation related to the first lies in the fact that, for Perniola the 1990s art world is still a market-based dimension. Borrowing Benjamin's notions from *The Work of Art in the Age of Mechanical Reproducibility*, Perniola maintains that although the neo-avant-gardes have moved away from the artistic 'aura' (that is, from the metaphysic idea of originality and uniqueness), they have replaced the auratic aspect with an economic aspect. In other words, for example, the iconic photographic prints of Warhol and Beuys may have, so to speak, 'killed God' (i.e. the metaphysical discourse of art); however, in doing so, they have replaced the previous God of art with the God of commerce and economy. Thus, Perniola notes that the neo-avant-gardes have extended the main tendency of capitalist societies, namely consumerist materialism, into the artistic field. In these terms, since the Second World War, the Western world has witnessed a general levelling of the symbolic, linguistic and cultural spheres within both ordinary life and the artistic environment. This tendency reached its peak, according to Perniola, with the 'return of the real' in the 1990s. Perniola contends that a 'flattening of the symbolic' (*livellamento del simbolico*) has occurred, involving both the neo-avant-gardes and the extreme realism of the 1990s: 'Today's extreme realism makes precisely this claim of showing the existent without any theoretical mediation' (AIS: 5).

In this sense, the neo-avant-gardes' transgression of the auratic element, the demystification of the metaphysical and auratic element of art, is instead a hyper-mystification: they do not actually deny the aura; rather, they mystify it, resurrecting it through the exaggerated economic evaluation of the artist's signature. The corollary of this phenomenon, Perniola argues, is that art critics and gallery owners have become mere advertisers and promoters. Extreme realism not only entails the artistic mystification of the neo-avant-gardes: it boosts it, since in pursuing an emotional shock in the viewer (through the exhibition of the real in its disgusting and abject elements), it re-enacts the same cultural and symbolic levelling implicit in the neo-avant-gardes. Considering reality in terms of disgust and abjection means interpreting it from a spontaneous, vitalistic and immediate perspective. In this sense, Perniola interprets 1990s' art in terms of 'idiocy', precisely because it implies remaining blind to far more complex manifestations of the notion of reality. For these arguments outlined, Perniola presents that disgust (*disgusto*) has taken the traditional place and role of taste (*gusto*).[1]

The extreme realism of the 1990s shifted from traditional notions of aesthetics such as the beautiful and the proportionate to the revolting, the abject and the disgusting. Hal Foster's claim (1996) is that contemporary art is characterized by reality in its traumatic and terrifying aspects. Nonetheless, for Perniola, displaying disgusting objects, secretions, worms, human insides, physical deformities and tumours does not necessarily mean entering the realm of transgression nor of the post-human. The disgusting is, in fact, linked with a 'surplus' of the vital, a hyperbolic grotesque manifestation of what is alive and expands itself to the detriment of what it surrounds: 'The disgusting is, precisely, the claim of the vital to swelling to the utmost and polluting everything that comes into contact with it ... [it] is a life impregnated with death that continues with greater obstinacy than ever its fight against form' (AIS: 7–8). Therefore, according to Perniola, the disgusting is not post-human but rather the supreme realization of the human. It is life without limitations, which grows against all form and shape. The disgusting is life itself, desperately striving to continue itself, which in turn ultimately destroys the world around it in furious vitalism. While much of post-human art is labelled as post-human, to Perniola, it does not reach *beyond* the human or *beyond* the organic but instead remains stuck within both categories.[2]

In addition, extreme realism does not differ much from the neo-avant-gardes from the second half of the twentieth century for another fundamental reason. It is part of a promotion system boosted by television, cinema, internet, graphics and design, sharing features of artistic fashion, namely the seasonal and ephemeral search of novelty, which transforms genuine ideas of provocation and transgression into a trend or a slogan. Hence, the real becomes the object of a weak, ephemeral fascination, perpetually overcome by the immediate artistic fashions replacing one another. It can thus create a shock but fails to open a new, disruptive dimension that undermines the fundamental assumptions of the individual. If the neo-avant-gardes have dissolved art into fashion, extreme realism has dissolved fashion into communication. Several years after *Art and Its Shadow*, Perniola published *Miracoli e traumi della comunicazione* (Miracles and Traumas of Communication), wherein he identifies a series of 'matrix events' (*eventi matrice*) that, due to their disruptive visual impact, have produced significant shifts in the viewer's perception of images, videos and media in general (cf. Dorfles 2014). Events such as the fall of the Berlin Wall, 9/11, Abu Ghraib's inmates' torture and Breivik's massacre at the Utøya Island have had such a huge impact on the collective imaginary that all the performances and exhibitions belonging to the realism of disgust seem to be pale imitations of a much more traumatic reality. In this sense, Perniola argues – in the wake of a statement by the composer Karlheinz Stockhausen – that the shock of the real has been overtaken by the shock of communication, implying that as soon as the media apparatuses and industries adopt a strategy similar to that of the artistic practices of the 1990s, the latter are replaced by a far more powerful and tentacular competitor: communication.[3]

Yet, I have also asserted earlier that Perniola, following Baroque literature, elaborates and develops the idea of beauty as *agudeza*, as something that stings, pierces and 'penetrates' minds and feelings. Does this mean that the viewer's shock evoked by extreme realism is close to Perniola's interpretation of the

Baroque? The answer is 'yes', I would argue, only if a crucial distinction is made within 1990s art between *realism as disgust* and *realism as difference*. The former entails a partial idea of the real, grounded upon vitalism and abjection. The latter involves a much more complex and enigmatic characterization, which will be dealt with in the following pages.

The excessive remainder of the artwork

Perniola's developments of contemporary art go hand in hand with his broader philosophical perspective, which is particularly sensitive to the notion of difference. To understand Perniola's interpretation of the notion of difference within his theory of art, it will be useful to provide a broader philosophical and conceptual clarification. At a theoretical level, a transition from Hegelian dialectic to the perception of difference occurred in Perniola's thought. As shown earlier, in *L'alienazione artistica*, Perniola shared the Situationist assumption – heir to the Hegelian-Marxist tradition – that art must undergo a triadic or dialectical transformation. Perniola deviates from this dialectical movement as he believes it fails to consider the negative, contradictory and conflictual element to its very end. In fact, by advocating a final synthesis, that is, a new unity after the dialectic contradiction, it tames the conflict, so to speak, into a greater final conciliation. Thus, the conflict within dialectics is thought of as something always already reconciled. Essential to traditional Hegelian aesthetics, according to Perniola, is the temporary nature of the negative moment: 'is the foreshadowing of an end to conflict, of peace to come, of an irenic moment when suffering and struggle are, if not definitively eliminated, at least temporarily suspended' (AIS: 14). In other words, the dialectic fails to see the surplus, the overabundance of the negative and conflictual element that allows this difference to emerge. The thought of difference is therefore understood by Perniola as 'the experience of a conflict greater than dialectical contradiction, toward the exploration of the opposition between terms that are not symmetrically polar with respect to one another' (AIS: 14). Perniola, to exemplify, adopts Freudian psychoanalytic theory. In fact, Freud elaborates the notion of the unconscious in opposition to the pre-conscious/conscious system. However, between these two elements, the opposition is not considered in a traditional way, i.e. according to the principles of identity and dialectical contradiction. Between the unconscious and the conscience, there is in fact an *asymmetrical opposition* (WE), as the former never manifests itself fully on the scene (despite being ever-present in each individual's daily life). The unconscious, in fact, appears indirectly through compromise formations, such as dreams, slips of the tongue, forgetfulness and so on. The difference, in this case, emerges as a type of thought in which notions such as asymmetry and non-identity – that is, of experiences far from the traditional philosophical logic, both Aristotelian and Hegelian – fall.

The point that Perniola precisely emphasizes is that there is a leap between dialectics and the conception of difference. The former is based on logical-theoretical speculation and has its roots in concepts such as non-contradiction and identity. The second is rather closer to the sphere of *feeling*. Feeling, unlike abstract speculation, is connected to a more empirical, bodily dimension, which also includes impure, disturbing, uncanny, ambivalent, psychopathological and equivocal phenomena. The sphere of feeling, unlike dialectics and logic, is not oriented towards completeness and final reconciliation. On the contrary, it is a type of sensitivity that opens the door to psychopathologies, drug addictions and perversions. Perniola is here influenced by several 'thinkers of the difference', such as Nietzsche, Heidegger, Bataille, Klossowski, Blanchot, Deleuze and Michelstaedter.

For the purpose of this chapter, I will concentrate on the notion of difference within the artistic domain, attempting to provide an answer to the following questions: what is the relationship between the artistic object and difference? How can the work of art be pondered within the problem of difference? From the very formulation of these two questions, a clear difference between Perniola's early and later writings can be highlighted. If between 1966 and 1972, the concept of 'artwork' involved the immobilization and the mummification of creative energies into a motionless, reifying and alienating object, the opposite holds true here: the work of art is pivotal, as it is able to convey the idea of difference. This change in Perniola is, I would argue, due to a new and more elaborate conception of the 'thing'. The status of the work of art as a thing is explicitly set out by Perniola himself in this passage:

> Contrary to the Platonic thesis that considers art as an imitation of nature, as mimesis, here the very status of the thing is attributed to the work of art, according to a tradition that has its roots in the culture of Ancient Egypt . . . what is striking in the ancient Egyptian experiences of art is the fact that it attributes to the works of art sensory faculties; the statues are given the power to see temple visitors. The borders between the organic and the inorganic are abolished, and the work of art appears as a non-organic living body.
>
> FA: 82

In Perniola's early writings, the thing is synonymous with reification and inert objectivity, if not even complicity with the capitalist mindset, devoted to the consumerist accumulation of goods and things. In the quoted passage, the thing is attributed other complex characteristics instead. I have already explored Perniola's thing theory previously, so I will only focus on some aspects pertinent to the artistic context here. The dimension of the thing, for Perniola, is presented by three key notions: the 'neutral', the 'external' and the 'radiant'. Neutral is intended by Perniola as a process of osmosis between the organic and the inorganic. From Palaeolithic engravings and ancient Egyptian religiosity to the reticular ecologies of current digital society, Perniola investigates phenomena where subjects and objects are neither entirely organic nor totally inorganic, but *transorganic*, referring to an interchange between what is alive and what is inert. This dimension, according to him, opens the doors to a neutral dimension of feeling, where subjectivity disappears and what is personal ('I feel') becomes impersonal ('it is felt').

The 'external' is characterized above all by the experience of becoming a thing. I specifically focused on the idea of becoming a mirror, namely a reflecting surface, capable of absorbing within it the world and its heterogeneous manifestations. Turning into a thing, therefore, indicates a disposition of acceptance towards the world, similar to the Stoic *amor fati* (love of fate). I have also developed, in the final chapter of Part Two, several affinities that Baudelaire's dandyism shares with Perniola's interpretation of the thing. The French dandy, in fact, embodies, in his aesthetically oriented lifestyle, the crucial features on which Perniola builds his theory of the thing. Finally, the thing is seen by Perniola not as a dull, fixed and stable entity, but as a dynamic one. Taking up Wittgenstein's and Freud's works, Perniola dwells on the 'radiation' of things, namely the fact that they can be at times surprising, and at other times repellent, disturbing or attractive. The thing in turn, far from being the fixation of alienated creativity into an object, as it was in *L'alienazione artistica*, is a new experiential territory to explore and further investigate for Perniola.

To think of artistic work as a 'thing' means taking into account the three fundamental components briefly summarized. In fact, for Perniola, the artwork is not a thing in the sense of a static, inert object, incapable of change – a bearer, so to speak, of the logic of identity. Nor is it the ultimate end of a process of reification of the individual. On the contrary, it can 'radiate', it can be 'uncanny', and it implies a transit between the organic and the inorganic. From the artwork, a surplus emerges, an excessive content that goes beyond surfaces and forms. The work of art is never just an *object*; it is a *thing*.[4] Thus, as per Perniola, the 'artistic thing' – as it could be named – does not involve an ascensional idealism or, on the contrary, a focus on earthly abjection (as was the case for most 1990s art). Neither loyalty to the 'aura' (that is, the metaphysical feature of the artwork) nor to the abject and the disgusting. Neither high nor low, but lateral. It implies that the artwork is an in-between entity that flourishes at the margins and not at the heights and the bottoms.

To clarify his thoughts, Perniola writes of *lights* and *shadows* regarding the artwork. On the one hand, there is the light, represented by all the discourses of the institutions, the market and the communication apparatuses cast upon the thing. In an interview released in 2001, Perniola focuses on the growing economic sides of cultural practices and activities. Museums all over the world continue to multiply exponentially and involve many other commercial fields. For instance, Bilbao's Guggenheim has become a strong enterprise from which not only artistic boutiques but tourism in general, including new hotels, restaurants and shops, flourishes. Thus, museums and exhibitions have become similar to carnivals, fairs or amusement parks. Perniola's concern, in this context, is not that art has become increasingly 'democratic', trying to establish a closer dialogue with the audience. It is rather a theoretical issue: if artists and artworks are involved in the ephemeral processes of production, fruition and destruction, that is, 'artistic fashions', what happens to the very idea of art in the end? If, traditionally, the Western idea of art represents a work that lasts longer than the author's life, which can be transferred to future generations, what happens with short-term oriented artworks and artistic practices? The major risk is that the capitalist mindset floods the artistic environment, transforming the artworks into artistic products or fetishes where quantity stands for more than quality. In other words, this is an environment in which money is far more important than creativity.

Perniola's response to this state of things is to highlight the necessity of keeping the 'other side' of art alive, keeping its oppositive facet always active. Figuratively speaking, wherever there is light, there must be shadow. Thus, Perniola argues that in spite and because of light, a shadow is projected at the margins of the artwork. The artwork has a 'remainder' (*resto*), an excessive element, which Perniola defines as its 'shadow'. The shadow represents the enigmatic core of the artwork, which survives beyond the light of economics and communication. It is in this precise enigmatic feature that Perniola sees the notion of difference, entailing 'the idea that in art and in philosophy there is something irreducible to the process of normalization and standardization in work in society' (AIS: 65). Erik M. Vogt claims that Perniola's idea of the remainder should be understood in terms of 'conflict and antagonisms' (2019b: 6), emphasizing the fact that the excessive core of the artwork lies primarily in its being *in opposition* with respect to the imaginary communication of neo-liberal society and its apparatus. Still, this remainder is what Perniola does not explain carefully within *Art and Its Shadow*. Renato Barilli, commenting on the book, states that the main thesis it proposes is 'definitely cryptic, evocative but scarcely proven' (2000: 33). In my opinion, looking for an understanding of the notion of 'shadow' exclusively within *Art and Its Shadow* might well leave the reader puzzled and confused. It is better understood through other texts, wherein Perniola focuses on the neutral, thingly and external dimensions of the material world (such as *The Sex Appeal of the Inorganic, Transiti, Enigmas* and *Del sentire*). From these texts, it becomes clearer that Perniola's goal is to elaborate on what he refers to as the 'third regime of art' (*terzo regime dell'arte*): against the economic homogenization of art and against the upward and downward movements of spiritualism and abjection, respectively, Perniola praises a third alternative. This alternative, at a closer look, comprises Perniola's overall effort to re-think contemporary society through several traditions of thought and authors (from Roman ritualism to Stoicism, Baroque literature and Jesuit thought). From this philosophical path, Perniola coined or developed several notions, such as 'enigma', 'transit', 'ritual without myth', 'simulacrum' and 'thing'. The idea of the 'shadow' is arguably the prosecution of this common thread within the art domain.

As I have asserted throughout this book, one of Perniola's main objectives is to investigate current phenomena and experiences without falling back on traditional metaphysical interpretations. For instance, besides the opposition between original and copy, he elucidates the simulacrum; besides the ideas of pure ritualism and mythological perspectives, he elucidates ritual without myth; besides the polarity between the organic and the inorganic, he elucidates the idea of a more complex and intertwining entity, the thing. This list, I argue, can cover all the main concepts that Perniola focused on throughout his writings. The same holds true for art: against the opposition between economy and spirituality and the polarity between 'aura' and mechanical reproducibility, he explores the idea of the artwork as an artistic 'thing' that possesses a 'shadow'. For Perniola, the shadow is within the orbital discourse of the difference because it implies considering the artwork as a thing, that is, as a radical heterogeneity, an experience that rejects quantitative and economic appropriations.

On the one hand, the work of art, entangled in the economic realms (the light), embodies the ultimate reduction of things in the pure value of exchange; however, on the other hand, it makes available the dimension of difference (the shadow). Upon scrutiny, Perniola's conclusion here can be seen as both the continuation and the reversal of the main thesis he developed in his early philosophical years. Earlier, I underlined how according to Perniola art, despite being an alienated manifestation of creativity, allows the conditions for such (partial) creativity to exist. In *Art and Its Shadow*, Perniola uses the notions of 'creativity' and 'alienation' far less and those of 'difference' and 'economy' much more. If the two terms are swapped, a similar conclusion appears at first glance. In fact, it is correct to claim that in both cases, Perniola considers the art realm as a complex intertwining of alienation/economy and creativity/difference. The crucial distinction lies in two specific points. The first is the distinctive meanings assigned to the notions employed. Creativity, for instance, is considered within a subjectivist horizon: the realization of one's own unique desire, whereas, difference is considered in the context of the experience of desubjectivation and suspension, i.e. of turning oneself into a thing. A major difference can also be found in the divergent proposal put forth after the analysis of the current trends. In his early writings, Perniola argues that it is necessary to elaborate on a project for the total realization of creativity within collective social life. In contrast, in his later writings, he does not propose the end of the economy by praising revolutionary creativity. He instead accepts the economic dimension of artistic objects, however stating that this dimension does not exhaust the work of art. Precisely what resists and goes beyond the economic side of the artwork, for Perniola, is what should be looked at.

What appears to be a constitutive ambiguity of the art world can be clarified by referring to a chapter in *Art and Its Shadow* entitled 'Idiocy and Splendour of Current Art'. Specifically, Perniola states that the extreme realism of the 1990s can be understood in two ways, namely idiocy and splendour. 'Idiotic' realism has already been analysed. It entails proposing as post-human what is actually only the culminating and destructive moment of the vital. In fact, by overlapping vitalism and realism, idiotic realism provides an ideological and partial version of the notion of the real. The real cannot simply be traced back to the empirical vital element but needs to be investigated taking into account ambiguous, disturbing, repellent and attractive experiences, where there is an exchange between the thingly and the organic elements and between the linguistic and the non-linguistic ones. Ultimately, post-human art can be positively regarded if 'realism' means a multifaceted and much more complex idea of reality. On the other hand, it can lead to a melting pot of futility and fuzziness. Therefore, here too, Perniola does not entirely criticize contemporary art but interprets and accepts it in its constitutive ambiguity, that is, with its possibility of being both idiocy and splendour, teeming with fringe, anti-metaphysical experiences and the risk of providing endless combinations of interchangeable futile objects.

Perniola's thought moves within the contemporary art world and at the same time outside of it; thus, the Italian philosopher tries to understand current logics (mercantile and communicative) while simultaneously trying to identify the potentially surprising, wonderful elements, capable of provoking amazement and uncanny experiences.

To complete the survey of Perniola's critique of contemporary art, it is worth briefly illustrating his standpoint in *L'arte espansa* (Expanded Art). Between 2000 and 2015, Perniola devoted several articles and issues of the *Ágalma* journal to contemporary art, still, his perspectives from *Art and Its Shadow* remained substantially unchanged (see AMN). For example, in *Ágalma* no. 9, entitled *Professione: Artista*, he focused on the so-called 'magic corporation', that is, the whole communicative and promotional apparatus of institutions, galleries, artists, critics and curators who are able to label something as art. He compares this practice to the sorceries, spells and enchantments of tribal and primitive societies and thus refers to it as a 'magic' corporation (MC: 5–6).

Nonetheless, according to Perniola, a turning point was in 2013 with the Venice Biennale, to which he devoted the last volume on contemporary art: *L'arte espansa*. Borrowing the title of a 1970 seminal work by Gene Youngblood – *Expanded Cinema* – Perniola claims that the current art world has been destabilized by the introduction of new horizons and the widening of its traditional boundaries. As per Perniola, it is the very assumption of making art that underwent a transformation. While the historical avant-gardes and the neo-avant-gardes were based on the notion of transgression, the orienting principle behind the 2013 Biennale was completely different, that of *encyclopedicity*. It is no longer a matter of founding manifestoes, artistic programmes or ephemeral fashions and artistic fetishes. The main point no longer lies in identifying a poetics around which one or more artists gather and with which they identify themselves. The criteria through which artists and works are included do not depend on a cohesive and shared perspective. The very distinction of whether something is art depends on a new operation of legitimization: encyclopedicity (on the reception of Perniola's *L'arte espansa* also see Trione 2015; Pappalardo 2015; Donà 2016; Velotti 2016; Taccone 2017; Juhl 2018; Marroni 2019; Bartoloni 2019).

Perniola devotes several pages to the analysis of the collection of the 157 extremely heterogeneous 'items' (*articoli*) of the Biennale to investigate the criteria for their inclusion in an 'encyclopedia'. There were both world-renowned artists, such as Cindy Sherman, Walter De Maria and Richard Serra, and people who have never self-identified as artists or who have never been part of the cultural and aesthetical worlds. Also considered together as artists there appear figures linked to the oneiric and the esoteric realms, such as Carl G. Jung, Rudolph Steiner and Aleister Crowley; adventurers, futurologists and embalmers; religious *ex voto* and Art Therapy works, just to name a few. Therefore, Perniola proposes that the authors included do not share a unique, comprehensive theme. Rather, several pivotal issues of aesthetics and art are put together: from Surrealism to the relationship between action and contemplation and from collection versus accumulation to the separation between art and life. Significantly, there is much less emphasis, compared to the 1990s, on realism.[5] Perniola conceives such a collection as a cultural operation heir for both the Baroque and the avant-garde milieus (especially the Situationist *détournement*), constituting the blooming and multiplication of spaces and meanings. To describe this procedure Perniola borrows the term *agency* from the British anthropologist Alfred Gell (1998):

> which implies a decentralisation of action from the individual to a very complex system of relationships, within which something or someone who is *fringe*, that is to say, marginal, even extraneous to the world of art, is admitted to be part of it, or s/he is already a recognized member but has never been treated according to an unusual, unconventional perspective ... It is a matter of moving, displacing, transforming what is given according to a procedure that belongs par excellence to the Baroque poetics theorized by Baltasar Gracián.
>
> AE: 45–6

The strategy which Massimiliano Gioni, the curator of the 2013 Biennial, adopted seems to recall a whole series of conceptual and aesthetic figures investigated by Perniola throughout his philosophical path. For instance, in the quoted passage, Perniola traces the 'making and unmaking of unlawful matches between things' in Gioni's work, which is typical of the Baroque attitude; on the same page, he also identifies the movement from same to same typical of the *transit* and the 'displacement' of the uncanny, which I developed while discussing the notion of the inorganic and Freud's *Unheimliche*. According to this theoretical standpoint, 'agency' (he employs the English term) implies that something might not necessarily be 'artistic' on its own. Perniola claims that there are no objective characteristics that define something as artistic, but rather it is agency through which fringe, marginal and surprising sides of productions, attitudes and experiences are explored, disseminated and developed.

Precisely because anything can be included in the sphere of art, even what was previously excluded, Perniola highlights the possibility of a risky outcome:

'drowning in an abyss of idleness and futility, in which not only the old idea of art disappears, but also every possibility of providing an orientation fades in a melting pot in which everyone is in harmony with everything' (AE: 48). In other words, Perniola is completely aware of the *ambiguity* of the fringe turning point of art. While, on the one hand, it finally seems to provide significant recognition to heterogeneous phenomena and manifestations of the surprising, the marvellous, the 'radiant' and the uncanny, at the same time, I would argue that it implies the possibility that, after all, expanding art implies expanding the already existing economic bubble. This bubble, therefore, becomes even more gigantic because it incorporates new territories hitherto excluded from traditional insider art. In other words, it can mark a move from the speculative bubble of the art world to the immensely larger speculative bubble of the art world*s* (plural).

This trend of ambiguity (also highlighted by Vogt 2020) is featured across Perniola's entire thought. The ambiguity lies in the fact that Perniola often seems to praise as well as reject the same argument. Another example emerges in *Del Sentire*. His examination of the status of the contemporary aesthetic experience leads him to conclude that our feeling may be defined as a 'feeling from outside', impersonal, neutral and close to a thing that feels. This, as shown previously, is positively welcomed by Perniola because, on the one hand, it links a plethora of experiences (from inorganic sexuality to virtual reality, drug addictions, perversions, etc.) to ancient and marginal traditions (Palaeolithic engravings, Egyptian architecture and Roman ritualism, among others ritualism, etc.); on the other hand, it opens up a post-metaphysical experiential horizon with new challenges and issues for philosophy, sexuality and everyday life. At the same time, however, he affirms that contemporary individuals live under the sign of 'sensology' (*sensologia*, DS: 5). Sensology is different from ideology but shares several essential features with it. Ideology, by providing a system of pre-given doctrines and opinions, comprises a pre-determined vision of the world that 'exonerates' the individual from the responsibility of thinking in a personal or critical way. Ideology 'thinks' in place of the individual, from whom nothing is then required, other than to trace what is 'already thought' (*già pensato*). Sensology, on the other hand, corresponds to an ideology of the senses, a socialization of personal feelings in a neutral and yet impersonal collectivity. In this sense, the individual cannot do anything but follow what is 'already felt' (*già sentito*) because his/her own affectivity is transferred from the subject to something external (on this topic also see Scrivano 1992; Vogt 2019a, 2019b, 2020; Borges Junior 2020). Perniola even states that our contemporary sensological feeling is a totalitarian feeling (DS: 16). Do these two conclusions not seem mutually exclusive? Should they not contradict each other? Which one does Perniola truly believe? I would claim that he is actually well aware of this ambiguity. He states that, to cope with a sensological world, the Marxist approach needs to be abandoned. The individual should not look for 'a reappropriation, a restitution, a restoration to the subject of what has been taken away' (E: 29). In other words, they should not fight what is 'already felt' with a nostalgic battle in favour of the 'I feel'. On the contrary, their attitude should be considered a mimetic rivalry with the opponent: 'treat the wound by means of the weapon that caused it' (E: 30). In other words, according to Perniola, the depersonalization of feeling must be carried through to its ends; we need to assume and radicalize phenomena that manifest themselves in society. Only in this way does the experience of the thing that feels not relapse into alienation but instead allow the individual to enter the phenomena explored in this book.[6]

11

Oscar Wilde: the In-Between Dandy

Finally, the third and last exemplary dandy scrutinized in this book is Oscar Wilde. Wilde was an internationally renowned dandy thriving at the end of the nineteenth century (especially well-known in Ireland, the United Kingdom, France and the USA). Like Baudelaire (and unlike Brummell), in addition to an aesthetically-oriented lifestyle, he published numerous writings. He was a poet, playwright, novelist, essayist and journalist. In the wide panorama of Wilde's writings, this book dwells specifically on his essays. In fact, the Irish dandy – while maintaining the typical witty essence of his most-acclaimed literary works – develops his perspective on art and society clearly and cohesively in his essays. By exploring his essays as well as the scholarly literature on the subject, I will show how Perniola's philosophy shares theoretical affinities with Wilde.

Recurrent dandy ideas in Oscar Wilde

To begin with, four core concepts of dandyism appear as a pattern in Wilde's works: first, the criticism of the bourgeois mindset; second, the privilege accorded to the artificial over the natural; third, the cult of exteriority, form and elegance as opposed to vulgarity and triviality; and fourth, the search for beauty in one's own age.

Wilde himself establishes a theoretical connection with Baudelaire. Specifically, in 'The Relation of Dress to Art' (released in the fashion magazine *Pall Mall Gazette*), Wilde focuses not only on the themes of clothing and aesthetics but also on the broader relationship between artists and their ages. To do so, he quotes the following passage from Baudelaire's *Salon of 1846*: 'The great colourists know how to create colour with a black coat, a white cravat and a grey background' (1995: 51). As suggested earlier in this book, Baudelaire considered the dandy a 'painter of modern life', that is, a figure capable of extracting beauty from the contingent and transient features of contemporaneity. This element of contingency is precisely what Baudelaire called 'modernity' and which Wilde too seems to have embraced in his own aesthetic perspective: 'the true artist does not wait for life to be made picturesque for him, but sees life under picturesque conditions always ... under certain conditions of light and shade, what is ugly in fact may in its effect become beautiful, is true; and this, indeed, is the real *modernité* of art' (1995: 51). Or again, in another passage within his *Lecture to Art Students*, he states: 'Do not wait for life to be picturesque, but try and see life under picturesque conditions' (1995: 129). Hence, the idea of an effectual beauty, which has the strength to arguably manifest itself concretely in the world, recurs several times in Wilde's work.

For Wilde (and for Baudelaire), beauty does not depend on objective canons, in which the harmony, proportions and unity of the parts play an essential role. The aesthetics of the dandies, like Perniola's, is not an objective but a strategic, worldly type of beauty that takes into account everyday life in its multiform manifestations. According to Perniola, Baudelaire's poetry is guided by the notion of *over-interest*, as opposed to the traditional idea of aesthetic *disinterest*. Wilde shares this anti-traditional and anti-academic standpoint when he writes: 'Art is not thought to be taught in Academies. It is what one looks at, not what one listens to, that makes the artist. The real schools should be the streets' (1995: 53). Wilde, by opposing academies and streets, alongside the use of his famous ironic witticism, stresses the idea that academies provide an overly abstract and ideal conception of beauty and that, conversely, the streets too can counterbalance the passivity of institutions. The streets represent the chance to see and participate with all the senses – not only hearing passively in the academies' lecture halls – in the atmosphere of modernity, grasping its architecture, design, styles, clothing and fashion. In this sense, as per Wilde, the streets work as 'real schools' that demand the dandy and the artist to adopt a lifestyle receptive of their own present. In this context, the first duty of the dandy entails being able to find and extract the conditions of beauty and that which is picturesque.

Another passage showing the influence of Baudelaire on Wilde can be traced to a lecture he delivered in New York on 9 January 1882, entitled 'The English Renaissance of Art'. Here Wilde, focusing particularly on the pre-Raphaelite movement, appears to be profoundly influenced by Baudelaire (although the latter is not explicitly mentioned). First, Wilde resorts to the critique of traditional philosophical aesthetics, stating at the very beginning of the lecture: 'I will not try to give you any abstract definition of beauty – any such universal formula for it as was sought for by the philosophy of the eighteenth century' (1995: 3). Wilde's polemic targets are above all thinkers belonging to the Enlightenment era, such as

Kant, who elaborated the conditions of possibility for the universality of the judgement of taste within the aesthetic field. Second, a few pages later, he echoes the Baudelarian distinction between the two elements of beauty: the eternal and the ephemeral. To summarize, Baudelaire believes beauty possesses two distinctive features. First, an eternal aspect corresponding to the artistic and aesthetic behaviour of man. Mankind has always produced heterogeneous manifestations of beauty, from Palaeolithic caves to contemporary art. At the same time, it has a relative aspect, peculiar to each age, which makes beauty endlessly unique and specific. In other words, beauty always exists, yet is never a mere repetition or reproduction of itself. Again, Wilde echoes Baudelaire's position: 'The artist is indeed the child of his own age, but the present will not be to him a whit more real than the past; for, like the philosopher of the Platonic vision, the poet is the spectator of all time and of all existence. For him no form is obsolete, no subject out of date ... There is indeed a poetical attitude to be adopted towards all things' (1995: 13). In this passage Wilde claims that the artist is 'child of his own age', thus reiterating the connection between modernity and beauty; in addition, he points out that, since man has always produced artistic 'forms', he also is invited to explore everything that has been done before him: 'For beauty is the only thing that time cannot harm. Philosophies fall away like sand, and creeds follow one another like the withered leaves of autumn; but what is beautiful is a joy for all seasons and a possession for all eternity' (1995: 21). In his poetic prose, Wilde departs from the Western perspective based on an idea of form linked to permanence (unlike, for instance, the Eastern Buddhist tradition based on impermanence). Fundamentally, although ancient Roman and Greek Gods, for instance, were replaced by other ones, Wilde continues to state that architecture, sculpture, poetry and art is what is capable of surviving the test of time. The 'forms' of the past serve as a testimony of human artistic behaviour through time. Forms, intended thus, are not to be merely considered as potentially endless structures, buildings or works. They also provide a glimpse of what Wilde calls the 'common intellectual atmosphere in all countries' (1995: 21). Hence, Wilde refers to a shared, recurring attitude towards beauty and artistic attitudes.

Wilde's notion of form does not refer only to figurative art. For example, in *The Truth of Masks*, he elaborates a philosophy of clothes by focusing on Shakespeare's theatre. If there is an archaeology of buildings, Wilde maintains, there also should be an archaeology of clothing. Whereas the former helps us to understand a historical period's aesthetics and architectonic techniques, the latter provides us with crucial information regarding the manners, rituals, clothing trends and broadly the lifestyles and social conditions peculiar to the time. Exteriority is understood by Wilde as a dimension worth exploring, as in its communicative richness, it provides information for the historian as well as for the dandy and the artist by bringing the past back to life:

> The ancient world wakes from its sleep, and history moves as a pageant before our eyes, without obliging us to have recourse to a dictionary or an encyclopaedia for the perfection of our enjoyment.
>
> Wilde 1987: 1006

Wilde claims that aesthetics should be appreciated and can be properly understood only if it involves human senses in their complexity. For instance, a book cannot stimulate hearing and does so for sight and touch only in a limited way. Thus, according to Wilde, based on visual abstraction, only a poor aesthetic experience is most likely to be produced. This further implies that aesthetics must not remain stuck within academies and encyclopaedias but should be actualized in life. For this very reason, Wilde saw in the dandyish attitude a proper lifestyle that could help the individual live an elegant life under the sign of aesthetics. His main objective was to *become* a work of art, not just to *produce* them.

Aesthetically oriented lifestyles are also cultivated by dandies to distinguish themselves from the bourgeois mentality. Wilde, like Brummell and Baudelaire before him, considers notions such as 'utility', 'profit', 'quantity' and 'function' to be at odds with dandyism. For example, he states, 'Each of the professions means a prejudice. We live in the age of the overworked, and the under-educated; the age in which people are so industrious that they become absolutely stupid. And, harsh though it may sound, I can't help saying that such people deserve their doom. The sure way of knowing nothing about life is to try to make oneself useful' (1987: 981). Just as Brummell and Baudelaire did, Wilde too despises the principle of utility. Being useful, for the dandies, means devoting the individual's efforts to a profession, a function, a job, and thus falling back on a series of duties and values that are not worth following within an aesthetically oriented lifestyle.

These claims are echoed in another essay by Wilde, *The Soul of Man Under Socialism*, which is devoted to, among other things, a critique of the late nineteenth-century capitalist society. Wilde, in fact, criticizes the very idea of private property. To him, an individual who employs all their time, energies and abilities to obtain property and then laboriously works to maintain is the literal expression of being a slave who loses the joy of living (1995: 1022). In other words, since all people potentially have creative energies according to Wilde, the duty of the state should be not to allow citizens to find employment and keep it for as long as possible, but to free them from the fatigue of working. Like Marx, who had criticized the alienation of the worker, Wilde borrows several core themes of nineteenth century's socialist and communist ideologies. He even goes further by praising technology and automated working machines as they can replace men in their jobs. These statements anticipate those of the Situationists (heirs to Marxist tradition) and of the collective creativity praised by Perniola in his early writings. In fact, here, too, the distinction between survival and life is outlined, that is, between an existence subjugated to a salary for survival, which never calls into question the status quo, and an existence that, according to both Wilde and the Situationists, is grounded upon an authentic realization of human creativity. In his invective against work and private property, Wilde anticipates the Situationist motto *'ne travaillez jamais'* ('never work') almost ninety years ahead of its materialization. Working in a capitalist society means – for this common thread of thought – approving and maintaining an oppressive apparatus, which comprises the collective realization of slavery, and not transgression and creativity.

Wilde speaks of socialism in so far as it leads to a new kind of individualism. Specifically, he distinguishes two types of individualism: one erroneous and one genuine (1987: 1022). The first is individualism understood in a pejorative sense or what is commonly understood by thinking only of oneself. This indicates individualism that confuses 'a man with what he possesses' (1987: 1022). In other words, the individualism present in capitalist societies implies a shift from being to having, that is, from having power over one's own life to simply being an accumulator of objects, capitals, properties, etc. Socialism then, which Wilde believes is the form of government that converts private property into public wealth (1987: 1019), transforms competition into cooperation for the benefit and well-being of everyone. However, the ultimate goal of socialism is, according to Wilde, to allow everyone to be fully and genuinely individualistic. At this point, the other form of individualism comes into play. According to Wilde, individualism does not mean being selfish; rather it is the opposite. Common morality praises altruism and deplores individualism. For Wilde, the opposite holds true. If altruism does not aim to subvert an oppressive order, it works only as a momentary palliative, an ephemeral relief that ultimately never casts questions regarding the poverty and misery of the masses. Instead, through socialism, freed from the burden of work and property, people can finally employ their time and skills authentically and above all put an end to poverty.[1]

So far, Wilde's claims possess, I would argue, a strong similarity with the Situationists and Perniola's *L'alienazione artistica*. In fact, both the Situationists and Perniola promoted the end of economic capitalist domination in the Western world in favour of a permanent revolution of everyday life based on individual creativity. The insurmountable difference between early Perniola and Wilde, however, stems from the fact that the former proposed an *overcoming* of art, while the latter an *expansion* of the artistic domain within everyday life. For early Perniola, Western art has always conveyed an alienated manifestation of creativity since it has always either been dependent on the ideologies of power or, failing that, independent only if isolated and harmless – that is, not able to provide concrete alternative perspectives. Therefore, art should have been overcome, and the creative drives should have been extended into the realm of everyday life. In contrast, Wilde proposes a transformation of life, so to speak, through the very eyes of art: 'Art is individualism' (1987: 1030). By linking individualism and art, he implies that people's guiding attitudes should follow the principle of art. It is in this very claim that Wilde's aestheticism appears. For Wilde, individuals themselves should become a work of art to make them and the surrounding world beautiful. In other words, the main purpose of Wilde's dandyism is to *realize* and *express* in one's own body (through elegance) and attitude (through individualism) what most artists only *produce* through objects (paintings, sculptures, among others). A young Perniola would have arguably considered this perspective within the artistic alienation inherent in Western aesthetics. In *The Soul of Man Under Socialism*, Wilde criticizes one kind of alienation, that of workers under capitalist systems; nonetheless, if we follow early Perniola's viewpoint, Wilde does not recognize another one: that of art itself.

Finally, the last recurrent core dandyish idea that emerges in Wilde's work is the despising of nature. I will focus on a passage that helps the reader understand why Wilde – and dandyism in general – does not appreciate the natural world. Like Baudelaire before him, Wilde links nature with survival, mere self-interest and above all the lack of proportions, comfort and design: 'the more we study Art, the less we care for Nature. What Art really reveals to us is Nature's lack of design, her curious crudities, her extraordinary monotony, her absolutely unfinished condition ... If Nature had been comfortable, mankind would never have invented architecture, and I prefer houses to the open air. In a house we feel all the proper proportions' (1987: 909).

First, Wilde considers nature as a series of natural and physical phenomena lacking 'style', that is, the human ability to go beyond raw reality in its immediacy and elevate, transform, and recombine it according to new aesthetic perspectives (see also Vincentini 1994). Nature privileges the individuals who, to survive, adapt themselves. In contrast, Wilde seeks rarer individuals who are able to build a 'higher' life over mere survival. Since he considers art to be the most significant expression of human behaviour, the ideal type of higher individual for him is the dandy. In fact, the dandies are those individuals who embody in their everyday lives an artistic and aesthetically oriented attitude. Hence, for Wilde, self-consciousness is crucial. Natural behaviours are, according to him, only instinctively driven and arrayed against this stands the 'self-conscious culture' of mankind (1987: 916). Nature can work as a first source of inspiration, but it is never the ultimate goal of art. It is only through the agency of humans that art can be expressed.

Although Wilde condemns the bourgeois and capitalist society of the time, it was thanks to that very society that he became the well-known and acclaimed dandy he was and continues to be. As Josephine Guy and Ian Small claim in their volume on Wilde and the culture industry in the late nineteenth century (2004), the American and European tours Wilde made in the early 1880s, where the bourgeoisie was the main audience, gave him an initial sparkle of international fame. In addition, despite condemning journalists, public opinion and 'the masses' in general, Wilde himself – as previously suggested – was a journalist for and editor of several fashion and popular culture magazines, read especially by the middle and upper classes. In other words, at first glance, Wilde shows several contradictions between his writings and his public image. The following pages investigate these contradictions to delineate the singularity of the dandy Oscar Wilde with respect to Brummell, Baudelaire and Perniola.

The subversion of writing

Scholars have debated the complex contradictory figure of Wilde since his first works were published. In the vast mass of his writings, several critiques have been elaborated. Most of these mainly focus on the contradictions between Wilde's statements, especially those condemning economy, journalism and the late nineteenth century's values, and his mediatic personality, in which fame, money, institutions and professions played an essential role.

Wilde did not devote his life solely to elegance and dandyism. Beyond cultivating dandyism in his persona, he was a writer, poet, editor, journalist, lecturer and critic. He had many occupations and institutionally recognized roles. For example, Wilde wrote for several magazines and journals, including *Woman's World*, the *Pall Mall Gazette*, the *Nineteenth Century* and the *Court and Society Review*, to which he contributed regularly, especially during the 1880s. He also embarked on a fifty-date tour across the US (1881–2), delivering lectures on disparate topics, from furnishing to art, clothing and make-up. As Regenia Gagnier (1987: 69) highlights, unlike Brummell, Wilde did not have a patron and although he came from a family of intellects (his mother was an Irish revolutionary and poet, his father a renowned ophthalmologist), he did not have a conspicuous inheritance. Gagnier continues, Wilde thus had to come to terms with the market and with the emerging media of the time (press, publicity, popular books, trend magazines). An institution such as the publishing market has various written and unwritten rules, depending particularly on the product's resonance with its audience and the number of units sold. Taking into account the opinion of the masses and the quantitative discourse is clearly at odds with the dandy's lifestyle. Nonetheless, as Guy and Small claim in their volume, many texts by Wilde were negotiated with the market industry (publishers, printers, theatre managers) and were therefore inevitably influenced by them (2004: 9). Guy and Small's study focuses on empirical data, paper material, letters and notes exchanged between Wilde and his editors. The authors conclude that Wilde had been writing for money all his life (2004: 21–2). Specifically, they point out how Wilde realized, beginning from his American lectures, that he could earn as much of a living from his knowledge as from his image. And there lies the main reason that, according to Guy and Small, Wilde commodified his personality to produce a popular and marketable image. Wilde was aware of the contradiction between his books and attitudes. He in fact states: 'Would you like to know the great drama of my life? It is that I have put my genius into my life – I have put only my talent into my works' (Wilde 1987: 689). Here, Wilde distinguishes genius from talent, placing a higher value on the former. For him, genius refers to his dandyism, namely his devotion to elegance and, in other words, his witty and ironic remarks (the aestheticization of lifestyle). Talent, on the other hand, is considered a by-product, a secondary result of his attitude, which helped him write books. It is no coincidence that Holbrook Jackson, commenting on this very sentence, claims, 'What he seemed to be doing all the time was to translate life into art through himself. His books were but incidents in this process' (2005: 362). Wilde attracted criticism from numerous scholars. Ellen Moers claims that he used dandyism for the purposes of notoriety (1960: 298) and should thus not even be considered a dandy but a go-getter (1960: 299). The drama critic James G. Huneker sees Wilde simply as a 'veritable *cabotin*' (2005: 368). G.K. Chesterton argues that Wilde was an artist and at the same time a charlatan. Specifically, Chesterton claims that Wilde's writings can be divided by two different criteria: the sentences in which the Irish dandy felt he was free to express himself (which

Chesterton considers valuable), and the ones in which he strived for attention and popularity (that for Chesterton mainly constitutes banal formulas and slogans) (2005: 339). In the article 'Oscar Wilde, commodity, culture' (2004), Dennis Denisoff argues that Wilde's main paradox stems from his consideration of art as an almost holy realm, at odds with market concerns; however, at the same time, he himself transformed art into a commodity to sell (2004: 119). In short, many critics see Wilde as the incarnation of mass industry and society. In this sense, Wilde contradictorily declared himself against the bourgeoisie, even while this expanding middle class was his main target and audience.

Although these briefly outlined criticisms have concrete empirical data to back them, I would argue that they can only be accepted in part. In this book, I follow Regenia Gagnier's perspective developed in *Idylls of the Marketplace: Oscar Wilde and the Victorian Public*. Gagnier's book offers a critical understanding of the relationship between Victorian 'culture industry' and the figure of Oscar Wilde. According to Gagnier, Wilde's work should be considered one of the first attempts to problematize and provide a concrete answer to the issue of art's place within a consumerist society (1987: 5). Wilde's attitude, according to Gagnier, was surprising and in some cases anticipated the artistic avant-gardes and countercultural practices of the twentieth century. Specifically, Gagnier's main claim is that although Wilde essentially wrote for a middle-class public and set his works within middle- and upper-bourgeois contexts and environments, he did not reflect middle-class values or fall under their influence. On the contrary, rather than considering Wilde as a poser, if not a middle-class pimp, Gagnier argues that he employed specific writing techniques to subvert his audience's cultural and moral codes. In other words, if it is true that Wilde's poetical imagination was imbued with the *clichés* of the dominant apparatuses, it is also true that he always added a subtle twist, in the form of an unexpected, surprising or uncanny substitutive word that radically transformed the meanings involved: 'His legendary wit consisted in practice of a talent for inverting Victorian truisms ... His mind was stocked with commonplaces, and seem to have been there for the sole purpose of their subversion' (Gagnier 1987: 7–8). For instance, in *The Soul of Man Under Socialism*, Wilde writes, 'Under individualism, people will be quite natural and absolutely unselfish' (1987: 1040); 'charity creates a multitude of sins' (1987: 1018); 'Democracy is the bludgeoning of people by the people for the people' (1987: 1026); 'In the interest of the rich, we must get rid of it [private property]' (1987: 1020). All of these statements, the tip of the iceberg of Wildean wit, are grounded upon a 'commonplace' on the one hand, and deployed to convey a new if not opposite meaning on the other. For instance, according to common morality, individualism means thinking only of oneself, therefore being an egoist. Wilde flips this truism by stating that egoism should be distinguished from individualism. For Wilde, the former entails asking or obliging other people to live according to how one lives or believes it is right to live. Therefore, it is a potentially authoritarian imposition that often leads to the censorship of differences and otherness. The latter does not place any obligation on others, but rather leaves the individual free to express their way of life. Thus, individualism does not mean selfishness – on the contrary, it implies the crucial right to express oneself. On the other hand, charity and altruism, understood by 'common sense' as two pivotal values, are both criticized by Wilde. In fact, for the Irish dandy, compassion and benevolence towards the afflicted can merely work as palliatives, which keep them in a state of survival, that is, in perennial misery and poverty. By not attempting any subversion of the status quo and focusing instead on transitory moments of altruism, Wilde understands charity as an aggravating factor of social difficulties and not as a genuine remedy. In this sense, ironically, it is closer to sin.

Wilde's work can be considered as a deconstruction of the categories of bourgeois thought from within, that is, within the mass apparatus advancing alongside the middle class at the time. To borrow Gagnier's words: 'Wilde's epigrams and paradoxes exploit the self-critical possibilities of the Victorian language and thought patterns' (1987: 32). In so doing, Wilde was able to be both critical of the dominant order and simultaneously be a prominent personality incessantly advertised and promoted within it. Gagnier notes that Wilde's style of writing foreran Debord's *détournement*, mainly considering the appropriation of a given content and in its re-organization in an unsettling way, possibly ironic, which loads it with a new subversive meaning.

Wilde's texts, far from echoing the middle-class mindset, were actually a subtle and complex combination of witticism, cynicism and subversion. His artistic attitudes, focusing on aesthetics and elegance, were never dissociated from the political element. There is another common aspect shared by Perniola and Wilde here: the way Perniola elaborated on the notion of strategic beauty, which links aesthetics and effectuality, Wilde too – akin to a modern Gracián – elaborated an acute, pungent, provocative, stylistically jewelled and seductive prose, which is never oblivious of the political and effectual elements. Wilde did not shy away from calling out what he perceived as a decay in customs, manners and generally art and literature. In an age where the technical reproducibility of objects was starting to impose itself, Wilde believed that the best strategy did not involve nostalgically searching for the lost aura. He remained within the field of a commodified arena and yet tried to elaborate and develop excessive elements of subversion.

Another connection with Perniola's reflection on art can be traced here. Perniola, despite criticizing neo-avant-gardes and commodity fetishism, does not propose a transcendent alternative, namely a return to the unique aesthetic authority of the artistic object's aura. Instead, he praises the so-called 'shadow of art' (AIS), which, I argue, corresponds to the irreducible elements of difference stemming from the work of art considered as a 'thing'. The shadow is that marginal and lateral side of art which the lights of economy and of communication cannot reach. Perniola's conception thus, I would argue, is similar to Wilde's. Although 'God is dead' as per Wilde, that is, although we can no longer rely on transcendent, supreme values and on art's aura, this is not a justification to remain stuck inside a nostalgic Passatist position or be submerged by triviality and vulgarity. If one can no longer be or live like Brummell, it does not mean that dandyism has to perish. Wilde, in so doing, represents a later phase of dandyism, which faces the huge transformations that European societies underwent throughout the nineteenth century. If it is true that Wilde explored the tools and the instruments of the time, namely the press and advertising systems, it was not to become a servant to these new technologies. Wilde did not use his era's new possibilities and opportunities to level his thought to an average middle-class standard. Rather, he used these very tools (for instance, through the insistent use of ironic *détournement*) *against* the dominant discourse.

Wilde's use of literary diversion, I would argue, shares an essential characteristic with Perniola's notion of 'shadow': Perniola claims that the work of art receives the light of the institutions while possessing a liminal, hidden area that is produced within this very light but cannot be revealed by it. Similarly, Wilde's *corpus* of publications is heavily invested in the light of consumer culture and middle-class popularity. In other words, Wilde's works exist within a capitalist context, but at the same time, they produce a flaw, a hole, a short circuit in the bourgeois imagery. They manage to guard and protect the qualitative aspect (creativity, opposition and difference) within a quantitative domain.

Both Perniola and Wilde refused to step back when confronted by the commodified and commodifying arena in which culture, art and aesthetics are continuously integrated. They did not search for the lost and transcendent 'aura' since the technologies of reproduction had transformed the very conception of art and artistry. Instead, they explored the new tools provided by this scenario by managing not to be swallowed by it with subtlety. In other words, both Wilde and Perniola said 'yes' to the present, trying to find the beauty in it, without celebrating the status quo but moving in between, at the margins, in alternative and subversive ways.

Dandyism and queerness

Over the past three decades, scholarship has focused on – often at odds in their premises and conclusions – the relationship between dandyism, body, gender and sexuality. Ian Kelly – following Captain Jesse's account on Brummell – contends that the English dandy possessed a 'neo-classical body' (Kelly 2005: 169) influenced by the ancient Greek and Roman statues. According to Kelly, the close-fitting style pioneered by Brummell was influenced by classical ideals of manliness. Brummell's simplicity in dressing, alongside his proportionate physique, leads Kelly to conclude that his dandyism did not share effeminate or androgynous features. On the contrary, Barbey d'Aurevilly states, 'Twofold and multiple natures, of an undecided intellectual sex, their Grace is heightened by their Power, their Power by their Grace, they are the hermaphrodites of History' (1897: 141). Thus, for Barbey, the dandies are in-between figures who display a combination of what is commonly associated with masculinity (power) and femininity (grace). These associations inevitably reinforce the normative differentiation between the sexes, implying that men are powerful, while women are soft, weaker and graceful. He thus seems to imply that being a hermaphrodite has to do with cross-dressing and manners, which we associate more with androgyny today. Daria Kent claims that the 'dandies' celibate tendencies and attitudes towards attraction is similar to today's asexuality' (2018: online source). Specifically, Kent indicates that the dandy can be considered a queer figure because they show a 'distaste' and distancing behaviour towards sex and reproduction. Kent suggests that the dandies, in their search for aesthetic perfection in their persona, cared mainly for fashion and elegance and not for worldly pleasures.

According to these authors, the dandy would not share a conspicuous affinity with Perniola's queer theory (noted especially in *Tiresia* and in *The Sex Appeal of the Inorganic*). As I mentioned earlier, Perniola's 'neutral sexuality' and the 'thing that feels' rather than being manly, androgynous or asexual are in fact precisely the opposite: genderqueer, against the idea of sexes as a harmonic balance and also capable of expressing a sexual interest in what is normally perceived to be unattractive.

Meanwhile, several scholars have given significant attention on the relationship between queerness and dandyism (such as Sontag 1967; Cohen 1993; Houk 1997; Eribon 2004; Greenwald 2008; Balász 2020) and others proposed the idea that dandies also were the first models of modern gay subjectivities, especially in terms of the conjunction between homosexuality and secrecy, seen and unseen, intimacy and disclosure (Sedgwick 1990; Feldman

1993; Sinfield 1994;). For instance, a figure such as Wilde possesses a gay identity 'fundamentally shaped by the dualism of secrecy and disclosure, but since telling is both prohibited and required, queer identity is always an internal contradiction between opacity and transparency, at once hidden and revealed' (Glick 2001: 129). Drawing on scholars such as Jack Halberstam and Elisa Glick, I claim that there are at least two significant aspects that make the dandy a queer figure, resonating with Perniola's theory. The first aspect can be seen in the dandy's praise of artificiality against nature and the second in the dandy's revolt against bourgeois normativity. The dandy's resentment of nature can be understood as an anti-Romantic standpoint that privileges forms and artificiality. As Halberstam presents, in his being against nature, the dandy can be considered a 'postnatural man, a defiant figure who finds himself outside nature and therefore against its most spectacular displays as exemplified by heterosexual love' (2020: 19). This also recalls Baudelaire's and Wilde's claim that nature is merely driven by survival and self-interest, which is equally evident in heterosexuality, understood to be a mechanism for the continuation of the species. The figure of the dandy/postnatural man, which Halberstam also takes from Huysman's *Against the Grain* and Wilde's *The Picture of Dorian Gray*, is understood as an eminently queer character. Rather than being asexual, as Kent suggests, the dandy seems to be driven by a non-heteronormative desire that refutes natural diktats and includes a postnatural lexicon within the sphere of sexuality. For the nineteenth-century dandy, this lexicon is made up of notions such as fashion, *maquillage*, make-up, mirrors and artificiality, while the latest queer literature expanded this list with the notions of the inorganic, thingness, technology and post-humanity, just to mention a few examples.

The queer dandy standpoint should not be understood merely as a fetishism for which what is made is superior to what is born. It is also a critique of the notion of morality with which bourgeois society has characterized the very idea of nature. Queerness, same-sex desire and non-reproductive sexual intercourse are stigmatized by the bourgeois mindset for being 'unnatural' and 'perverted' and therefore closer to pathological if not criminal behaviours. An increasing body of literature over the past few decades has explored the violent and repressive underpinnings of the Western idea of nature, in sight of possible new understandings and relationships between humans and non-human entities (such as Morton 2010; Latour 2005; Haraway 2016). These authors echo the dandy's perspective, for whom nature is 'an anachronism, part of a past' to which the dandy 'does not wish to return and a hallmark of the morality to which he is indifferent' (Halberstam 2020: 20). Against the keywords of the bourgeois mindset previously analyzed, such as money, profit and function, the morality encoded with the idea of nature is also abhorred by dandies. Thus, the dandies share a central aspect of queerness: the 'politics of style', which is a subversive and controversial attitude to heterosexual norms, industriousness and utilitarianism (Glick 2001).

It is also notable that there is a crucial difference between Perniola's queer theory and the three exemplary dandies explored in this book. In fact, while Perniola's idea of the thing that feels and of neutral sexuality implies an experimental gender fluidity that undermines the very category of biological sexes in light of queering post-human agency, Brummell, Baudelaire and Wilde still enjoy the privileges that their respective societies offer them. In other words, although the three of them despise both the declining aristocracy and the emergent middle class, they nonetheless rely on them in terms of visibility, income, institutions and social recognition. They at once condemn the patriarchal heteronormativity dominant in the society of their time and contribute to its continuation. However, what I propose here slightly differs from these arguments. The dandy's revolt can be understood as a 'subversion from within', meaning that their effort does not constitute a *total* revolution of everyday life but a challenge that occurs in the very environment criticized and deplored. For the dandies, the aesthetic element was in fact never oblivious to the political one, or what I call through Perniola's philosophy a 'strategic beauty'. Neither guided by a nostalgia of the past nor by a utopian project, the dandies did not recede in the face of the increasingly commodified arena of the emergent mass capitalism. Rather, they challenged its views and normativity by elaborating their subversive perspectives within and beyond it.

Mona Lisa vamp

To further develop the affinity between Perniola's statements on art theory and Wilde's perspective, these pages focus on Wilde's essay *The Critic as Artist*. Written when he was thirty-seven years old, it shows Wilde's idea of art on the one hand and his peculiar conception of the role of art criticism on the other.

The Critic as Artist is a dialogue between two friends, Gilbert and Ernest, divided into two parts. Gilbert is Wilde's spokesperson, while Ernest asks questions and sometimes summarizes the arguments. The essay focuses on the status of art criticism. Wilde, through Gilbert's voice, unfolds his philosophy of criticism, explaining the critic's role, function and, in general, the relationship between criticism and art. Gilbert is often pressured by Ernest who expresses his doubts (a literary device Wilde uses to outline his standpoint with more precision). I will not provide a step-by-step explanation of all the arguments presented. My aim is not to summarize the text but to develop Gilbert's (Wilde's) pivotal positions in order to compare them with Perniola's thought.

At the beginning of the essay, Ernest claims that the art critic is a fairly new figure. According to him, when classic art flourished in ancient Greece (fifth–fourth centuries BCE), there were no such figures. Gilbert immediately contradicts Ernest by claiming that the Greeks were indeed highly developed in critical skills. From philosophy to theatre, poetry and literature, Gilbert maintains that the Greeks possessed a critical spirit that was hardly ever attained again in the following centuries. Thus, from the beginning of the essay, Wilde links criticism with the broad ability to think critically, that is, to have a disposition capable of grasping distinctions, imagining, interpreting and judging in the aesthetic domain. To refine these intellectual skills, according to Wilde, the critic needs to possess heterogeneous and deep knowledge. Paradoxically, he claims that the critic should know more than the artist (Wilde 1987: 961). In fact, the artist, for Wilde, is basically an individual of action: they *act* upon a canvas, a block of marble, a piece of wood. And the same applies to the realm of history. According to Wilde, it is much harder to talk about history than it is to actually do it. For instance, Wilde argues that it is easier to shoot a political leader than to understand such an event and its broader historical implications. In the same way, he points out the paradox that it is easier to make art than to discuss it. Since doing and feeling are not the work of education, refinement and intellectual cultivation, there is not a great deal of merit in them according to Wilde: also animals share them with humans. On the contrary, it is only through appropriate language and refined sensitivity ('self-conscious culture') that it is possible to discuss something, write a novel or analyze historical events. The Irish dandy writes, 'The world is made by the singer for the dreamer' (1987: 964). In other words, for Wilde, the critic should not be interested in reality in its vitalistic immediacy, but in the re-combination of empirical sources and their elevation in a new complexity under the sign of aesthetics:

> ... it is rather the beholder who lends to the beautiful thing its myriad meanings, and makes it marvellous for us, and sets it in some new relation to the age, so that it becomes a vital portion of our lives, and a symbol of what we pray for, or perhaps of what, having prayed for, we fear that we may receive ... For when the work is finished it has, as it were, an independent life of its own, and may deliver a message far other than that which was put into its lips to say.
>
> Wilde 1987: 968

Wilde makes clear in this passage that he is more interested in the aftermath of a work's accomplishment rather than its actual creative process. The beholder is not the active figure of the artist who paints, carves, sculpts and so on, but another figure, that of the critic, whom Wilde considers also to be a creator. The critic produces a different creation from the existing one by adding something that the artist may not have thought of, imagined or even understood.

Wilde leverages Leonardo's *Mona Lisa* to explain his position (1987: 968). He speculates that perhaps Leonardo 'was merely the slave of an archaic smile' (1987: 968). With this provocative line, Wilde means that although his painting is crucial for the history and theory of art, nonetheless, while painting it, Leonardo might not have 'contemplated', for example, 'the animalism of Greece, the lust of Rome, the reverie of the Middle Age ... the return of the Pagan world, the sins of the Borgias' (1987: 968). Thus, as per Wilde, Leonardo might have not taken into account all the quoted expressive elements that were later imagined, added and created by critics in the following centuries. Therefore, criticism cannot confine itself to the mere 'discovery' of the intentions of the author but should build new creative interpretations upon the artwork.

Wilde states that the highest form of criticism is 'the record of one's own soul' (1987: 966). This sentence seems to apparently convey the idea of a strong subjectivity, an identity that finds an ultimate expression through the work of criticism. Juxtaposed with Wilde's praise of individualism, this perspective seems at odds with both dandyish desubjectivation and Perniola's interpretation of the Stoic–Jesuit indifference previously explored. Yet Wilde does not convey the idea of a strong, unitary identity that displays the certainties of the Cartesian *cogito* and modern science. On the contrary, Wilde has an empty subjectivity in mind that is capable of welcoming what comes from the outside: 'we must surrender ourselves absolutely to the work in question, whatever it may be, if we wish to gain its secret' (1987: 986). This sentence, I would argue, is pivotal not only to the aims of this section but also to the overall book. It contains a recurrent dandyish standpoint and has an additional element close to Perniola's theory of art. This sentence refers specifically to desubjectivation on the one hand and to a hidden dimension of the artwork on the other ('its secret').

In Part One, I investigated the so-called 'election of the difference' in Jesuit thought. To be able to attune oneself in the surrounding world and grasp the ever-changing and unpredictable historical manifestations, the individual should live 'like a corpse' following the Ignatian motto *perinde ac cadaver*. It is precisely this approximation to the inert, thingly, inorganic dimension of death that allows the disappearance of personal identity as well as the possibility to understand the subtle phenomena and experiences through which one passes. Brummell, the 'subject without guarantee' (Coblence 1988: 157) which disappears in his everyday ritual clothing, approaches the inorganic dimension of the 'puppet' and at the same time manages to become the most renowned *arbiter elegantiarum* of English Regency.

In Part Two, I elucidated Perniola's conception of the thing. I outlined the terms under which becoming a thing, specifically becoming a mirror (that is, a reflecting surface), implies gathering in what comes from outside by muting one's own beliefs and vitalist drives according to Perniola. Following this common thread, I also showed the terms under which Baudelaire believed that the dandy should become, metaphorically speaking, a mirror as large as the entire urban setting. In so doing, the dandy is capable of extracting the peculiar beauty that emerges from the transient, fugitive and contingent atmospheres of the modern urban environment.

Further, I claim that Wilde can be inscribed in the same theoretical and experiential direction. 'Surrender oneself to the work' means precisely abandoning one's subjective drives to an external object, that is, withdrawing oneself and letting one's work speak through oneself. Only in this way, Wilde points out, is it possible to glean the work's 'secret'.

Not only does Wilde praise a de-subjectivated, decantered dimension of human subjectivity, but he also adds that a specific surplus element, which in this passage is called 'secret', and which Perniola, I would argue, refers to as 'shadow'. As made clear in the text, Wilde frequently uses, with respect to the artistic object, connotations surprisingly close to those of 'shadow', 'remainder' and 'residue'. For example, he speaks of the 'mystery', the 'wonder' and the 'ultimate secret' of the work of art (Wilde 1987: 970). Wilde rejects the idea that the artwork has just a single message, an individual meaning or representation to convey: 'The critic ... will look upon Art as a goddess whose mystery it is his province to intensify, and whose majesty his privilege to make more marvellous in the eyes of men' (1987: 972). The critic carries out a process in which the work of art is only a starting point. In fact, they do not remain satisfied with the supposed intentions of the artist and go beyond them towards a new creation. In this sense, Wilde considers the critic *as* an artist since by deepening and discovering symbols, meanings and expressions in the artwork, the critic continues the creation begun by the artist. In fact, Wilde states that 'the critic will always be reminding us of great works of art are *living things*' (1987: 973, emphasis added). I emphasize living things here because, I would argue, the combination of *life* and *things*, namely between organic and inorganic, between movement and inertia, is at the heart of Perniola's philosophy. A form is alive since it is never simply the result of a single intention; it does not convey a unilateral and individual single message or meaning. In other words, an artwork cannot be merely understood as a concrete manifestation of the artist's ideas, poetics and dreams; we should not explain and focus on the artwork as a projection of the artist's life or as the result of their unconscious drives unleashed. It is not a matter of colonizing works of art with reductive hermeneutical perspectives. Rather, Perniola and Wilde wish to give the artworks their own voice, so to speak, which go beyond the artists' intentions and cannot be subsumed merely within an allegoric point of view. Poetically, exploring Leonardo's *Mona Lisa*, Wilde refers to this 'life' of the artwork in this way:

> ... whenever I pass into the cool galleries of the Palace of the Louvre, and stand before that strange figure 'set in its marble chair in that cirque of fantastic rocks, as in some faint light under sea', I murmur to myself, 'she is older than the rocks among which she sits; like the vampire, she has been a diver in deep seas, and keeps their fallen day about her: and trafficked for strange webs with Eastern merchants; and, as Leda, was the mother of Helen of Troy, and, as St Anne, the mother of Mary; and all this has been to her but as the sound of lyres and flutes, and lives only in the delicacy with which it has moulded the changing lineaments, and tinged the eyelids and the hands'. And I say to my friend, 'The presence that thus so strangely rose beside the waters is expressive of what in the ways of a thousand years man had come to desire;' and he answers me, 'Hers is the head upon which all "the ends of the world are come," and the eyelids are a little weary'.
>
> 1987: 967–8

Wilde compares the *Mona Lisa*'s condition as an artwork to that of a vampire. The vampire, as Perniola also pointed out in *The Sex Appeal of the Inorganic*, 'is a being halfway between life and death' (SAI: 75), that is, an in-between, intermediary entity, not completely alive nor entirely dead. To consider the artwork as a manifestation of the idea of the 'undead' means introducing the dimension of the thing. In fact, the artwork is not understood merely as an object, namely a fixed entity, potentially signifying the reified expression of alienated creativity. It possesses the life of things; it is, as Wilde writes, a living thing, an entity susceptible to transformation and mutation as soon as it comes to existence. The *Mona Lisa*, taken as an exemplar of a living thing by Wilde, shows the precise terms by which an artwork is able to go beyond itself and its creator's intentions.

Building on Perniola's notion of transit, Paolo Bartoloni understands the works of several contemporary artists such as Urs Fisher, Jeff Koons, Jan Fabre and Ai Weiwei (especially concerning their urban exhibitions in the city of Florence) as 'cumulative images':

> What I mean by cumulative image is that experience of perception and emotional and cognitive impact produced by the coming together of different genres, styles and tastes in one place. The outcome of this process of combination, as Perniola has alluded to in his work, is not so much measured according to the aesthetic validity of its individual components as on their coming together as an event.
>
> Bartoloni 2019: 106

Through Perniola's conceptual tool kit, Bartoloni contends that it is possible to explore and experience a 'new language of combination' with respect to contemporary art, which is the result, for instance, of divergent interpretations of 'living things' accumulating over time and of the different contexts and environments they accompany. The rose, the rocks, the smile and the waters of the *Mona Lisa*, for instance, hold together, gather in and accumulate centuries of readings and understandings, but also historical events, 'desires' and 'merchant traffic'. This perspective implies a fundamental characteristic, also pointed out by Bartoloni, who refers to Perniola's concept of transit. In fact, it is precisely by allowing the 'coming together of different genres, styles and tastes' that differences emerge. For instance, although the *Mona Lisa* has always been the same painting, the same oil on the same poplar panel, it is not a mere sameness which is at stake. Novelty and originality paradoxically stem from sameness: difference is unfolded by an unfamiliar configuration of the same entity. Perniola's notion of transit and, might I add, Wilde's conception of the artwork as a living thing also involve 'taking a step back' in the traditional understanding of the artwork (Bartoloni 2019: 106). This step back implies focusing neither on the greatness of an artwork, nor on its transgressive and revolutionary purposes and not even on its communicative and promotional ends. It means welcoming alternative experiences of art itself, made possible by the very artistic categories that Perniola's philosophy unfolds.

Conclusion

This book discussed Perniola's philosophy and the phenomenon of dandyism oriented around the idea of an aesthetic challenge. What does this challenge mean? Against what or whom is it aimed? Can it be compared to a revolt or a revolution? As I wrote in the chapter dedicated to Brummell, the dandies' attitude should not be considered revolutionary in the traditional sense since the dandies did not question the status quo openly and violently with an aim to transform it from its core. The dandies lived according to a daily ritual of aestheticization within the urban world of the middle class and high society. Therefore, they accepted the rules appropriate to those environments, while playing with these very rules at the same time: they 'dared with tact'. Revolutions, in contrast, canonically involve a break, a jump, a rupture between the new and the old. The dandy challenge implies instead the emergence of novelty and difference within the pre-existing social configuration through a critique 'from within' of the very realms loathed.

The dandies investigated in this book were not representatives of the aristocracy and nobility, nor of the emerging bourgeoisie. Although often surrounded by the aristocrats and bourgeois, they moved *in between* social classes and roles. Their lifestyles entailed, on the one hand, relying on the status quo and its institutions and, on the other, a peculiar aesthetic challenge to society's ideologies, normativity and myths. Brummell, Baudelaire and Wilde repudiated the utilitarian bourgeois mindset and its ideas, from work to money, from family to love, sexuality and beauty. They instead elaborated on the cultivation of beauty in the face of the general downgrading of taste due to the growing industrialization of goods and lifestyles. The dandies did not passively witness and complain about the vulgarization of manners and of existence in general. Their lives instead show a continuous search for beauty, elegance, artificiality and *amor fati* within the very society they despised. Brummell elaborated a clothing ritual wherein his subjectivity disappeared in the folding of his fabrics; Baudelaire praised the idea of becoming a mirror as large as society;

Wilde urged his listeners to find what was picturesque in their own epoch by leaving the academies and walking the streets.

These attitudes, as I point out in this book, represent a challenge to society that can be compared in parallel to Perniola's philosophy. Neither the dandies nor Perniola follow a revolution or a utopia but are rather interested in the development, unwrapping and unfolding of what is already present. The transit, as 'the movement from the same to the same', means precisely the idea that difference, innovation, change and surprise do not stem from the cult of novelty for its own sake but from a re-combination of what already exists. In this sense, Perniola's dandy philosophy calls and challenges the individual not only to criticize or refute certain aspects of society, but also to be open to the manifestation of a rich, profound, deep, and inexhaustible layered world, which involves a reconfiguration of our everyday life in its entirety.

This book encompasses a variety of themes belonging not only to philosophy and aesthetics but also to literature, critical theory, sociology of communication and art. In so doing, it is informed by an interdisciplinary approach that can foster a debate across a plethora of research areas. First, it provides an interpretation of Perniola's philosophy from his early to mature writings. Second, whereas only a few scholars have ascribed a philosophical dignity to dandyism (see especially Gagnier 1987; Coblence 1988; Schiffer 2008), my book is intended for the enhancement and deepening of the discussion on dandyism within philosophy, especially in the area of aesthetic theory. By comparing Wilde's aesthetics with Perniola's, I show how the essays of a late Victorian Irish dandy are still in dialogue with post-Second World War European society.

My book also shows that dandyism is not only a historical and philosophical phenomenon but also has a geographical dimension. The figures selected all belong to different geopolitical settings: Brummell the English Regency; Baudelaire, 1848's revolutionary Paris; Wilde, between Dublin and London at the end of the nineteenth century; and Perniola, an Italian intellectual between the twentieth and twenty-first centuries. Nonetheless, they all shared a dandyish attitude towards life. By linking these figures, I want to underline the development of dandyism in a European context across time. This can be the starting point for future investigations into dandyism, not as a nation-dependent phenomenon but instead as a movement encompassing post-industrial Europe.

Furthermore, dandyism and Perniola's thought have not solely attracted scholarly interest. Dandyism is an aesthetically oriented lifestyle that still appeals to many clubs and small circles globally, with exhibitions, websites, blogs, podcasts and YouTube channels. At the same time, pop stars and artists, not to mention philosophers and psychoanalysts, are often broadly labelled as 'dandies', mostly on the basis of elegance and wit. Perniola's works have influenced artists, performers, dancers and musicians (see, for instance, RiLaben, Di Ponio and Pensa). Hence, a study devoted to dandyism and philosophy can become a central theoretical work of reference for further research in the field.

Given the number of similarities and the relevance of the affinities between Perniola and dandyism, I was surprised that Perniola did not make this observation himself. As stated above, he devoted only two pages to dandyism in general and a sparse few to Baudelaire's poetics. He never wrote on Brummell, nor on Wilde, despite the striking connection detectable. My analysis of Perniola's private archive showed that he did not possess a copy of Wilde's essays, only an edition of *The Picture of Dorian Gray* and a collection of aphorisms. He might have found resonances with his thoughts if he had read Wilde's prose instead.

In conclusion, this book arrives at the crossroads of different debates, specifically concerning contemporary philosophy, the phenomenon of dandyism and the relationship between aesthetics and lifestyle. Perniola's understanding of Italian culture and tradition takes a different path (EIC, EIN, IE) than the so-called Italian Thought and away from the theorists who recurrently focus and develop the theme of biopolitics (such as Giorgio Agamben 1998). Perniola's reflections, instead of accounting for the politicization of a 'bare life', revolve around its opposite – life's entrance into a neutral dimension. This dimension does not imply that life is undressed or reduced to its biological and animal terms; it is rather clothed, coated, covered and layered within the realm of things and artificiality. While Agamben isolates, so to speak, the minimum degree of life needed to discuss contemporary biopolitical scenarios, Perniola explores life in its interaction with artificiality and anti-naturalistic phenomena (from Palaeolithic engravings to contemporary drug addictions). For Perniola, life is already and always clothed, covered with the fabrics of language, institutions and the broader symbolic realm. Therefore, his philosophy can be considered an autonomous attempt to explore the human and non-human conditions of the current world, parallel to and not to be confused with that of the Italian Thought pursuers.

Furthermore, one of the main purposes of this research is to witness how philosophy – far from being an abstract discipline, enclosed within itself and its arguments, valid and effective only at a purely theoretical level – represents a crucial challenge for the individual: to constantly interpret the surrounding world and carefully shape their attitudes, manners and everyday choices. By investigating Roman ritualism, Stoic exercises, the Jesuit and Baroque traditions, dandyism, and the avant-gardes of the twentieth century – guided by Perniola's philosophy – I wish to show how, against the misological ('hatred of reasoning') drift of contemporary social and political fields, a co-belonging has always existed, that is, a somewhat explicit link between philosophy, aesthetics and life. Dandy philosophy is the philosophy that trains the individual to live well, challenging the status quo while accepting and loving fate.

Notes

Introduction

1. On Perniola's literature on these topics see AH, BN, CA: 135–68, DIP, EIC, IYR, JJ, KP, LR, LTC, OMP, PS. On its reception see, for instance, Miranda 1983; White 1984; Borradori 1989; Lumley 1990; Motta 1998; Sinnerbrink 2006; Covarrubias 2012; Sargento 2015; Friberg 2017; Zhou 2018; Carandente 2018; Scrivano 2018; Compagno 2018; Ágalma 2020; Manfreda 2021; Duarte 2021; Somhegyi, forthcoming).

1 The Suicide of Literature

1. This, as I shall argue, is also a fundamental aspect of the dandy aesthetic lifestyle. In another chapter, I will demonstrate in what terms the dandy can be viewed as a mirror figure who reflects the surrounding world by following an oppositive and subversive stance towards bourgeois normativity.
2. This perspective echoes the slogan *l'art pour l'art* (art for art's sake), which gained traction in nineteenth-century bohemian France and expresses the intrinsic value of art beyond any didactic, political or utilitarian function.
3. On Beckett's vitalism and especially its relationship with the philosophy of Henri Bergson, see Milz 2008.
4. Walter Pedullà, in an article on Perniola's perspective, contends that the metanovelists also could be understood as mystics: 'The spiritualistic pride of striving to be an absolute, the Romantic ambition of *l'art pour l'art*, the aestheticizing illusion that commits art to the task of clarifying autonomously the meaning of life' (1966: 13), would bring the metanovelists closer to the edges of mysticism, rather than into a coherent phase of literature after the traditional novel.

2 To Love or Smash Images? The Dimension of the Simulacrum

1. On Perniola's idea of simulacrum in relation to 1980s artworld see Nittve 1989.
2. An idiom might help in better understanding the desubjectivation implied by the notion of the simulacrum: 'The suit does not make the man'. This idiom is grounded

on a metaphysic framework for which appearances are deceiving. What appears is something like a mask, hiding a deeper and truer reality – the 'true' face of an individual. Perniola's understanding of the simulacrum, in contrast, as his interpretation of the Roman rituals suggests, treats it as a dimension that does not contemplate any realm 'beyond'. What we are given is a realm of surfaces and appearances, but this realm can be seen with disdain only, in so far as a hierarchically superior 'original' world is taken for granted.

3 As Gianni Vattimo singles out, Perniola develops the culture of the simulacrum, especially to its religious ends: 'Those who have accepted that everything is appearances, in fact, found themselves in a similar condition to those who have religiously renounced the world and that, precisely for this reason (it is the history of the successes of the Company of Jesus), can devote themselves to mundane activities with an attention and lucidity unknown to those who instead still have interest, passion and beliefs in values' (1980: 3).

4 As Robert Burch put it: 'Possessed of this new sensitivity, one can still care for and enjoy what is given, but always only "moderately", as if, so to speak, it were always already taken away' (2002: 187).

5 On this matter, Pier Paolo Poggio points out the following: 'It is here that the space that can only be filled by the cultural operator is opened up, realizing the transition to the simulacral dimension. The end of ideological politics offers only two possibilities: either the refusal of the world as it is – the end of all the old representations and of the possibility itself of building a representation, here looking for an original referent on which to erect a new dynamic of life – or the disenchanted but not quietist acceptation of the results of *historical time*' (1980: 136).

3 Action at the End of Action: Rituals without Myths

1 According to Perniola, Husserl elaborates a theoretical-contemplative phenomenology which, despite striving to encompass the entirety of everyday life, does not include the political-practical field but only the moral one. The concept of politics for Perniola is oriented towards effectiveness (the tangible effects of something on reality); on the other hand, morality is developed over regulatory ideas (normative ethics, utopian justice and so on). This is why Perniola is always suspicious when the moral discourse is brought into the philosophical field, because, he argues, it is inherently powerless over reality. Thus, Perniola moves from what he refers to as the 'monastic attitude' of Husserlian phenomenology to practical issues and political commitment, namely from a theory of knowledge to a theory of action: 'I have always been dissatisfied with the far too contemplative approach adopted by phenomenology, with its wholly theoretical attitude and the subjective transcendentalism associated with it' (EE: 162).

2   For Perniola's ritual without myth in the context of popular culture and theory of communication also see Pfaller 2003 and Vogt 2019a, 2020.
3   As Wasim Salman states, 'It should be noted that humanism is not an alternative to metaphysics but its continuation. Perniola's religious thought focuses on the issue of humanism and anti-humanism, or identity and difference, underlining that the experience of difference is not an exclusive prerogative of the Protestant Reformation; it is also an essential aspect of Catholicism' (2021: 134).
4   Loyola recurrently states: 'that particular sin or defect which he [the practitioner] wants to correct and amend' (2017: First Week); or 'asking account of his soul of that particular thing proposed, which he wants to correct and amend' (2017: First Week) or 'when that same bad thought comes to me and I resist it, and it returns to me again and again, and I always resist, until it is conquered' (2017: First Week). As these passages highlight, Loyola neither clarifies nor provides concrete examples of flaws and sins.
5   The dandies, in fact, believed that each age has its own beauty, which can be extracted, so to speak, and cultivated within one's own manners and lifestyle.
6   Focusing on the relationship between philosophy and action in Perniola's theory, Maurizio Ferraris contends that 'Philosophy, by not having foundationalist concerns, is no longer in the pathetic condition of perennial belatedness which affected the owl of Minerva' (1986: 21).
7   Hayden White, commenting on Perniola's philosophical strategy, states that 'it can be seen in this operation an exercise of de-familiarisation. It is like if Perniola is an ethnographer who returns from a remote land to talk about an exotic culture of a civilisation still unknown' (1984: 120). White seems to suggest that Perniola intertwines the methods of philosophy with those of ethnography and anthropology to study ancient Western practices and show their underground and intimate correspondence with what we usually refer to as a 'post-metaphysical' world. The notion of neo-ancient also has been recently investigated by Erik M. Vogt, who drew a parallel between Perniola's perspective and that of Jacques Rancière (see Vogt 2019a, 2019b).

4   George Bryan Brummell: the Ritual Clothing

1   The exact amount of the fortune inherited by Brummell is uncertain but is estimated to have been around £30,000, worth nearly £2.5 million today (Kelly 2005: 157).
2   The parallel between Brummell as a puppet and the Jesuit thought should not lead one to believe that puppets are more attuned to God than humans. In this case, the parallel is drawn to emphasize the disappearance of one's own contingent necessities and accidents. In other words, both 'living as a corpse' from the Ignatian tradition and the figure of the puppet share this 'elemental' feature of reduction and cutback of one's own subjectivity.

5 What Is It Like to Be a Thing?

1. Parts of this chapter were first published within the journal article 'The Adventures of the Thing: Mario Perniola's Sex Appeal of the Inorganic' (see Bianchi 2020a).
2. There are many occurrences of the word 'thing' in *The Society of the Spectacle*. Each instance reinforces Debord's Marxist point of view on reification, which is at odds with Perniola's philosophy. For instance, Debord writes about the 'domination of society by "intangible or tangible things"' (2005: 17); or: 'It is things that rule and that are young, vying with each other and constantly replacing each other' (2005: 31); or again: 'The things that the spectacle presents as eternal are based on change, and must change as their foundations change' (2005: 35); coming to the conclusion that historical life has been reduced into the 'economic history of *things*' (2005: 44) where time is a '*time of things*' (2005: 83).
3. In this sense Bartoloni argues that 'In Perniola humans are both individuals and things, and their status is always already a negotiation of this fusion between organic and inorganic: no longer entirely organic and partly thing-like' (Bartoloni 2011: 157).
4. As Steven Shaviro claimed in an article on Perniola's concept of thing, 'Perniola invents a new ontological category, that of the 'thing that feels': something that is utterly apart from the duality of subjectivity (which we usually equate with sentience) on the one hand, and of insentient objects on the other' (2005: online source).

6 A Queering Agency: Perniola's *The Sex Appeal of the Inorganic*

1. On this matter, I do not entirely agree with the following claim made by Frida Beckman: 'Perniola's formulation elucidates that it is orgasm as a governing rule rather than the orgasm in itself that needs to be rejected' (2013: 61). On the one hand Beckman is right in pointing out that Perniola criticizes orgasm understood as the underlying principle orienting sexual intercourse; yet, on the other, Perniola also asserts that 'It is hard to avoid the impression that something one wants quickly to return to zero cannot, indeed, be worth more than zero' (SAI: 3). Perniola wishes to emancipate sexuality from nature precisely by cutting off the state deprived of tension which follows the orgasm.
2. Perniola's theory of neutral sexuality – as Antonio Pomposini has argued – should in fact not be confused with other post-human perspectives, such as the new materialist vitalism of Rosi Braidotti, which heavily relies on the vitality of matter (Pomposini 2019: 263).

3 As James Swearingen and Joanne Cutting-Grey put it, 'Sexuality, belonging no longer to the experience of the subject as a feeling which the subject possesses, undergoes dispersion in the impersonal "it" which feels' (2002: 3).
4 In certain respects, Perniola's argument is related to the heterophenomenology issues raised, for instance, by Daniel Dennett and Thomas Nagel with his *What is it Like to be a Bat*? Echoing the latter, Perniola delivered a lecture at the Universidade de São Paulo in 2014, called *Come si sente una pianta?* (How does a plant feel itself? cf. SISV), inquiring on the possibility of a 'vegetal feeling' against the binary and heteronormative standpoint. Unlike Nagel and Dennett, however, Perniola does not analyze heterophenomenology 'from the point of view' of the philosophy of science, which focuses especially on the duality internalism/externalism. He is more interested in the experimental types of feeling that open new experiential fields for humans and non-humans, linking aesthetics, literature, philosophy and sexuality (also see Camaiti-Hostert n.d.; Lozano 1999; Torres Ruiz 2002; Alzuru 2003; Sandford 2004; Hognerund Træland 2013; Markin 2018).
5 Massimo Verdicchio, commenting on Perniola's *The Sex Appeal of the Inorganic*, argues: 'What is at stake is no longer the subject but the philosophical-sexual thing which triumphs over individual subjectivities and over the world of instrumentality and expectations' (2001: 36).
6 It is not a coincidence that in the *Diagnostic and Statistical Manual of Mental Disorders*, as Sergio Benvenuto points out, perversions are regarded as *disorders* and not diseases or illnesses (Benvenuto 2016: XV).
7 The ideas of a permanent excitement and of suspension, linked to the 'thing that feels' and the figure of the vampire, appears closely related to Indian, Chinese and Japanese mystical sexuality to me, where – especially in the Daoist alchemist tradition and in Tantric Buddhism – sexual intercourse is also understood in terms of preservation of the climax and retention of the orgasm (also see Robinet 1988; van Gulick 2003; Moeller 2006: 21–32; Raveri 2014: 289–92, 394–6).
8 On the significance of the notion of transit in Perniola's philosophy, Robert R. Shane highlights that transit 'is not only an aesthetic tool, but also a political and ethical one. Perniola's erotics recognize that the interaction between bodies in erotics or love is inherently political, but he also provides a way out of traditional relations of dominations' (2004: online source). In addition, on the relationship between the transit and love see Nicolini 2018.
9 I began to delve into this issue with Zsuzsanna Balázs in our article entitled 'Esperienze queer nel Tiresia di Mario Perniola' (Queer Experiences in Mario Perniola's Tiresias, 2021).
10 Upon closer examination, a fascination with queer issues is present throughout Perniola's career. Already in 1959, in his youthful *Programma Manifesto*, he says, 'You will magnify my privilege of coinciding with the woman I love' (PM: 9). After *Tiresia*, published in

1966, many other works also show a tendency to explore different understandings of gender and non-heteronormative sexualities, from *Transiti* and *The Sex Appeal of the Inorganic* up until his posthumously published autobiography, written during the last year of his life and tellingly titled *Tiresia contro Edipo* (Tiresias Against Oedipus). Throughout his work, Perniola returns to the same coherent set of themes and experiences again and again – bringing out of them queer and subversive instances.

11 Giuliano Compagno indicates that 'an aesthetic experience as synthesis between a post-human empathy and a subjective abstraction asserts itself; a philosophy that, through the rejection of the concept of pleasure, seeks the core of an extreme-thought which is given from what is external, and that from the external draws its own energy' (1996: 144).

12 Luigi Antonio Manfreda points out a connection between Perniola and Deleuze: 'In this living–non-living interweaving, in the life–death co-belonging, one can sense in the background the Deleuzian monism and, even before that, the Spinozian one: there are no final parts; the real is compact, continuous' (2020: 30).

13 On the concept of 'fold' in Perniola and Deleuze, see Hevrøy and Ohldieck 2015.

7 Beauty is Like a Blade: Towards a Strategic Theory of Aesthetics

1 This chapter has been partially published as 'Mario Perniola's Aesthetics between Stoicism, the Baroque and the Avant-Gardes' in *The Polish Journal of Aesthetics* (see Bianchi 2020b).

2 As Gianni Carchia points out, the Stoics abolish the distinction between form and content: because there is no place to be, so to speak, for ideas within Stoic theory, the material world is not a copy or residue of something greater (Carchia 2006: 139).

3 Hence, for the Stoics, Socrates' life was a model of virtue. In fact, as noted by James Woelfel, Socrates lived 'committed to the pursuit of virtue and calm and fearless in the face of opprobrium and death' (Woelfel 2011: 124).

4 Interestingly enough, James Bond Stockdale (1923–2005) a US Navy admiral and aviator, stated that he managed to survive seven years of imprisonment and tortures during the Vietnam War thanks to Stoic philosophy and Epictetus' *Handbook*. See Sherman 2007: 1–17.

5 The occurrences of Gracián's reflections in Perniola's writings are as follows: T: 180–4, E: 125–39, D: 25–35, DS: 71–9, SS: 112–13, EIC: 199, 204.

6 As Hidalgo Serna notes: '*ingenium* counterposes two separate things over against each other and with images objectifies relationships or similarities between them which are already present' (1980: 253).

8 Charles Baudelaire: Greatness without Convictions

1 In a short piece titled 'A Defence of Cosmetics', Max Beerbohm, an exemplar dandy of the first half of the twentieth century, wrote a passage that exemplifies the kind of *amor fati* of self-confidence in one's time that should shape the dandy's attitude: 'Artifice must queen it once more in the town, and so, if there be any whose hearts chafe at her return, let them not say, "We have come into evil times," and be all for resistance, reformation or angry cavilling. For did the king's sceptre send the sea retrograde, or the wand of the sorcerer avail to turn the sun from its old course? And what man or what number of men ever stayed that reiterated process by which the cities of this world grow, are very strong, fail and grow again? Indeed, indeed, there is charm in every period, and only fools and flutterpates do not seek reverently for what is charming in their own day. *No martyrdom, however fine, nor satire, however splendidly bitter, has changed by a little tittle the known tendency of things*. It is the times that can perfect us, not we the times' (1981: 48).
2 The French poet continues his invective against business in general using other metaphors and examples. For instance, he argues, young men become increasingly independent not because they leave their houses for a militant, adventurous or aesthetic lifestyle, but because they decide to start a new trade, hopefully to become rich and perhaps even to compete with their fathers (1996: 1405). When money and the spirit of trade become an essential passion within one's life, Baudelaire suggests that it colonizes their dreams and goals, turning everyone into guardians of safe boxes (1996: 1405).
3 Perniola's fourth and last journal *Ágalma*, founded in 2000, can be ascribed to this trend, as it explores a wider array of cultural products and phenomena within aesthetics. Its subtitle is telling: *Rivista di studi culturali e di estetica* (Journal of cultural studies and aesthetics). On this issue, Perniola is recognized as one of the main contributors to the development of cultural studies and, broadly, material and visual culture in Italy (cf. Ruggieri 2021).
4 As Giovanni Macchia noted, Baudelaire's attacks on nature should also be seen within his anti-romantic standpoint: 'the romantic poet . . . substituted the actor with the man; what marked the so-called triumph of sincerity and freedom was equal to substituting nature to art, identifying art with life' (1975: 128).
5 Baudelaire's claims are expressed through fragments, projects and incomplete works, and are often stated in a provocative way. Interestingly, several insights emerging from his works are still under discussion within recent studies on aesthetics and evolution. For example, Stephen Davies (2012), who applies theories of evolution to art in order to discuss its origins and functions, asserts that non-human animals do not produce art (2012: 27). For instance, during the mating season, when a peacock unfurls its tail and exhibits the brilliance of its feathers, when a bee dances and a

nightingale sings, all of these activities should not be confused with beauty or aesthetic behaviour. In fact, what looks beautiful to us is much more likely to appear to the animals as *good*, in terms of fitness and ability to survive in a world where the strongest eats the weakest. Moreover, the songs and the performances of non-human animals, despite appearing and sounding appreciable, are extremely repetitive, monotonous and stereotypical. Thus, Davies argues that these performances cannot fall under the concept of art, as they lack the complexity of the aesthetic creations produced by human beings (2012: 97).

9 The Artistic Alienation and the Situationist International

1 Inspired by the Situationist environment and by an anti-Leninist perspective, the Communist group named Ludd was active between 1969 and 1970 especially between Genoa and Milan (see Lippolis and Ranieri 2018; Jappe 2019).
2 For example, Perniola writes, 'If we speak of cave paintings and magic is connected to them, then the magic of the primitive man must be studied' (AA: 10). According to Perniola, art emerges from and depends on its social and historical expressions. *L'alienazione artistica* does not provide any set definition for art because any essentialist or metaphysical characterization would be at odds with its constitutive historical – and thus mobile relative to a given period – aspect.
3 It is no coincidence that the complexity of the text is highlighted by Pierre Sansot in his preface to the French edition published in 1977: 'This work is a melange of youthful enthusiasm and immense culture, of radical criticism and of positive imagination' (1977: 7).
4 In so doing, Perniola borrows Debord's analysis from *The Society of the Spectacle*, trying to apply its premises and methodologies to outline the ways in which the ancient Greek's epic poems are also embedded within a spectacular-type system of power.
5 Perniola uses the word 'meaning' often in *L'alienazione artistica* without providing a clear definition. He mainly associates it with the idea of 'authenticity', implying that an action can be considered 'meaningful' if it expresses and realizes human creativity in a non-alienated way.
6 *Détournement*, as Jappe notes (1999: 61), is a practice that allows us to understand an essential characteristics of the concept of society according to the Situationists. In fact, the construction of situations does not imply utopianism in the sense of a search for the revolutionary moment in a future that is yet to come. Contrarily, the premises for the revolution are all *ready-made*, to borrow a notion typical of Dadaist avant-garde. It is merely a matter of recombining the present to reassemble it in order to open up new possible experiences and ways of existence. The situation,

therefore, implies a choice in favour of the present and its not-yet-uncovered possibilities, which await practices and exemplary actions to be elaborated and developed (on this notion also see Bunyard 2018).

7   Perniola comes back to the Renaissance turning point several decades after *L'alienazione artistica*. Although the causes of this turning point are explained in the same way, his evaluation of it substantially changes. Specifically, while in 1971 he considers this paradigm shift as a significant step in the process of artistic alienation, in 2002 he regards it as the emergence of the 'learned artist', who learns and teaches in academies: an artist who 'cannot be ignorant' (CTP: 128).

8   See for instance these passages which exemplify Alberti's standpoint on the idea of a manufacturing capitalism: 'to increase my tranquillity, I would like to have something secure, something I could see improving under my hands from day to day. Perhaps I would have men working wool or silk or something similar. This kind of business is less trouble and much less nerve-racking than trade. I would gladly take on an enterprise like that' (1994: 66); or 'I would select with care and have good and honest employees. I would keep a close check on things, too, and go over even minor transactions. Even though I already knew the answers, I should ask questions just to appear watchful. I would not do this in such a way as to seem over-suspicious and distrustful but in a way that might influence my agents to avoid becoming careless' (1994: 67).

9   Perniola uses the term 'merchant' (*mercante*) ambiguously, referring to both artisan workshops and to actual Renaissance artists. To avoid confusion, I mark the distinction between the two by referring to Renaissance artists as proto-bourgeois entrepreneurs.

10   'Save the surplus of things, and keep it safe' (Alberti 1994: 93).

11   'I have found it wise to set aside a certain amount for outside use, for investments and purchases' (Alberti 1994: 77).

12   Commenting on *L'alienazione artistica*, Robert W. Kretsch wrote that Perniola's survey is against 'the ultimate neo-Platonic belief that artistic creativity can arise only in an ideal, separate world' (1972: 570).

13   Pierre Dalla Vigna recently wrote an introduction reviewing Perniola's engagement with the journals and the political movements of the time (2019). The entire series of five issues that constituted *Agaragar* has been recently republished by PGreco (see Agaragar 2020)

14   Perhaps this should also be reminded to all those scholars who study punk and other counterculture movements: do these scholars realize that an authentic punk attitude despises institutions and their outputs? Or maybe they believe that they can 'teach' their potential readers to feel revolutionary for a day, throwing their Starbuck's coffee onto the wall? Quoting a saying from the mysteries, Plato writes in his *Phaedo*: 'The thyrsus-bearers are many ... but the inspired few' (1959: 15).

15 Here, a standpoint of Perniola's previously analyzed theory returns: similar to the metanovelists who were closed in their self-awareness and continuously referred to themselves and their consciousness, the SI members claimed to possess the monopoly of the critical consciousness of the time. The SI seemed to have expanded the metanovelists' individual hyperconsciousness to the group. Precisely for this reason, ultimately, the Situationists themselves became the executioners, judges and victims of their own criticisms.

10 A Shadow and Its Art

1 On Perniola's notion of disgust, also see Vattimo 1999 and Ryynänen 2021.
2 As Massimo Recalcati indicated, Perniola shows how abject art can actually be understood as a 'psychotic realism'. According to Recalcati, several artists, such as Gina Pane, Orlan, Franko B. and Stelarc, act out the horror of the body without the 'symbolic "veiling" of the unconscious ... an abusive invasion of the real with no mediation' (2007: 78); in doing so, the work 'loses its formal identity, falls apart, psychotically collapses in an absence of organization' (2007: 214).
3 On Perniola's theory of communication, see Descamps 2004; Abruzzese 2004; Groys 2006; Vogt 2020, Di Felice 2020.
4 As Farris Wahbeh points out, commenting on Perniola's conclusions in *Art and Its Shadow*: 'Perniola reconceptualises the art object as an entity that plays a larger role in human interaction, that interacts with the human body' (2006: 493). Or, to use Alberto Bertozzi's remarks: 'What makes Perniola's discourse worth reflecting upon, I maintain, is the fact that it is a completely different direction for aesthetics: neither upward, towards harmonious beauty, nor downward, toward a mystification of its apparent opposite (i.e. ugliness and abjection) but towards the "beside" of the thing' (2005: 376).
5 In this sense, the numerous references to authors and works related to the magical, supernatural and oneiric worlds evince a return to Surrealism and the abandonment of themes related to the notion of the real.
6 A quotation from Perniola's autobiography well exemplifies his overall attitudes towards the decades he explored and studied: 'I have never shared the nihilistic aspect of 1968, of 1977, of postmodernism, of posthumanism, of neoliberalism, of the cultural studies and of multiculturalism. Not willing to lose contact with the world, I was involved in the movement of the 1968 (but following Guy Debord, who was an advocate of classical culture par excellence), in the movement of 1977 (but alongside Fachinelli and his ecstatic mind), in postmodernism (but with Lyotard and not with Vattimo), in posthumanism (but with *The Sex Appeal of the Inorganic* which is an eminently philosophical and non-consumerist approach), in neoliberalism (but

with Luc Boltanski and his third spirit of capitalism), in cultural studies (but with *Ágalma*'s Italian perspective and not according to the English model) and in multiculturalism (but respecting all the cultures thought and lived in their autonomy and not in a melting-pot)' (TCE: 54–5).

11 Oscar Wilde: the In-Between Dandy

1 More specifically, in his essay, Wilde does not develop a traditional idea of socialism as a government-centred political system but more as an anarchic and libertarian approach. He believes, as suggested, that socialism should be understood only as a phase that will lead to individualism.

References

Abruzzese, A. (2004), 'La comunicazione cattiva', *Il Manifesto*, 13 April: 14.
Ágalma (2020), *Mario Perniola. Enigma, storia, scrittura*, 39, Monographic issue devoted to Mario Perniola's thought.
Agamben, G. (1998), *Homo Sacer: Sovereign Power and Bare Life*, trans. D. Heller-Roazen, Redwood City (CA): Stanford University Press.
Agaragar (2020), *Rivista 'Situationista' italiana (1970-1972). Fondata e diretta da Mario Perniola*, Complete collection of the issues of the journal *Agaragar*, Milan: Pgreco.
Alberti, L.B. (1994), *The Family in Renaissance Florence*, vol. 3, trans. R. Neu Watkins, Long Grove: Waveland Press.
Alzuru, P. (2003), 'Sentir y perversión en la estética de Mario Perniola', *Estética*, 7: 45–52.
Ando, C. (2008), *The Matter of the Gods*, Berkeley: University of California Press.
Ayala, J.M. (2005), *Diccionario de conceptos de Baltasar Gracián*, Madrid: Catedra.
Aylesworth, G. (2015), 'Postmodernism', *Stanford Encyclopedia of Philosophy*. Available online: https://plato.stanford.edu/entries/postmodernism/ (accessed 17 January 2022).
Balázs, Z., (2020), 'Yeats's Queer Dramaturgies: Oscar Wilde, Narcissus, and Melancholy Masculinities in Calvary', *International Yeats Studies*, 4 (1): 15–44.
Balázs, Z. and E. Bianchi (2021), 'Esperienze *queer* nel *Tiresia* di Mario Perniola', in E. Bianchi and M. Di Felice (eds), *Le avventure del sentire. Il pensiero di Mario Perniola nel mondo*, 67–89, Milan-Udine: Mimesis.
Barbey d'Aurevilly, J.-A. (1897), *Of Dandyism and of George Brummell*, trans. D. Ainslie, London: J.M. Dent & Company.
Barilli, R. (2000), 'Una "terza via" per l'arte alla ricerca dell'aura perduta', *Corriere della Sera*, 1 October: 33.
Bartoloni, P. (2007), 'The value of suspending values', *Neohelicon*, 34: 115–22.
Bartoloni, P. (2011), 'Thinking Thingness: Agamben and Perniola', *Annali D'Italianistica*, 29: 141–62.
Bartoloni, P. (2016), *Objects in Italian Life and Culture: Fiction, Migration, and Artificiality*, London: Palgrave Macmillan.
Bartoloni, P. (2019), 'Transit and the Cumulative Image: Perniola and Art', *Ágalma*, 39: 99–108.
Baudelaire, C. (1964), *The Painter of Modern Life and Other Essays*, trans. J. Mayne, London: Phaidon.
Baudelaire, C. (1996), *Opere*, eds and trans. G. Raboni and G. Montesano, Milan: Meridiani Mondadori.
Baudelaire, C. (2011), *Œuvres Complètes*, M. Jamet (ed.), Paris: Robert Laffont.

Baudrillard, J. (1978), 'La prècession des simulacres', *Traverses*, 10: 3–37.
Beard, M., J. North and S. Price (1998), *Religions of Rome*, vol. 1, Cambridge: Cambridge University Press.
Beckett, S. (2009), *Three Novels: Molloy, Malone Dies, The Unnamable*, New York: Grove Press.
Beckman, F. (2013), *Between Desire and Pleasure. A Deleuzian Theory of Sexuality*, Edinburgh: Edinburgh University Press.
Beerbohm, M. (1981), 'A Defence of Cosmetics', in K. Beckson (ed.), *Aesthetes and Decadents of the 1890s: An Anthology of British Poetry and Prose*, 47–62, Chicago: Chicago Academy Publishers.
Bellarmino, R. (1837), *De Controversiis Christianae Fidei*, vol. 3, Naples.
Bellarmino, R. (2016), 'The Art of Dying Well', in *Saint Robert Bellarmine. Collection* [eBook edn], trans. J. O'Sullivan, London: Aeterna Press.
Benjamin, W. (2002), *The Arcades Project*, trans. H. Heiland and K. McLaughlin, Cambridge: Harvard University Press.
Benjamin, W. (2006), *The Writer of Modern Life. Essays on Baudelaire*, trans. H. Eiland, E. Jephcott and R. Livingstone, London: Penguin.
Benvenuto, S. (2016), *What are Perversions? Sexuality, Ethics, Psychoanalysis*, London: Karnac.
Berardi, F. (1973), *Cultura, lavoro intellettuale e lotta di classe*, Naples: Guida.
Berardi, F. (1974), *Scrittura e movimento*, Venice: Marsilio.
Berardi, F. (2012), 'Un falso Perniola', *Alfabeta 2*, 16. Available online: https://www.alfabeta2.it/2012/02/09/un-falso-perniola/ (accessed 3 September 2021).
Bertozzi, A. (2005), review of M. Perniola *The Sex Appeal of the Inorganic*, *Philosophy in Review*, 25: 374–7.
Beuve-Mery, A. (2009), 'Guy Debord: National Treasure?', trans. BNB, Available online: https://libcom.org/library/guy-debord-national-treasure-16062009 (accessed 3 September 2021).
Bianchi, E. (2019), 'Reality as Stratification of Surfaces. Mario Perniola's Philosophy of Transit', *European Journal of Psychoanalysis*. Available online: https://www.journal-psychoanalysis.eu/reality-as-stratification-of-surfaces-the-concept-of-transit-in-mario-perniolas-philosophy/ (accessed 3 September 2021).
Bianchi, E. (2020a), 'The Adventures of the Thing: Mario Perniola's Sex Appeal of the Inorganic', *AM Journal of Art and Media Studies*, 22: 23–34.
Bianchi, E. (2020b), 'Mario Perniola's Aesthetics between Stoicism, the Baroque and the Avant-Gardes', *The Polish Journal of Aesthetics*, 59: 29–42.
Bianchi, E. and M. Di Felice, eds (2021), *Le avventure del sentire. Il pensiero di Mario Perniola nel mondo*, Milan-Udine: Mimesis.
Blush, S. (2001), *American Hardcore: A Tribal History*, Port Townsend, WA: Feral House.
Borges Junior, E. (2020), 'Teoria da Forma Algorítmica. Entre uma estética e uma ética dos algoritmos: relações entre imagem, fruição e ação', PhD diss., Escola de Comunicações e Artes, Universidade de São Paulo.

Borradori, G., ed. (1989), *Recoding Metaphysics. The New Italian Philosophy*, Evanston: Northwestern University Press.

Bottani, L. (1983), review of M. Perniola, *La società dei simulacri*, in *Filosofia*, 34: 296–301.

Bredin, H. (1972), review of M. Perniola, *L'alienazione artistica*, in *The British Journal of Aesthetics*, 1: 88.

Breuil, H. (1952), *Quatre cents siècles d'art pariétal*, Montignac: Centre d'Études et de Documentation préhistoriques.

Brown, B. (2001), 'Thing Theory', *Critical Inquiry*, 28 (1): 1–22.

Bukdahl, E.M. (2017), *The Recurrent Actuality of the Baroque*, Denmark: Controluce.

Bullough, E. (1912), '"Psychical Distance" as a Factor in Art and an Aesthetic Principle', *British Journal of Psychology*, 5 (2): 87–118.

Bunyard, T. (2018), *Debord, Time and Spectacle. Hegelian Marxism and Situationist Theory*, Leiden and Boston: Brill.

Burch, R. (2002), 'The Simulacrum of Death: Perniola Beyond Heidegger and Metaphysics?', in J. Swearingen and J. Cutting-Gray (eds), *Feeling the Difference, Extreme Beauty. Aesthetics, Politics, Death*, 180–93, New York and London: Continuum.

Butler, J. (1990), *Gender Trouble: Feminism and the Subversion of Identity*, London and New York: Routledge.

Callon, M. (1986), 'Some elements of a sociology of translation: domestication of the scallops and the fishermen of St Brieuc Bay', in J. Law (ed.), *Power, Action and Belief: A New Sociology of Knowledge?* 196–223, London: Routledge.

Camaiti-Hostert, A. (n.d.), 'Sexy Things', *Threads*. Available online: http://www.altx.com/ebr/ebr6/6cam.htm (accessed 3 September 2021).

Capovin, R. (2020), 'Un'uscita dagli anni Settanta. Perniola e i simulacri', *Ágalma*, 39: 19–28.

Carandente, A., ed. (2018), *Secondo tempo. Libro cinquantesimo. Numero monografico dedicato a Mario Perniola (1941–2018)*, Naples: Marcus.

Carassus, E. (1971), *Le mythe du dandy*, Paris: Armand Colin.

Carassus, E. (1990), 'Dandysme et Aristocratie', *Romantisme*, 70: 25–37.

Carchia, G. (2006), *L'estetica antica*, Rome: Laterza.

Carravetta, P. (2012), 'What Is "Weak Thought"? The Original Theses and Context of *il pensiero debole*', in G. Vattimo and P.A. Rovatti (eds), *Weak Thought*, 1–38, Albany: SUNY Press.

Chesterton, G.K. (2005), 'On Wilde as a Great Artist and Charlatan', in K. Beckson (ed.), *Oscar Wilde. The Critical Heritage*, 339–41, London and New York: Routledge.

Cicero (1991), *On Duties*, trans. M. T. Griffin and E. M. Atkins, New York: Cambridge University Press.

Coblence, F. (1988), *Le Dandysme, obligation d'incertitude*, Paris: PUF.

Cogan, J. (2014), 'The Phenomenological Reduction', *Internet Encyclopedia of Philosophy*. Available online: http://www.iep.utm.edu/phen-red/ (accessed 3 September 2021).

Cohen, E. (1993), *Talk on the Wilde Side: Toward a Genealogy of a Discourse on Male Sexuality*, London and New York: Routledge.

Collins, R. (1998), *The Sociology of Philosophies. A Global Theory of Intellectual Change*, Cambridge: Harvard University Press.

Comi, I. (2008), *George Bryan Brummell*, Lecco: Stefanoni.

Comi, I. (2014), *Breve riflessione sul dandy e sul samurai*, Lecco: Stefanoni.

Compagno, G. (1996), *Troppo vicino, troppo lontano*, Milan-Udine: Mimesis.

Compagno, G. (2018), *Era Mario Perniola*, Milan-Udine: Mimesis.

Conrad, J. (2005), *Lord Jim*, San Diego: Icon.

Contreras-Koterbay, S. (2021), 'Affrontare *Il sex appeal dell'inorganico* nell'era della New Aesthetic', trans. M. Dianetti, in E. Bianchi and M. Di Felice (eds), *Le avventure del sentire. Il pensiero di Mario Perniola nel mondo*, 45–65, Milan-Udine: Mimesis.

Costa, M. (1973), review of M. Perniola, *I situazionisti – Agaragar*, in *NAC* (Spring): 41.

Covarrubias, I. (2012), '¿Es posible pensar la política como simulacro?' *Revista de Filosofía*, 133: 269–75.

Cox, C. and D. Warner (2004), *Audio Culture. Readings in Modern Music*, London and New York: Bloomsbury.

Dalla Vigna, P. (2019), 'Alla ricerca dell'intellettuale collettivo. Mario Perniola e le riviste da *Tempo presente* ad *Agaragar*', *Ágalma*, 39: 34–45.

Davies, S. (2012), *The Artful Species*, Oxford: Oxford University Press.

De Donato, F. (1995), 'Mario Perniola e il neo-antico. Quindici anni di ricerche tra lo studio dell'antichità e l'antropologia culturale', in M. Perniola (ed.), *Il pensiero neo-antico. Tecniche e possessione nell'arte e nel sapere del mondo contemporaneo*, 119–22, Milan-Udine: Mimesis.

De la Boullaye, H.P. (1956), 'Sentir, sentimiento y sentido, dans le style de saint Ignace', *Archivum Historicum Societate Iesu*, 25: 416–30.

De Ribadeneira, P. (1583), *Vida del Padre San Ignacio de Loyola, Fundador de la Compañía de Jesús*, Madrid.

Debord, G. (1990), *Comments on the Society of the Spectacle*, trans. M. Imrie, London and New York: Verso.

Debord, G. (2005), *The Society of the Spectacle*, trans. K. Knabb, London: Rebel Press.

Deleuze, G. (1969), *Logique du sens*, Paris: Minuit.

Deleuze, G. (1983), 'Plato and the Simulacrum', trans. R. Krauss, *October*, 27: 45–56.

Deleuze, G. and F. Guattari, (2000), *Anti-Oedipus. Capitalism and Schizofrenia*, trans. R. Hurley, M. Seem and H.R. Lane, Minneapolis: University of Minnesota Press.

Deleuze, G. and F. Guattari (2013), *A Thousand Plateaus*, trans. B. Massumi, London and New York: Bloomsbury.

Deleuze, G. and C. Parnet (2007), *Dialogues II*, trans. H. Tomlinson and B. Habberjam, New York: Columbia University Press.

Denisoff, D. (2004), 'Oscar Wilde, commodity, culture', in F.S. Roden (ed.), *Palgrave Advances in Oscar Wilde Studies*, 119–42, London: Palgrave Macmillan.

Descamps, C. (2004), 'Pour l'esthétique', *La Quinzaine Littéraire*, 887: 18.

Di Felice, M. (2010), *Paesaggi Post-Urbani*, Milan: Bevivino.
Di Felice, M. (2017), *Net-attivismo*, Rome: Edizioni Estemporanee.
Di Felice, M. (2020), 'Per un'altra comunicazione: cinque passi nel pensiero comunicativo di Mario Perniola', *Ágalma*, 39: 46–55.
Di Rienzo, C. (2020), 'Ágalma, tra estetica e politica. Omaggio a Mario Perniola', *Italian Thought Network*. Available online: https://italianthoughtnetwork.com/contrappunti/ (accessed 3 September 2021).
Di Stefano, E. (2018), *Che cos'è l'estetica quotidiana*, Rome: Carocci.
Donà, M. (2015), 'Arte, artificio, arbitrio', *L'Espresso*, 10 December: 111.
Dorfles, G. (2014), 'L'impossibile che cambia la vita. Così fatti eccezionali hanno destabilizzato istituzioni e costumi', *Corriere della Sera*, 3 June: 25.
Duarte, R. (2021), 'Perniola's Tropicalism', *Ágalma*, 42: 83–92.
Dumoulié, C. (2002), *Il desiderio*, trans. S. Arecco, Turin: Einaudi.
Eco, U. (1966), 'Il metagruppo di La Spezia', *L'Espresso*, 26 June: 20.
Eliade, M. (1975), *Il mito dell'eterno ritorno*, trans. G. Cantoni, Rome: Borla.
Epictetus (1983), *Handbook of Epictetus*, trans. N. White, Indianapolis: Hackett.
Eribon, D. (2004), *Insult and the Making of the Gay Self*, Durham, NC: Duke University Press.
Esslin, M. (1980), *Meditations: Essays on Brecht, Beckett, and the Media*, London: Methuen.
Holland, E.W. (2013), *Deleuze and Guattari's A Thousand Plateaus*, London and New York: Bloomsbury Academic.
Fabris, A. (2000), 'Na espiral do simulacro', in M. Perniola, *Pensando o Ritual*, 9–21, São Paulo: Studio Nobel.
Favardin, P. and L. Bouëxière (1988), *Le dandysme*, Lyon: La Manufacture.
Feldman, J. (1993), *Gender on the Divide: The Dandy in Modernist Literature*, Ithaca, NY: Cornell University Press.
Ferraris, M. (1986), 'Perniola in situazione', *Alfabeta*, 85: 21.
Ferroni, G. (1996), *Dopo la fine: sulla condizione postuma della letteratura*, Turin: Einaudi.
Foster, H. (1996), *The Return of the Real*, Cambridge: MIT Press.
Friberg, C. (2007), 'Towards a Sensibility of Everyday Life', paper presented at *The Limits of Aesthetics*, Nordiska Sällskapet för Estetik, 31 May–2 June.
Friberg, C. (2017), '"Now before it is too late" – Ultracontemporary art as a response to contemporary political apathy', *Copenaghenbiennale*, 4 January. Available online: http://www.copenhagenbiennale.org/carsten-friberg (accessed 3 September 2021).
Gagnier, R. (1987), *Idylls of the Marketplace. Oscar Wilde and the Victorian Public*, Redwood City: Stanford University Press.
Gasquet, A. (2018), 'Prefacio. Within & Outside: somewhere off the beaten tracks', in M. Perniola, *La risa filosofica*, Buenos Aires: Las Cuarenta.
Gell, A. (1998), *Art and Agency: An Anthropological Theory*, Oxford: Clarendon.

Gide, A. (2021), *Marshlands* [eBook edn], trans. D. Searls, New York: New York Review Books.
Giudici, G. (1998), 'Gli "esercizi spirituali" come testo poetico', in Ignazio di Loyola, *Esercizi Spirituali*, 125–33, Milan: SE.
Glick, E. (2001), 'The Dialectics of Dandyism', *Cultural Critique*, 48: 129–63.
Gnoli, A. (2011), '"Il cavaliere figlio del 68", Quei pamphlet paradossali', *La Repubblica*, 24 November: 55.
Gracián, B. (1969), *Agudeza y arte de ingenio*, vol. 2, E.C. Calderón (ed.), Madrid: Clásicos Castalia.
Greeley, A. (2000), *The Catholic Imagination*, Oakland: University of California Press.
Greenwald, J.L. (2008), 'The Gay Man's Burden: Wilde, Dandyism, and the Labors of Gay Selfhood', presented at 'Undergraduate Humanities Forum 2007–2008: Origins'. Available online: https://repository.upenn.edu/uhf_2008/5/?utm_source=repository.upenn.edu%2Fuhf_2008%2F5&utm_medium=PDF&utm_campaign=PDFCoverPages (accessed 3 September 2021).
Groys, B. (2006), 'I corpi di Abu Grahib', *Ágalma*, 11: 16–23.
Guy, J. and I. Small (2004), *Oscar Wilde's Profession*, Oxford: Oxford University Press.
Hadot, P. (1988), *Esercizi spirituali e filosofia antica*, trans. A.M. Marietti, Turin: Einaudi.
Hadot, P. (1995), *Philosophy as a Way of Life*, trans. M. Chase, Oxford UK and Cambridge USA: Blackwell.
Halberstam, J. (1998), *Female Masculinities*, Durham, NC: Duke University Press.
Halberstam, J. (2020), *Wild Things. The Disorder of Desire*, Durham, NC: Duke University Press.
Haraway, D. (2016), *Staying with the Trouble: Making Kin in the Chthulucene*, Durham, NC: Duke University Press.
Harman, G. (2002), *Tool-being: Heidegger and the Metaphysics of Objects*, Chicago: Open Court.
Harman, G. (2011), *The Quadruple Object*, Winchester: Zero Books.
Harrison, T. (1999), 'The Michelstaedter Enigma', *Differentia: Review of Italian Thought*, 8/9: 125–41.
Hazlitt, W. (1934), *The Complete Works of William Hazlitt*, Vol. XX, P.P. Howe (ed.), London and Toronto: J.M. Dent & Sons.
Heidegger, M. (1967), *What is a Thing?* trans. W.B. Burton and V. Deutsch, Chicago: Henry Regnery Company.
Heizer, R.F. and A.M. Baumhoof (1976), *Prehistoric Art of Nevada and California*, Berkeley: University of California Press.
Hevrøy, S.A. (2013), 'Fatum and Fragility. Mario Perniola's Philosophy of Death', in L. Steffen and N. Hinerman (eds), *Death, Dying, Culture: An Interdisciplinary Interrogation*, 89–96, Leiden and Boston: Brill.
Hevrøy, S.A. and H.J. Ohldieck (2015), 'Folds, Vitality, Fragility: Gilles Deleuze and Mario Perniola', *Ágalma*, 30: 74–82.
Hickman, M.L. (1978), 'Views of the Floating World', *MFA Bulletin*, 76: 4–33.

Hognerund Træland, K. (2013), 'Fra uorganisk til organisk sansning. Om estetick sensualitet som svar på økologisk fremmedgjøring', MA diss., Bergen University.
Houk, D. (1997), 'Self Construction and Sexual Identity in Nineteenth-Century French Dandyism', *French Forum*, 22 (1): 59–73.
Huneker, J.G. (2005), 'On Wilde as an Imitator', in K. Beckson (ed.), *Oscar Wilde. The Critical Heritage*, 367–8, London and New York: Routledge.
Huxley, A. (1950), *Themes and Variations*, New York: Harper & Brothers.
Ignatius of Loyola (2017), *Spiritual Exercises* [eBook edn], San Francisco: Ignatius Press.
Illouz, E. (2013), *Why Love Hurts. A Sociological Explanation*, Cambridge: Polity.
Jackson, H. (2005), 'On Wilde as Dandy and Artist', in K. Beckson (ed.), *Oscar Wilde. The Critical Heritage*, 355–63, London and New York: Routledge.
Jappe, A. (1999), *Guy Debord*, trans. D. Nicholson, Berkeley and Los Angeles: University of California Press.
Jappe, A. (2019), 'Ludd, o il Sessantotto trascendente', *Comunismo e Comunità*. Available online: http://www.comunismoecomunita.org/?p=6052 (accessed 3 September 2021).
Jesse, C. (1844), *The life of George Brummell, Esq., commonly called Beau Brummell*, vol. 2, London: Saunders & Otley.
Jouve, N. (1980), *Baudelaire. A Fire to Conquer Darkness*, London: Palgrave Macmillan.
Juhl, C. (2018), 'Conditions for an Ontology of Freedom with an Art-Theoretical Aim. Discussing the Philosophical Work of Mario Perniola in the 1990s', *Ágalma*, 37: 113–23.
Kelly, I. (2005), *Beau Brummell. The Ultimate Dandy*, London: Hodder.
Kelly, M. (ed.) (1998), *Encyclopedia of Aesthetics* (4 vol.), New York and Oxford: Oxford University Press.
Kent, D. (2018), 'Redefining the Dandy. The Asexual Man of Fashion', *Making Queer History*. Available online: https://www.makingqueerhistory.com/articles/2018/4/7/redefining-the-dandy-the-asexual-man-of-fashion (accessed 3 September 2021).
Klossowski, P. (1998), *Nietzsche and the Vicious Circle*, trans. D.W. Smith, Chicago: University of Chicago Press.
Kretsch, R.W. (1972), review of M. Perniola, *L'alienazione artistica*, *The Journal of Aesthetics and Art Criticism*, 4: 570–1.
Lasch, C. (1979), *The Culture of Narcissism*, New York: W.W. Norton.
Latour, B. (2005), *Reassembling the Social*, Oxford: Oxford University Press.
Lewis-Williams, D. (2006), 'Shamanism: a contested concept in archaeology', *Before Farming*, 4: 1–15.
Linder, M. and J. Scheid (1993), 'Quand croire c'est faire. Le probleme de la croyance dans la Rome ancienne', *Archives de Sciences Sociales des Religions*, 81: 47–62.
Lippolis, R. and L. Ranieri (2018), *La critica radicale in Italia. Ludd 1967–1970*, Turin: Nautilus.
Lozano, J. (1999), 'El *sex-appeal* de lo asqueroso', *Revista de libros* (November): 7–8.

Lumley, R. (1990), *States of Emergency: Cultures of Revolt in Italy from 1968 to 1978*, London and New York: Verso.

Macchia, M. (1975), *Baudelaire*, Milan: Rizzoli.

Manfreda, L.A. (2020), 'Paesaggi plastici', *Ágalma*, 39: 29–33.

Manfreda, L.A. (2021), 'Iconoclastia e rappresentazione. Su Bataille letto da Perniola', in E. Bianchi and M. Di Felice (eds), *Le avventure del sentire. Il pensiero di Mario Perniola nel mondo*, 159–69, Milan-Udine: Mimesis.

Manovich, L. (2013), *Software Takes Command*, New York and London: Bloomsbury Academic.

Manovich, L. (2020), *Cultural Analytics*, Cambridge: MIT Press.

Margat, C. (2003), review of M. Perniola, *Le sex-appeal de l'inorganique*, *Art Press*, 296: 63.

Marino, P. (2010), review of M. Perniola, *The Sex Appeal of the Inorganic*, *Journal of the History of Sexuality*, 19: 170–2.

Markin, P. (2018), 'Perniola's Sex Appeal of the Inorganic as the Underlying Principle of Art and Capitalism', *Open Culture*, 11 May 2018. Available online: https://oc.hypotheses.org/966 (accessed 3 September 2021).

Marroni, A. (1981), review of M. Perniola, *Dopo Heidegger*, *Itinerari*, 3: 237–9.

Marroni, A. (1986), 'Una filosofia del transito', *Il cannocchiale*, 3: 164–72.

Marroni, A. (1992), 'Sotto il segno dell'enigma', *Tempo presente*, 133/134: 101–6.

Marroni, A. (2019), *L'arte ansiosa*, Milan: Mondadori.

Marx, K. (1982), *Capital*, vol. 1, trans. B. Fowkes, London: Penguin.

Marx, W. (2005), *L'adieu à la littérature. Histoire d'une dévalorisation XVIII–XX siécle*, Paris: Minuit.

Matos, O. (2000), 'O triunfo da cópia', *Folha de S. Paulo*, 9 December. Available online: https://www1.folha.uol.com.br/fsp/resenha/rs0912200014.htm (accessed 3 September 2021).

Meillassoux, Q. (2008), *After Finitude: An Essay on the Necessity of Contingency*, trans. R. Brassier, London and New York: Continuum.

Meyer, M.P. (2019), *Archery and the Human Condition in Lacan, the Greeks, and Nietzsche: the Bow with the Greatest Tension*, Washington, DC: Lexington Books.

Michelstaedter, C. (2004), *Persuasion and Rhetoric*, trans. R.S. Valentino, C. Sartini Blum and D.J. Depew, New Haven and London: Yale University Press.

Milz, M. (2008), 'Echoes of Bergsonian Vitalism in Samuel Beckett's Early Works', *Samuel Beckett Today / Aujourd'hui*, 19: 143–54.

Miranda, M. (1983), review of M. Perniola, *L'"instant éternel". Bataille et la pensée de la marginalité*, *Cahiers internationaux de sociologie*, LXXV: 359–61.

Mizzau, M. (1968), 'Il metaromanzo', *Il Verri*, 26: 94–7.

Moeller, H.G. (2006), *The Philosophy of the Daodejing*, New York: Columbia University Press.

Moers, E. (1960), *The Dandy. Brummell to Beerbohm*, New York: Viking.

Montale, E. (1966), 'Entra in scena il metaromanzo', *Corriere della Sera*, 9 October: 11.

Montandon, A. (ed.) (2016), *Dictionnaire du dandysme*, Paris: Honoré Champion.
Moretti, G. (2020), 'Estetica e Comparatistica. Riflessioni per un rapporto rinnovato', *Comparatismi*, 5: 63–7.
Morgenthaler, F. (1980), *Homosexuality, Heterosexuality, Perversion*, New York: Analytic Press.
Morton, T. (2010), *The Ecological Thought*, Cambridge, MA: Harvard University Press.
Morton, T. (2013), *Hyperobjects: Philosophy and Ecology After the End of the World*, Minneapolis: University of Minnesota Press.
Most, G.W. (2002), 'Heidegger's Greeks', *Arion: A Journal of Humanities and the Classics*, 10 (1): 83–98.
Motta, R. (1998), 'O útil, o sagrado e o mais-que-sagrado no xangô de Pernambuco', *Horizontes Antropológicos*, 4 (8): 168–81.
Natta, M.-C. (2011), *La Grandeur sans convictions. Essai sur le dandysme*, Paris: Éditions du félin.
Nicolini, A. (2018), 'A Thing That Feels. Love and Seduction in Mario Perniola's Philosophy of Transit', *Ágalma*, 36: 97–106.
Nietzsche, F.W. (2003), *Beyond Good and Evil: Prelude to a Philosophy of the Future*, trans. R.J. Hollingdale, London: Penguin Classics.
Nigianni, C. and M. Storr (eds) (2009), *Deleuze and Queer Theory*, Edinburgh: Edinburgh University Press.
Nittve, L. (1989), 'Ritual Ecstasies', *Artforum International* (January): 82–7.
Orlandini, S. (1972), 'A proposito di alienazione artistica', *Arte e società* (May): 27–8.
Panella, G. (1983), review of M. Perniola, *Dopo Heidegger*, *La critica sociologica* (April): 155–60.
Pappalardo, D. (2015), 'La trasformazione delle opere in "arte"', *La Repubblica*, 13 September: 51.
Pasolini, P.P. (1972), 'Outis', *Nuovi argomenti*, 29/30: 149–50.
Patella, G. (2001), 'L'estetica e la sfida degli studi culturali', in L. Russo (ed.), *La nuova estetica italiana*, 235–42, Palermo: Aesthetica Preprint.
Patella, G. (2019), 'Una filosofia dell'intermedio. Ricordo di Mario Perniola', *Rivista di estetica*, 70: 171–6.
Patella, G. (2020), 'La civiltà estetica tra acutezza e strategia. Mario Perniola maestro riluttante', in A. Marroni and U. Di Toro (eds), *Maestri ribelli*, 162–79, Verona: Ombre Corte.
Paulhan, J. (2006), *The Flowers of Tarbes: or, Terror in Literature*, trans. M. Syrotinski, Champaign: University of Illinois Press.
Pedullà, W. (1966), 'Nuovi mistici della letteratura', *L'Avanti*, 29 September 1966: 3.
Perniola, M. and G. Vattimo (1990), 'Arte e illusione', in G. Vattimo (ed.), *Filosofia al presente*, 54–67, Milan: Garzanti.
Pfaller, R. (2003), 'Little Gestures of Disappearance. Interpassivity and the Theory of Ritual', *Journal of European Psychoanalysis*. Available online: http://www.psychomedia.it/jep/number16/pfaller.htm (accessed 3 September 2021).

Plato (1959), *Phaedo*, trans. F.J. Church, New York: The Liberal Arts Press.
Plutarch (1967), *Lives*, trans. B. Perrin, Cambridge, MA: Harvard University Press.
Poe, E.A. (1982), *The Complete Tales and Poems* [ePub edn], London: Penguin.
Poggio, P.P. (1980), review of M. Perniola, *La società dei simulacri*, *Studi Bresciani*, 3: 135–6.
Pomposini, A. (2019), 'Entre lo orgánico y lo inorgánico: la experiencia del hacerse cosa en Perniola y Braidotti', *Estudios de Filosofía*, 17: 150–72.
Raveri, M. (2014), *Il pensiero giapponese classico*, Turin: Einaudi.
Recalcati, M. (2007), *Il miracolo della forma*, Milan: Bruno Mondadori.
Reynolds, S. (1906), 'Autobiografiction', *Speaker*, 6 October: 28–30. Available online: https://blogs.kcl.ac.uk/maxsaunders/autobiografiction/transcription-of-reynolds-essay/ (accessed 3 September 2021).
Rilke, R.M. (1955), *Del Poeta*, trans. G. Pintor, Turin: Einaudi.
Robinet, I. (1988), 'Sexualité et taoïsme', in M. Bernos (ed.), *Sexualité et religions*, 51–71, Paris: Les Éditions du Cerf.
Rousseau, J.-J. (1990), *The Confessions and Correspondence, including the letters to Malesherbes*, C. Kelly, R.D. Masters and P.G. Stillman (eds), trans. C. Kelly, Hanover and London: University Press of New England.
Rovatti, P.A. (1981), 'Noi, dietro la maschera', *La Repubblica*, January 2: 42.
Ruggieri, M. (2021), 'Eco and Gramsci: Unexplored Connections in Cultural Studies', *Italian Studies*, 10 June. Available online: https://www.tandfonline.com/doi/full/10.1080/00751634.2021.1923177 (accessed 3 September 2021).
Rüpke, J. (2007), *The Religion of the Romans*, trans. R. Gordon, Cambridge: Polity.
Ryynänen, M. (2017), 'Chopin's Heart: The Somatic Stimulation of Our Experience of Thingness in Everyday Popular Culture', in C. Friberg and R. Vazquez (eds), *Experiencing the Everyday*, 190–205, Aarhus: Aarhus University Press.
Ryynänen, M. (2021), 'Disgusting, Enigmatic, Inorganic. Mario Perniola, the Dank Humanities, and the Role of the Philosopher in Contemporary Culture', *Ágalma*, 41: 123–31.
Sabatini, A. (1966), 'Il metaromanzo e il paradosso della narrativa', *Il cannocchiale*, 4/6: 185–91.
Saito, Y. (2010), *Everyday Aesthetics*, Oxford: Oxford University Press.
Sandford, S. (2004), 'Let's Talk About Sex', *Radical Philosophy*, 127: 35–40.
Salman, W. (2021), 'La dimensione religiosa nel pensiero di Mario Perniola', in E. Bianchi and M. Di Felice (eds), *Le avventure del sentire. Il pensiero di Mario Perniola nel mondo*, 117–37, Milan-Udine: Mimesis.
Sansot, P. (1977), 'Préface', in M. Perniola, *L'aliénation artistique*, 7–19, Paris: 10/18 U.G.E.
Sapori, A. (1952), *Le marchand italien au moyen âge*, Paris: Armand Colin.
Sargento, P. (2015), *Forma, matéria e presença*, Lisbon: Chiado.
Sartre, J.-P. (1967), *Baudelaire*, trans. M. Turnell, New York: New Directions.
Sartre, J.-P. (2003), *Being and Nothingness: An Essay on Phenomenological Ontology*, trans. H.E. Barnes, London and New York: Routledge.

Saunders, M. (2010), *Self Impression. Life-Writing, Autobiografiction, & the Forms of Modern Literature*, Oxford: Oxford University Press.
Scheid, J. (2011), *Quando fare è credere*, trans. B. Gregori, Rome: Laterza.
Schiffer, D.S. (2008), *Philosophie du dandysme: Une esthétique de l'âme et du corps*, Paris: PUF.
Schmitt, R. (1959), 'Husserl's Transcendental–phenomenological Reduction', *Philosophy and Phenomenological Research*, 20: 238–45.
Scrivano, F. (1992), review of M. Perniola, *Del sentire*, Il verri, 3/4: 193–7.
Scrivano, F. (2018), 'Il filosofo combattente per il "sentire"', *Il Manifesto*, 10 January. Available online: https://ilmanifesto.it/il-filosofo-combattente-per-il-sentire/ (accessed 3 September 2021).
Sedgwick, E.K. (1990), *The Epistemology of the Closet*, Berkeley: University of California Press.
Serna, E.H. and O. Olson (1980), 'The Philosophy of "Ingenium": Concept and Ingenious Method in Baltasar Gracián', *Philosophy & Rethoric*, 13 (4): 245–63.
Shane, R. (2004), 'Ritually Thinking the Eye: An Aesthetics and Ethics of Vision After the Work of Mario Perniola', paper presented at *IAPL 28th Annual Conference 'Virtual Materialities'*, 19–25 May, Syracuse (NY).
Shaviro, S. (2005), 'The Sex Appeal of the Inorganic', *The Pinocchio Theory*. Available online: http://www.shaviro.com/Blog/?p=440 (accessed 3 September 2021).
Sherman, N. (2007), *Stoic Warriors: The Ancient Philosophy Behind the Military Mind*, Oxford: Oxford University Press.
Shildrick, M. (2009), 'Prosthetic Performativity: Deleuzian Connections and Queer Corporealities', in C. Nigianni and M. Storr (eds), *Deleuze and Queer Theory*, 115–33, Edinburgh: Edinburgh University Press.
Sholtz, J. and C. Carr, eds (2021), *Deleuze and the Schizoanalysis of Feminism*, London and New York: Bloomsbury Academic.
Silva, U. (1980), 'Cari simulacri', *Il Messaggero*, 25 June: 16.
Silverman, H.J. (2001), 'Foreword', in M. Perniola, *Ritual Thinking. Sexuality, Death, World*, 9–14, Amherst, NY: Humanity Books.
Sinfield, A. (1994), *The Wilde Century: Effeminacy, Oscar Wilde, and the Queer Moment*, New York: Columbia University Press.
Sinnerbrink, R. (2006), 'Cinema and Its Shadow: Mario Perniola's *Art and Its Shadow*', *Film Philosophy*, 10 (2): 31–8.
Sombart, W. (1925), *Il capitalismo moderno*, trans. A. Cavalli, Florence: Vallecchi.
Sombart, W. (2017), *Economic Life in the Modern Age*, N. Stehr and R. Grundmann (eds), London and New York: Routledge.
Somhegyi, Z. (forthcoming), 'Valuing and Revaluing the City. Interpreting Art and Urban Regeneration with Mario Perniola', *Ágalma*, 43.
Somhegyi, Z. and M. Ryynänen, eds (2020), *Aesthetics in Dialogue. Applying Philosophy of Art in a Global World*, Pieterlen and Bern: Peter Lang.

Sontag, S. (1967), *Against Interpretation and Other Essays*, New York: Farrar, Straus & Giroux.
Stevenson, A. (ed.) (2010), *Oxford Dictionary of English*, Oxford: Oxford University Press.
Swearingen, J.E. and J. Cutting-Gray, eds (2002), *Extreme Beauty: Aesthetics, Politics, Death*, London and New York: Continuum.
Taccone, S. (2017), *La radicalità dell'avanguardia*, Verona: Ombre Corte.
Tatarkiewicz, W. (1970), *Ancient Aesthetics*, vol. I, trans. A. Czerniawski and A. Czerniawski, Paris, Mouton and Warsaw: Polish Scientific Publishers.
Tatarkiewicz, W. (1974), *Modern Aesthetics*, vol. III, trans. C.A. Kisiel and J.F. Besemeres, Paris, Mouton and Warsaw: Polish Scientific Publishers.
Torres Ruiz, M.Á. (2002), 'Sexo inorgánico en el ciberspacio: relaciones entre ciencia y pornografía', *Desacatos*, 9: 23–56.
Trione, V. (2015), 'Motti di spirito, provocatori e creatori che non creano. Ma non è piú una cosa seria', *Corriere della Sera*, 8 November: 29.
Ussama, Y. (2020), 'Tweeting During the Covid-19 Pandemic: Sentiment Analysis of Twitter Messages by Donald Trump', *Digital Government: Research and Practice*, 2 (1): 1–7.
Van Gulick, R.H. (2003), *Sexual Life in Ancient China. A Preliminary Survey of Chinese Sex and Society from ca. 1500 B.C. till 1644 A.D.*, Leiden and Boston: Brill.
Van Sevenant, A. (2021), 'Dualettica estetica', in E. Bianchi and M. Di Felice (eds), *Le avventure del sentire. Il pensiero di Mario Perniola nel mondo*, 105–15, Milan-Udine: Mimesis.
Vattimo, G. (1980), 'La società manipolata', *La Stampa*, 14 August: 3.
Vattimo, G. (1999), 'Il disgusto estetico', *L'Espresso*, 28 January: 90.
Vattimo, G. and P.A. Rovatti (2012), *Weak Thought*, trans. P. Carravetta, Albany: SUNY Press.
Velotti, S. (2016), 'L'occasione mancata dell'arte espansa', *Exibart*, 17 February. Available online: https://www.exibart.com/politica-e-opinioni/loccasione-mancata-dellarte-espansa/ (accessed 3 September 2021).
Verdicchio, M. (2001), 'Reading Perniola Reading: An Introduction', in M. Perniola, *Ritual Thinking. Sexuality, Death, World*, 15–42, Amherst, NY: Humanity Books.
Vincentini, I. (1994), 'Grande stile', in M. Perniola (ed.), *L'aria si fa tesa*, 72–80, Genoa: Costa & Nolan.
Virgil (2007), *Aeneid*, trans. F. Ahl, Oxford: Oxford University Press.
Vogt, E.M. (2019a) *Zwischen Sensologie und ästhetischem Dissens. Essays zu Mario Perniola und Jacques Rancière*, Berlin: Turia & Kant.
Vogt, E.M. (2019b), 'Aesthetics Qua Excess: Mario Perniola and Jacques Rancière', *AM Journal of Art and Media Studies*, 20: 1–10.
Vogt, E.M. (2020), 'A Plea for Reinstituting the Symbolic Order', *Ágalma*, 40: 103–11.
Wahbeh, F. (2006), review of M. Perniola, *Art and its Shadow* and *The Sex Appeal of the Inorganic*, *The Journal of Aesthetics and Art Criticism*, 64 (4): 493–5.

White, H. (1984), 'The Italian Difference and the Politics of Culture', *Graduate Faculty Philosophy Journal*, 10 (1): 117–22.
Whitley, D. (2007), *Introduction to Rock Art Research*, Walnut Creek: Left Coast Press.
Wilde, O. (1987), *The Complete Works of Oscar Wilde*, Leicester: Gallery Press.
Wilde, O. (1995), *The Uncollected*, J.W. Jackson (ed.), London: Fourth Estate.
Wittkower, R. and M. Wittkower (2006), *Born Under Saturn: The Character and Conduct of Artists*, New York: NYRB.
Woelfel, J. (2011), 'The Beautiful Necessity: Emerson and the Stoic Tradition', *American Journal of Theology and Philosophy*, 32 (2): 122–38.
Yoshioka, H. (2019), '"Technological Singularity"' in the Light of Kant's Theory of Art: Reconsidering Artificial Intelligence from an Aesthetic Point of View', paper presented at *21st International Congress of Aesthetics*, Belgrade, Serbia, 21–26 July.
Zeran, A. (2014), 'The Evolution of Indifference: Locating Stoic Influence in Jules Barbey d'Aurevilly's "Du Dandysme et de Georges Brummell" and Charles Baudelaire's "Le Peintre de la vie moderne"', MA diss., University of Western Ontario. Available online: https://ir.lib.uwo.ca/etd/1860 (accessed 3 September 2021).
Zhou, X. (2018), 'Perniola's Studio', *Rivista di estetica*, 69: 119–23.

Index

20th Century Aesthetics (Perniola) 1

A Tale of the Ragged Mountains (Poe) 96
A Thousand Plateaus (Deleuze & Guattari) 121
Abel, Lionel 15
Abruzzese, Alberto 220 n.3
absence 70, 73, 117
Adams, Henry 31
addiction 5, 96, 99, 102–3, 177, 184, 209
Adorno, Theodor W. 140, 155–6
Aeneid (Virgil) 169
aesthetics 1, 2, 6, 11, 14–15, 25, 33, 36, 108, 129–30, 142, 145–7, 154–5, 164–5, 174, 183, 197, 200–1, 208, 215 n.4
    aestheticism 192, 194, 196
    anti- 139, 141
    Baroque 5, 128, 131–3
    behaviour 136, 218 n.5
    as challenge 8, 207
    cultural turn of 140–1
    difference 97
    disinterest 141, 188
    experience 184, 216 n.11
    Hegelian 176
    horizon 123, 138–41
    lifestyle 3, 8, 136, 148–50, 168, 178, 187–8, 193, 198, 209–10, 211 n.1, 217 n.2; *see also* dandyism, strategic beauty, warrior
    and literature 29–30
    Mamurial (*mamuriale*) 36–7; *see also* Rome
    objectivism 135, 137
    over-interest (*sovra-interessamento estetico*) 96, 188
Against the Grain (Huysman) 199
Ágalma (journal) 2, 26, 138, 182, 211 n.1, 217 n.3, 221 n.6
Agamben, Giorgio 209
Agaragar (journal) 2, 153, 155, 167, 219 n.13

agudeza 128–30, 132, 137, 139, 175
    see also Gracián
aisthēsis 129
Akutagawa, Ryūnosuke 17
Alberti, Leon Battista 158–9, 219 n.8
Alcibiades 135
Alfabeta (journal) 66
alienation
    artistic 3, 7, 22, 155, 162–4, 181, 185, 191–2, 219 n.7; *see also* art
    and commodification 83, 86–7, 90, 95
    and dandyism 75
    literary 19–20, 22; *see also* metaliterature
Alzuru, Pedro 215 n.4
amor fati 8, 125, 146, 178, 207, 217
    see also love
Ando, Clifford 53
androgyny 116–17, 198
    see also gender, queer
android/s 106
animal/s 47, 84–5, 88, 90, 100–1, 107, 111, 120, 139, 201–2, 209, 218 n.5
Antichrist, The (Nietzsche) 57
anti-hedonism 6, 99, 101, 121
    see also pleasure/beyond pleasure
anti-intellectualism 65–7
Anti-Oedipus (Deleuze & Guattari) 121
Apollinaire, Guillaume 114
appearance/disappearance 3–5, 33, 35, 37, 39–40, 57, 63, 73–5, 77, 127, 130, 202, 212 n.1, 212 n.2, 213 n.2
appropriateness (*decorum*, *prepon*) 126–8, 137, 146
Arcades Project (Benjamin)
archaeology of clothing 189
archetype 50
architecture 5, 47, 95–6, 130, 136, 140, 184, 188–9, 192
aristocracy 73–5, 142–3, 200, 207
Aristotle 56, 177

art
  as agency 183
  alienation 4, 22, 153, 155–7, 161, 163–4, 192, 219 n.7
  autonomy 158–60
  Baroque 44
  Biennials 182–4
  Conceptual 172
  and crafts 158–60
  creativity 153, 157, 162, 219 n.12
  criticism 200–4
  Dadaist 153
  and economy 163–4, 179–81, 184; *see also* commodity/commodification
  Egyptian 104
  as encyclopedicity 182
  expanded (*espansa*) 182
  fashion 175, 179; *see also* clothing, cosmetics, make up
  as ghetto 160–1
  as historic category 155, 161–2
  as idiocy 174
  as inspiration 137
  Land 172
  market 172, 195
  Minimal 172
  and modernity 187–90
  and nature 192–3
  New Realism 172, 175–6
  objectivism 37
  as occasion 137
  of living 42, 128–9, 132; *see also* lifestyle *under* beauty
  Outsider 141
  overcoming 161–2, 167, 172, 176, 192
  Palaeolithic 88–9
  Pop 172
  as profession 171, 174
  pseudo-participation 156; *see also* separation, spectacle
  remainder 179–80
  Renaissance 158–9
  revolution 154–5, 162, 165
  Rock 88, 130
  Roman 36–7
  shadow (*ombra*) 3, 8, 179–80, 197
  Situationist 153, 165–6, 169
  spiritual torment 160
  as splendour 174, 181
  Surrealist 153–4
  Therapy 183
  third regime of (*terzo regime dell'arte*) 180
  as transgression 171–2
  urban 170
Art and Its Shadow (Perniola) 173, 175, 180–2, 220 n.4
Art of Worldly Wisdom, The (Gracián) 128
Artaud, Antonin 14, 16–19, 24, 121
artificiality 3, 6, 8, 41, 43–4, 64, 77–8, 83–4, 89, 95, 102, 106–7, 135, 142, 145–6, 148, 187, 199, 207, 209
  see also cosmetics, inorganic, neutral
artworld 47, 159, 161, 164, 170–4, 177, 180–4
artwork
  aura 173, 179–80, 197
  object 153, 163, 177, 205
  reproducibility 43
  as thing 4, 8, 177–8, 180, 197, 204–5
asexuality 198–9
  see also gender, queer
Asimov, Isaac 106
assemblage 123
atopos 113, 115, 123
Augustine of Hippo 51
author 4, 11, 15–20, 22–4, 27–8, 30–1, 179, 202
Ayala, Jorge M. 139
Aylesworth, Gary 34

Balázs, Zsuzsanna 198, 215 n.9
Balzac, Honoré de 24
Barbey d'Aurevilly, Jules A. 69, 72–3, 80, 143, 147, 198
Barilli, Renato 180
Baroque 1, 4–6, 14, 34, 38, 41–7, 56, 64, 74, 93, 122–3, 127–30, 132–3, 137, 142, 150, 175–6, 180, 183, 209
Barthes, Roland 15, 23, 26
Bartoloni, Paolo 2, 24, 86–6, 182, 204–5, 214 n.3
Bataille, Georges 3, 21–2, 111, 130, 170–1, 177

Baudelaire, Charles 2, 6, 109, 123, 127, 130, 133, 187, 193, 207–9
  aesthetics/anti-aesthetics 96, 111, 140–2, 150, 190, 200; *see also* surnaturalism
  artificiality 3, 145–6
  beauty 135–7, 148, 189; *see also* strategic beauty
  clothing 143
  dandyism 5, 8, 94, 135–9, 142, 147–8, 178; *see also* theories of dandyism
  detachment 148–9; *see also* Stoicism
  inspiration 103
  make-up 146–7; *see also* cosmetics
  modernity 138–9, 144, 188
  mirror/s 144–5, 203, 207; *see also amor fati*, becoming
  money 139, 142, 144, 217 n.2; *see also* bourgeoisie
  nature 139, 145–6, 192, 199, 217 n.4, 217 n.5
Baudrillard, Jean 2, 33–5
Baumgarten, Alexander G. 129
Baumoff, Martin A. 88
Beard, Mary 53–4
beauty 94, 139, 146, 148–50, 207
  Baroque 128–9, 131, 137, 175
  as challenge 137, 143
  and evolution 218 n.5
  ideal 104, 126, 143
  and melancholy 144
  and modernity 8, 135–8, 141–2, 187–9, 197, 203, 213 n.5
  objective 8, 104, 135, 189, 220 n.4
  as *prepon*; *see* appropriateness
  racism of 8, 104
  Stoic 124, 126, 137
  strategic (*bellezza strategica*) 3, 5, 6, 123, 127, 132, 170, 196, 200
  in *The Sex Appeal of the Inorganic* (Perniola) 99, 102, 118
  and truth 63
Beckett, Samuel 4, 14–17, 19–25, 29, 211 n.3
Beckman, Frida 120, 214 n.1
becoming 36, 99, 113, 115, 120, 122, 125
  indifferent 45
  mirror 92–4, 136–7, 145, 178, 203, 207

  nothing 46, 132
  simulacrum 5
  thing 6, 79, 91, 146, 178, 203
Beerbohm, Max 72, 217 n.1
Bellarmino, Roberto 42, 46
Benjamin, Walter 42, 83–5, 103, 109–10, 144, 173
Benvenuto, Sergio 108–110, 215 n.6
Berardi, Franco 25, 163–4
Berlusconi o il '68 realizzato (Perniola) 25
Bernini, Gian Lorenzo 46
Bertozzi, Alberto 220 n.4
Beuve-Mery, Alain 170
Bianchi, Enea 91, 214 n.1, 216 n.1
Biffures (Leiris) 19
biopolitics 209
blackness 143
  see also clothing
Blade Runner (Scott) 106
Blanchot, Maurice 14–16, 19, 22–3, 177
blog/s 24–5
Blush, Steven 105
body 36, 58, 78–9, 83, 89, 99, 102, 104, 111, 118, 121, 126, 146, 177, 192, 198, 220 n.2, 220 n.4
  without organs 112, 118, 121–2
Boethius 113
Boileau, Nicolas 24
Boltanski, Luc 221 n.6
Book of the Courtier, The (Castiglione) 128
Borges Junior, Eli 184
Borradori, Giovanna 211 n.1
Bottani, Livio 45–6
Bouëxière, Laurent 138–9
bourgeoisie/bourgeoise 5, 8, 75–6, 115, 138, 142–3, 147, 154, 157–60, 162–3, 165–6, 187, 190, 193, 195–7, 199, 207, 211 n.1, 219 n.9
Brecht, Bertold 15
Bredin, Hugh 161, 163
Breivik, Anders 175
Breton, André 16
Breuil, Henri 88
Breve riflessione sul dandy e sul samurai (Comi) 149
bricolage 108
  see also perversion/s

Brown, Bill 85
Brummell, George Bryan 2–3, 5, 8, 69–72, 128, 135, 143, 187, 193–4, 197, 208–9, 213 n.1
  and aristocracy 74–6
  and bourgeoisie 74–6, 190, 207
  desubjectivation 77–80, 203, 213 n.2
  detachment 80
  form 74
  and history 76–7; *see also storiette*
  mirror/s 5, 72–3, 130; *see also* artificiality, becoming
  ritual clothing 5, 72–4, 77–8, 80, 142, 203, 207
  and Romanticism 76–7
  sexuality 198–200
Buddhism 13, 28, 189, 215 n.7
Bukdahl, Else Marie 34, 42–5
Bullough, Edward 103
Bunyard, Tom 219 n.6
Burch, Robert 34, 45, 63, 212 n.4
Burke, Edmund 129
bushidō 149
Butler, Judith 116, 120
Byzantine 38, 40

Cabanne, Pierre 163
Callon, Roger 85
Camaiti-Hostert, Anna 215 n.4
Camus, Albert 21
Capital, The (Marx) 169
capitalism 7, 47, 87, 100, 119, 157–9, 162, 164–6, 168–9, 174, 177, 179, 190–3, 197, 200, 219 n.8, 221 n.6
Capovin, René 34, 47
Carandente, Alessandro 211 n.1
Carassus, Émilien 69, 75–6
Carchia, Gianni 216 n.2
Carr, Cheri L. 121
Carravetta, Peter 65
Castiglione, Baldassarre 128
castration 118–21
Catholicism 38, 55, 59, 61, 64, 128, 213 n.3
Catiline 135
ceremony 50, 53–4, 64, 126
  see also ritual without myth
challenge 8, 35, 94, 129, 132, 138, 144, 154, 207–9

Chance (Conrad) 17
Chesterton, G.K. 194–5
Chiaromonte, Nicola 2, 15
Cicero 124, 126–7
cinema 2, 15, 87, 112, 140, 165, 168, 173, 175, 182
Clinamen (journal) 2
clothing 3, 5, 70, 72–80, 83, 102, 110, 142–5, 148, 150, 187–9, 194, 203, 207, 209
Cloud system 107
Coblence, Françoise 69, 71–2, 77–9, 147, 203, 208
Coffinhal, Jean-Baptiste 63
Cogan, John 52
Cohen, Ed 198
Coleridge, Samuel T. 103
Collins, Randall 140
Comi, Ivano 69, 71, 73, 149
Comments on the Society of the Spectacle (Debord) 39
commodity/commodification 7–8, 83, 86–7, 158, 160, 169, 172, 194–7, 200
communication 2, 11, 28, 95, 139, 175, 179–80, 197, 208, 213 n.2, 220 n.3
Compagno, Giuliano 211 n.1, 216 n.11
Complete Gentleman, The (Gracián) 128
comradery 99–100
  see also sexuality
conatus 120
concepto 128, 130–2
  see also Gracián
Confessions (Rousseau) 4, 23
Conrad, Joseph 4, 16–18, 24
Contreras-Koterbay, Scott 51
Contro la comunicazione (Perniola) 139
convenient, *see* appropriateness
copy 33–4, 36–8, 40–3, 45, 50, 57, 64, 91, 107, 111, 123, 180, 216 n.2
  see also original, repetition, simulacrum
corpse 45, 78–9, 83, 112, 202, 213 n.2
cosmetics 146, 149, 217 n.1
  see also make-up
Costa, Mario 163
Covarrubias, Israel 211 n.1
Covid-19 25

Cox, Cristoph 106
Critic, The (Gracián) 128
Critic as Artist, The (Wilde) 200
Crowley, Aleister 183
cumulative image 205
Cutting-Grey, Joanne 215 n.3
cyberpunk 99
Cyberpunk 2077 (CD Project Red) 106
cyborg/s 89, 106-7

Dadaism 7, 153, 162-3, 172, 218 n.6
Dalla Vigna, Pierre 219 n.13
dance 74, 140, 209, 217 n.5
dandyism 1-3, 5, 34, 37, 56, 62, 69, 71, 79, 83, 127, 133, 141, 150, 178, 201
   artificiality 142, 199
   beauty 6, 135-7, 148, 170, 187-8, 203
   and bourgeoisie 75-6, 138, 142-3, 147, 187, 190, 193, 195-7, 199, 207, 211 n.1
   as challenge 94, 138-9, 144, 147, 200, 207, 210
   and culture industry 193-5
   clothing 72-4, 143, 189-90
   cosmetics 145, 149, 217 n.1
   definition of 72-3
   desubjectivation 78-80, 202
   detachment 138, 142, 147-8
   form 74
   grand style 150, 168-9
   and mirrors 94, 130, 138, 145-6
   modernity 6, 80, 136, 138, 142, 203, 207-10, 211 n.1
   and nature 145-7, 192-3, 199
   queerness 198-200; *see also* gender, queer
   and Romanticism 76-8, 199
   and samurai 149
   sexuality 198-200
   sprezzatura 73
   Stoicism 147-8
   theories of 135-40, 187-93
   wit 8, 77, 128, 196-7
   and work 75, 138, 190-1
Dante 12, 168
Daoism 215 n.7
Davies, Stephen 217 n.5, 218 n.5
De arte bene moriendi (Bellarmino) 42
De Brosses, Charles 110

De Carlo, Mario 28
de Chirico, Giorgio 88
De controversiis christianae fidei (Bellarmino) 42
De Donato, Federico 65
De Maria, Walter 182
De Quincey, Thomas 103, 141
Deafheaven (band) 106
death 12-13, 34, 46, 60-1, 78-9, 91, 149-50, 154, 163, 202, 216 n.12
   see also simulacrum
Death Stranding (Kojima Productions) 106
deathcore music 105
Debord, Guy 1-2, 7, 39-40, 86-87, 130, 155, 157, 162, 166-70, 196, 214 n.2, 218 n.4, 220 n.6
decorum, see appropriateness
Del sentire (Perniola) 92-3, 180, 184
Del sentire cattolico (Perniola) 59-60, 65
Del terrorismo come una delle belle arti (Perniola) 4, 11, 26
Deleuze, Gilles 33-4, 57, 111-12, 118-22, 177, 216 n.12
   see also body without organs, gender, queer
Della Casa, Giovanni 128
demythologization (*demitizzazione*) 53, 57
   see also ritual without myth
Denisoff, Dennis 195
Dennett, Daniel 215 n.4
derealization (*derealizzazione*) 35
   see also simulacrum
Derrida, Jacques 2, 15
Descamps, Christian 220 n.3
Descartes, René 51, 84-5
desire 5, 13-14, 54, 60-1, 77, 79-80, 92, 99, 101-2, 108-10, 116, 118-22, 124-5, 148, 153-5, 162-3, 172, 181, 199, 205
desubjectivation 4, 35, 37, 45-6, 54, 61, 125, 127, 142, 181, 202, 211 n.2
detachment 3-4, 31, 77-8, 83, 103, 138, 142-3, 147-9, 168-9
détournement 8, 106, 157, 167, 170, 183, 196-7, 218 n.6
dialectic 55-6, 97, 117, 162, 164-5, 176-7
Di Felice, Massimo 85, 94-5, 220 n.3
Di Ponio, Joseph 209

Di Rienzo, Caterina 45
Di Stefano, Elisabetta 140
Dialogues II (Deleuze) 121
Dick, Philip K. 106
Diderot, Denis 24, 51
difference 3–4, 55, 77, 90, 114–15, 164, 205, 208, 213 n.3
  aesthetics of 97
  and art theory 176–7, 179–81, 197
  and diversity 56
  election of (*elezione della differenza*) 46, 48, 60–2, 79, 125, 202
  and history 45–6, 60–1, 127
  and indifference 45–6, 60–1, 64
  Italian 55–6
  sexual 112, 116–17
  and value 57
Ding 86
  see also thing/s
discretion 14, 132
disgust 173–6, 179, 220 n.1
disinterest 125, 141–2, 188
  see also aesthetics
distinction 114, 136, 143, 148, 150, 201
Donà, Massimo 182
Dopo Heidegger (Perniola) 62, 65
Dorfles, Gillo 175
drift (*dérive*) 167
drone music 106
drugs 5, 94, 96, 99, 102–4, 141, 147, 177, 184, 209
Duarte, Rodrigo 2, 211 n.1
Duchamp, Marcel 163
Dumoulié, Camille 119

Ecclesiastes 168
echolalia 25
Eco, Umberto 2, 15
Education of Henry Adams, The (Adams) 31
effectiveness (effectuality) 3–6, 29, 39, 44, 47, 52, 54, 57, 62, 64–5, 83, 93, 123, 126–7, 129–30, 149, 154–7, 161, 168–9, 188, 196, 212 n.1
Egypt 5, 53, 89, 104, 129–30, 177–8, 184
eîdos 74
elegance 3, 8, 69, 72, 135–6, 143, 187, 192–4, 196, 198, 207, 209
  see also appearance, form

Eliade, Mircea 49–50
Eliot, T.S. 114
Ellis, Bret E. 30
emo music 105
emotions 25–6, 30, 58, 74, 8, 86, 96, 105, 124, 148, 168, 174, 205
enantiodromia 113, 132
enigma 7–8, 88–9, 111, 114–16, 165, 179–80
Enigmas (Perniola) 89–90, 92, 122, 180
Enlightenment 61, 156, 188
Eno, Brian 105
Enragés 166
Epictetus 124, 127, 216 n.4
epoché 51–4, 61, 83, 101–2, 104
epos 156
Eribon, Didier 198
Erlebnis 21
Errata (journal) 167
Esslin, Martin 22
Estetica italiana contemporanea (Perniola) 1
Estetica News (journal) 2
ethics 108, 129, 145, 149, 212 n.1, 215 n.8
everyday life 5, 7, 13, 21, 24, 39, 51–2, 56, 60, 74–6, 78, 85, 88, 91–2, 94, 100, 129, 137–8, 155, 157, 160–2, 164–5, 168, 172, 184, 188, 192–3, 200, 203, 208–9, 212 n.1
evocatio 37–8, 53, 55
  see also Rome, ritual without myth
Ex Machina (Garland) 106
excitement 6, 84, 100, 102–3, 108, 110–11, 120–21, 215 n.7
Expanded Cinema (Youngblood) 182
Explosions in the Sky (band) 106
exteriority 3, 6, 8, 73–4, 91–5, 103, 138, 142, 187, 190
  see also artificiality, inorganic, neutral, thing/s
extraneousness 50, 55, 97, 102–3
  see also uncanny

Fabre, Jan 204
Fabris, Anateresa 41
Fachinelli, Elvio 220 n.6
fashion 5, 46, 70–3, 83–4, 137, 140–1, 175, 179, 182, 188, 198–9
  see also modernity

Favardin, Patrick 138-9
feeling (*sentire*) 1, 48, 84, 96-7, 116, 123, 165, 177
    Catholic 55, 58-9
    cosmic 92, 99, 111-12, 120
    and difference 56
    from the inside (*sentire dal di dentro*) 90, 92, 95, 102-3, 105, 110
    music 105-6
    from the outside (*sentire dal di fuori*) 61, 102-3, 184
    ritual (*sentire rituale*) 55
    sexuality 104-7, 215 n.3
    Stoicism 124
    strong (*forte sentire*) 12-14
    suspended, impersonal 6, 87-9, 91, 93, 102-3, 105-6, 109-10, 112, 178, 185; *see also* inorganic, neutral
    see thing that feels *under* thing/s
    vegetal 215 n.4
Feldman, Jessica R. 198
Fellini, Federico 15
Ferraris, Maurizio 213 n.6
Ferroni, Giulio 24
fetishism 47, 83-4, 86, 108-11, 179, 182, 197, 199
Feuerbach, Ludwig 169
Fichte, J. Gottlieb 23
Fisher, Urs 204
Flares (Baudelaire) 135, 148
Flowers of Evil, The (Baudelaire) 143
Foster, Hal 174
Franklin, Benjamin 159
Franko B. 220 n.2
Freud, Sigmund 5-6, 21, 28, 96-7, 108, 110-11, 117-18, 120-2, 141, 170-1, 178, 183
Friberg, Carsten 25, 61, 211 n.1
futility 75, 181, 184

Gadamer, Hans-Georg 65
Gagnier, Regenia 8, 194-6, 208
Gasquet, Axel 1
Gelassenheit 63
Gell, Alfred 183
gender
    binary restriction of 116-17
    and dandyism 198-200
    fluidity 115-16; *see also* queer
    and neutral sexuality 99, 114, 117-18, 216 n.10
    performative 120
    theories 112, 122
    transgender 115
Genet, Jean 15
genius 130
genos 156, 161
Gentile, Giovanni 21
George IV 70-1, 73
Ghost in the Shell (Oshii) 106
Gide, André 4, 16-18
Gioni, Massimiliano 183
Giordano Bruno 113
Giudici, Giovanni 58
Glick, Elisa 199-200
Gnoli, Antonio 25
God Is an Astronaut (band) 106
Godard, Jean-Luc 15
Godspeed You! Black Emperor (band) 106
Gracián, Baltasar 14, 125, 128-32, 137, 139, 170, 183, 196, 216 n.5
Gramsci, Antonio 62, 67
Grass, Günter 30
greatness 138, 150, 205
Greeley, Andrew 55
Greenwald, Jordan L. 198
Grillo, Beppe 25
grindcore music 105
Groys, Boris 220 n.3
Guattari, Félix 111-12, 118-22
    see also body without organs, gender, queer
Guicciardini, Francesco 14, 62
Guy, Josephine 193-4

habitus 50, 74, 126, 147, 169
Hadot, Pierre 125
Hagakure (Tsunetomo) 149
Halberstam, Jack 116, 199
Haraway, Donna 199
hardcore music 105
Harman, Graham 85
harmony 36-7, 55, 73-4, 92-3, 116, 119, 123, 127, 129, 132, 137, 140, 143, 145, 184, 188, 198, 220 n.4
    see also appropriateness, symmetry/asymmetry

Harrison, Thomas 13
Hazlitt, William 77–8
Hegel, G.W.F. 56, 62, 84, 89, 97, 140, 155, 162, 169, 176–7
Heidegger, Martin 34, 62–5, 84–6, 113, 170, 177
Heizer, Robert F. 88
Heraclitus 64, 113, 132
hermaphrodite 115, 198
Hero, The (Gracián) 128
heroism 76, 129, 138, 140, 144
  see also warrior
Hesiod 114
heteronormativity 6, 8, 116, 121, 199–200, 215 n.4, 216 n.10
  see also queer
heterophenomenology 111, 215 n.4
Hevrøy, Stein A. 63, 149, 216 n.13
Hickman, Money L. 113
historical avant-gardes 1, 7–8, 123, 133, 153, 155, 164, 166, 169, 171, 183, 195, 218 n.6
historiettes 26, 30
Hognerund Træland, Kristine 215 n.4
Holland, Eugene W. 121
Homer 64, 114, 156
homoeroticism 115
  see also gender, queer
homosexuality 64, 108, 115–16, 198
  see also gender, queer
Houk, Deborah 198
Huneker, James G. 194
hunting magic 88
Husserl, Edmund 51–2, 212 n.1
Huxley, Aldous 46, 103
Huysman, Joris-Karl 199
hyperreality 35, 48
hyperuranium 91, 124

iconoclasm/iconophily 38–42, 57, 140
  see also image theories *under* simulacrum
identity 5, 7, 36–7, 41, 43, 45, 53, 56, 60–2, 77, 79, 92, 94, 97, 101–2, 115–16, 119–20, 154, 157, 176–8, 199, 202, 213 n.3, 220 n.2
ideology 4, 8, 63, 66, 184
Idylls of the Marketplace (Gagnier) 195

Ignatius of Loyola 14, 34, 42, 44–5, 55–62, 78–9, 125, 128, 170, 202, 213 n.2, 213 n.4
ignorance 39, 66–7, 219 n.7
  see also anti-intellectualism, misology
Il metaromanzo (Perniola) 2, 4, 11, 14–15, 22
Il re nudo (journal) 167
Illouz, Eva 35
imaginary wholeness 118
imagination 44, 55, 130, 141, 145, 195
imitation (*mimesis*) 36, 79, 137, 177
In girum imus nocte et consumimur igni (Debord) 168
indeterminate international (*internazionale indeterminata*) 48
indifference 25, 45–6, 53, 58, 60–2, 64, 77, 83, 125, 127, 147, 149, 199, 202
individualism 191–2, 195–6, 202, 221 n.1
ingenio 128, 130–2, 139, 216 n.6
  see also Graciàn
inorganic 3, 5, 6, 8, 61, 79, 83–4, 87–92, 94–7, 99–111, 116–18, 146, 149, 165, 177–8, 180, 183–4, 199, 202–3, 214 n.3
  see also artificial, neutral, sexuality
International Congress of Aesthetics (IAA) 140
irony 30, 69, 77
Italian Thought 209

Jackson, Holbrook 194
James, Henry 15–16, 24
James, William 49
Jappe, Anselm 166–7, 218 n.1
je ne sais quoi 73, 128
Jentsch, Ersnt 97
Jesse, Captain William 69, 73, 77, 198
Jesuit Order 14, 34–5, 38, 41–8, 53, 55–8, 65–6, 74, 78–9, 112, 127–8, 147, 180, 202, 209, 213 n.2
Jesus 38, 44, 58, 128
jouissance 119
Joyce, James 30
judgement 5, 14, 51, 56, 58–9, 103, 108, 124–5, 131, 141, 189
Juhl, Carsten 182
Julius Caesar 135

Jung, Carl G. 183
Jünger, Ernst 103

Kant, Immanuel 56–7, 84, 97, 110, 129–30, 140–1, 189
Kelly, Ian 69–73, 75, 198, 213 n.1
Kelly, Michael 140
Kent, Daria 198–99
Kenzaburô, Ôe 30
Klossowski, Pierre 2, 33–4, 110, 130, 177
Kojève, Alexandre 169
Koons, Jeff 204
Krauss, Friedrich S. 108
Kretsch, Robert W. 219 n.12
Kurosawa, Akira 17

L'adieu à la littérature (William Marx) 29
L'alienazione artistica (Perniola) 7, 22, 153, 155, 156, 158–9, 161–2, 164–5, 167, 171, 176, 178, 191, 218 n.2, 219 n.7
L'arte espansa (Perniola) 182
L'avventura situazionista (Perniola) 1
L'erba voglio (journal) 56, 167
La società dei simulacri (Perniola) 33–5, 47–9, 171–3
Lacan, Jacques 117–20, 122
Landolfi, Tommaso 14
landscape 77, 84, 90, 142, 154
Lasch, Christopher 35
Latour, Bruno 85, 199
Lavoisier, Antoine-Laurent 63
Lefebvre, Henri 169
Leiris, Michel 4, 17, 19
Leonardo da Vinci 202, 204
Leopardi, Giacomo 13
Lettrist International 165
Lévi-Strauss, Claude 49, 51, 108
Lewis-Williams, David 88
libertinism 99–100
Linder, Marc 54
Lippolis, Leonardo 218 n.1
literature 2, 4, 11, 72, 112–13, 123, 140, 187, 196, 208, 211 n.1, 215 n.4
    autobiografiction 30
    autobiography 6, 11, 23, 27, 30–1, 87, 122, 216 n.10, 220 n.6
    Baroque 142, 150, 175, 180
    experimental 17
    Greek 64, 156, 158, 201

inner experience 21, 30
Japanese 113
literary devices 27, 30, 200
meta- 15–16, 18, 22, 25–6, 211 n.4
minimalism 29
minor 4, 26, 28–30
Modernism 30
Naturalism 4, 16, 26
novel 4, 6, 11, 14–24, 26, 29–31
psychoanalysis 21, 97
queer 115, 199
Romanticism 23–4
sci-fi 5, 106–8
self-reference 15, 17, 21, 23, 26
spontaneity (immediacy, transparency) 21, 23–4
Logic of Sense, The (Deleuze) 121
logos 123–4, 127, 147, 149
London 5, 69–73, 208
London Psychogeographical Committee 165
Lord Jim (Conrad) 17
love 8, 12–13, 46, 93–4, 104, 125, 136, 199, 207, 215 n.8
Lozano, Jorge 215 n.4
Ludd 153, 167, 218 n.1
Lukács, György 155, 169
Lumley, Robert 211 n.1
Lyotard, Jean-François 220 n.6

Macchia, Giovanni 217 n.4
Machiavelli, Niccolò 12, 80, 168
Macrobius 35, 37
Maffesoli, Michel 2
make-up 7, 146, 149, 194, 199
    see also artificiality, cosmetics
Malone Dies (Beckett) 19
Mamurius Veturius 36–7
Manfreda, Luigi A. 211 n.1, 216 n.12
Mannerism 128, 132, 160
Manovich, Lev 95
Marcus Aurelius 124, 127
Margat, Claire 111
Marino, Patricia 101
Markin, Pablo 214 n.4
Marroni, Aldo 62–3, 182
Marshlands (Gide) 18
Marx, Karl 5–6, 86–7, 97, 110–1, 155, 158, 161, 169, 176, 185, 191, 214 n.2

Marx, William 22, 24, 29–30
masochism 84, 108–10, 122
mass media 35, 38–9, 41, 47–8, 66, 87, 157
mathcore music 105
Matos, Olgaria 41
matrix events (*eventi matrice*) 175
Meillasoux, Quentin 85
melancholy 143–4, 149, 160–1
Melville, Herman 169
Metal Gear Solid (Konami, Kojima Productions) 106
metalcore music 105
Metropolis (Lang) 106
Meyer, Matthew P. 119
Michelangelo Buonarroti 160
Michelstaedter, Carlo 12–14, 177
Miller, Henry 16, 24
Milz, Manfred 211 n.3
Miracoli e traumi della comunicazione (Perniola) 175
Miranda, Michel 211 n.1
mirror/s 5–6, 16, 72, 79, 92–4, 130, 136–8, 144–6, 178, 199, 203, 207, 211 n.1
see also *amor fati*, becoming
Mirror or the Metamorphosis of Orante, The (Perrault) 93
mirror stage 118–19
misology 210
Mizzau, Marina 15
modernity 6, 64–5, 136–8, 141, 144, 146, 148, 188–9
Moeller, Hans-Georg 215 n.7
Moers, Ellen 69–72, 75–7, 143, 194
Molloy (Beckett) 19
money 107, 138–9, 142, 144, 154, 158–9, 179, 193–4, 200, 207, 217 n.2
Montaigne, Michel de 21, 168
Montale, Eugenio 2, 15, 22
Montandon, Alain 3
Moravia, Alberto 2
Moretti, Giampiero 56
Morgenthaler, Fritz 108
morphé 74
Morton, Timothy 85, 199
Most, Glenn 63–4
Motta, Roberto 211 n.1
Movement for an Imaginist Bauhaus 165
music 84, 96, 99, 104–6, 140, 209
My Bloody Valentine (band) 106

My Heart Laid Bare (Baudelaire) 135, 139, 143, 148
myth 4–5, 26, 49–55, 74–6, 92, 114–16, 156, 207

Nadeau, Maurice 15
Nagel, Thomas 215 n.4
Napoleon 62, 72
narcissism 35, 92–3, 95, 145
Natta, Marie-Christine 69, 119, 135, 147–8
nature 4, 6, 8, 23, 64, 76, 83, 92, 100, 112, 121, 130, 139, 142, 145–8, 172, 177, 192–3, 199–200, 214 n.1, 217 n.4
necrophilia 108
negative 97, 162, 164, 176
neo-ancient (*neo-antico*) 65, 213 n.7
neo-avant-gardes 171–5, 182, 197
neo-Classicism 75, 198
neo-Idealism 21
neo-Platonism 51, 219 n.12
neo-Stoicism 123, 138, 147
neutral 5–6, 52, 77, 83–4, 87–92, 95, 99, 101–112, 116–18, 120, 125, 127, 145, 147–49, 178, 180, 184, 198, 200, 209
see also artificiality, inorganic, feeling, sexuality
Nicolini, Andrea 215 n.8
Nietzsche, Friedrich 23, 28, 33–4, 36, 39, 57, 62, 65, 130, 140–1, 170–1, 177
Nihei, Tsumotu 106
nihilism 22, 26, 63, 65, 220 n.6
Nittve, Lars 211 n.1
North, Frederick 70
Numa Pompilius 35–6
Nuovi Argomenti (journal) 153

Object-Oriented Ontology 85–6
Oedipus 119–21
Of Dandyism and of George Brummell (Barbey d'Aurevilly) 72, 147
Ohldieck, Hans J. 216 n.13
opposition 8, 34, 36, 41, 43, 45, 66, 77, 83, 90–1, 101, 116–17, 126–7, 132, 144, 147, 150, 164, 176, 179–80, 197
orgasm 6, 99–102, 118, 120–1, 214 n.1, 215 n.7
see also sexuality

Origin of the German Tragic Drama, The (Benjamin) 42
original 33–8, 40–6, 50, 63–4, 91, 93, 107, 111, 157, 173, 180, 205, 212 n.2
 see also copy, simulacrum
Orlan 220 n.2
Orlandini, Sergio 163
ornament 128, 144
Ovid 114

Painter of Modern Life, The (Baudelaire) 135, 143, 148
Palaeolithic 5, 88–9, 129, 136, 178, 184, 189, 209
Pane, Gina 220 n.2
Panella, Giuseppe 62
Pappalardo, Dario 182
Parallel Lives (Plutarch) 35
paraphilia 108
Pareyson, Luigi 2, 14, 168
Paris 143–4, 166, 170, 208
Paris Spleen (Baudelaire) 143
Parmenides 64
parody 147–8
Pascal, Blaise 21, 27
Pasolini, Pier Paolo 2, 114
Patella, Giuseppe 128, 130, 140
Paulhan, Jean 24
Pedullà, Walter 15, 211 n.4
Pensa, Marika 209
Perrault, Charles 93
persuasion 12–13
Persuasion and Rhetoric (Michelstaedter) 12–13
perversion/s 1, 6, 83–4, 86, 94, 102, 104, 108–12, 177, 184, 215 n.6
Pfaller, Robert 213 n.2
Phaedo (Plato) 219 n.14
Phaedrus (Plato) 104
phenomenology 51–2, 54, 212 n.1
Philosophical Investigations (Wittgenstein) 96
Picture of Dorian Gray, The (Wilde) 199, 209
picturesque 188, 208
Pinard de La Boullaye, Henry 58
Pirandello, Luigi 15, 19
plants 47, 84, 90, 120, 215 n.4
Plato 33–38, 40, 91, 104, 117, 120, 123–4, 135, 177, 189

pleasure/beyond pleasure 6, 12, 99–103, 109–10, 114–15, 121, 129, 138, 143, 157, 198, 216 n.11
 see also desire, excitement
Plutarch 35–6
Poe, Edgar Allan 6, 96, 112, 141
poetry 11, 14, 90, 103–5, 109, 139, 141, 156, 158, 188–9, 195, 201
Poggio, Pier Paolo 212 n.5
politics 1–3, 7, 14, 16, 24–5, 28–9, 33, 35, 38–9, 51–2, 54, 65–7, 80, 90, 105, 116, 121, 123, 127–8, 153–4, 156, 161–2, 165–6, 168–9, 196, 200–1, 208–10, 211 n.2, 212 n.5, 215 n.8, 219 n.13, 221 n.1
Polykleitos 36
polymorphic perversity 120
Pomposini, Antonio 214 n.2
Pope Alexander VII 46
Pope Urban VIII 46
populism 26, 56, 63, 66
post-black music 106
post-hardcore music 105
post-humanism 108, 174–5, 181, 199–200, 214 n.2, 216 n.11
postmodernism 1, 48, 67, 136, 173, 220 n.6
post-rock music 106
prepon, *see* appropriateness
Programma Manifesto (Perniola) 11–13, 215 n.10
progressive rock 105
Protestantism 40, 64, 213 n.3
Proust, Marcel 21
pseudo-community 156–7, 161
 see also separation, Situationist International, spectacle
psychic distance 203
psychoanalysis 5, 21, 92, 96–7, 108–12, 118–22, 171, 176–7, 209
psychogeography 167
psychosis 220 n.2
punk 105
puppet 79, 149, 203, 213 n.2
purity/impurity 18, 23, 39, 52, 56, 137, 177

queer 6, 11, 84, 215 n.10
 and dandyism 150, 198–200
 identities 114–16, 198–200
 performativity 116

philosophies 114, 120–2
and transit (*transito*) 118
Quindici (journal) 167

Rancière, Jacques 213 n.7
Ranieri, Paolo 218 n.1
rapcore music 105
Rashōmon (Kurosawa) 17
Raveri, Massimo 215 n.7
Recalcati, Massimo 220 n.2
reification, *see* alienation
Remarks on the Philosophy of Psychology (Wittgenstein) 96
Renaissance 46, 128, 155, 158–60, 162, 219 n.7
repetition 5, 25, 35, 43, 50–2, 54, 104, 106, 189
  see also copy, original, simulacrum
replicants 106–7
Return of the Real, The (Foster) 174
revolt 20, 138–9, 144, 150, 199–200, 207
revolution 1, 7, 29, 39, 72, 75, 94, 138, 153–7, 159, 162–9, 181, 192, 194, 200, 205, 207–8, 218 n.6, 219 n.14
Reynolds, Stephen 30
rhetoric 12–13
Ribadeneira, Pedro de 59
Rigaut, Jacques 94
RiLaben 209
Rilke, Rainer M. 90, 104
Rimbaud, Arthur 27
Ritual Thinking. Sexuality, Death, World (Perniola) 2, 49
ritual without myth (*rito senza mito*) 2–5, 49–55, 57, 61–2, 64, 74, 78, 80, 126–7, 165, 180, 213 n.2
Rivière, Jacques 18–19
Rivista di estetica (journal) 155
Robertson Smith, William 49
Robinet, Isabelle 215 n.7
rock music 105
Romanticism 4, 8, 23–6, 76–7, 112, 141, 146, 199, 211 n.4, 217 n.4
Rome 1, 3, 35–8, 47–8, 53–5, 64–6, 74, 79–80, 112, 114, 123–4, 126–30, 169, 180, 184, 189, 198, 202, 209, 213 n.2
Rousseau, Jean-Jacques 4, 23–4, 26, 146
Rovatti, Pier Aldo 37, 65
Ruggieri, Marco 217 n.3

Rüpke, Jörg 53–4
Rushdie, Salman 30
Ryōi, Asai 113
Ryynänen, Max 2, 80, 140, 220 n.1

Sabatini, Angelo 15, 24
Sache 86
  see also thing/s
sadism 108–10
Saito, Yuriko 140
Salman, Wasim 213 n.3
Salon of 1846, The (Baudelaire) 135, 144, 187
samurai 149
Sandford, Stella 215 n.4
Sandman, The (Hoffmann) 97
Sansot, Pierre 160, 163, 218 n.3
Sapori, Armando 159
Sargento, Pedro 211 n.1
Sartre, Jean-Paul 21, 85, 145
Saturnalia (Macrobius) 35
Saunders, Max 27, 30–1
Scheid, John 37, 53–4
Schlegel, Friedrich 23
Schmitt, Richard 52
Schopenhauer, Arthur 13
Schulze, Klaus 105
screamo music 105
Scrivano, Fabrizio 184, 211 n.1
secrecy 37, 39–40, 64, 115, 198–9, 202–3
Sedgwick, Eve K. 198
seduction 37, 48, 128–9
seemly, *see* appropriateness
Sehnsucht 76
Seneca the Younger 124
senses 44–6, 58, 61, 74, 106, 129, 145, 184, 188, 190
sensology (*sensologia*) 184–5
separation 7, 155, 157, 160–5, 172, 183
Serna, Hidalgo 131, 216 n.6
Serra, Richard 182
setsuwa 26, 30
Sex Appeal of the Inorganic, The (Perniola) 1, 5–6, 80, 83–4, 88, 96, 99, 101–4, 107–9, 112, 114, 116, 120, 180, 198, 204, 215 n.5, 216 n.10, 220 n.6
sexuality 1, 6, 84, 96, 207, 215 n.4
  as accumulation (climax) 100
  as appetite (hunger) 100–1

artificial 83
beyond gender 116; *see also* gender
excitement 84
as familiarity 100
functionalism 100-101
inorganic/organic 5, 84, 99, 102–3, 106, 114, 117–18, 184
and knowledge 99-100
neutral 104, 106–11, 120, 198, 214 n.1, 215 n.3
non-heteronormative 116, 121, 199–200, 215 n.4, 216 n.10
see also queer
Shakespeare, William 189
Shane, Robert R. 78, 215 n.8
Sherman, Cindy 182
Sherman, Nancy 124–5, 127, 216 n.4
Shildrick, Margrit 118, 120
Shoegaze music 106
Sholts, Janae 121
Silone, Ignazio 2
Silva, Umberto 34
Silverman, Hugh J. 128
simulacrum 2–5, 64, 165, 180, 211 n.1
    Baroque emblem 37–8
    and dandyism 78–9
    and death 45–6, 61, 78–9
    and history 29
    and image theories 38–44; *see also* iconoclasm, iconophily
    and Internet of Things 47–8
    Jesuit thought 44–6, 55, 57
    and mass media 41
    perversions 111
    and ritual thinking (*pensiero rituale*) 50, 53, 69
    Roman culture 35–7, 212 n.2; *see also* Rome
    theories of 33–5
simulation 4, 34–5, 46, 78, 107, 149
Sinfield, Alan 199
Sinnerbrink, Robert 211 n.1
situation 140, 157, 160, 165, 167
Situationist International 1, 7–8, 39, 87, 106, 140, 153, 156–7, 160, 162, 165–72, 176, 183, 191, 218 n.1, 218 n.2, 218 n.6, 220 n.15
Small, Ian 193
social media 4, 13, 23–6, 29, 47

Socialism ou Barbarie (journal) 169
Societas Raffaello Sanzio 1
Society of the Spectacle, The (Debord) 86, 169, 214 n.2
Socrates 113, 216 n.3
software ecologies 94–5, 178
soldier 127, 148–9
Sombart, Werner 159
Somhegyi, Zoltán 140, 211 n.1
Sontag, Susan 198
Sophocles 13, 64, 114
Soul of Man Under Socialism, The (Wilde) 190, 192, 195
species 74
specularism (*specularismo*) 3, 6, 84, 92–5, 142
spectacle 7, 35, 39–40, 86–7, 156–7, 163, 165, 167–70, 214 n.2, 218 n.4
Spiritual Exercises (Loyola) 34, 42, 44, 57, 60, 79
spiritualism 6, 8, 18, 30, 36, 88–91, 94, 97, 101–2, 104, 106–7, 127, 130, 160–2, 180, 211 n.4
Spleen II (Baudelaire) 109
sprezzatura 73, 128
Steiner, Rudolph 183
Stelarc 220
Stendhal 24, 141
Stockdale, James Bond 127, 216 n.4
Stockhausen, Karlheinz 175
Stoicism 1, 3, 6, 29, 78, 80, 112, 123–7, 129–32, 137–8, 147–9, 178, 180, 202, 209, 216 n.2
storiette 2–4, 11, 26–31
Streben 76
Sturm und Drang 76
sublime 1, 24, 76, 97, 112, 139
subjectivity 5–6, 14, 21, 22, 27, 30, 35, 51, 53, 61, 75–80, 84, 88–9, 92–3, 97, 100–2, 109, 111, 120, 122, 132, 142, 145, 147, 167–8, 178, 181, 198, 202–3, 207, 213 n.2, 214 n.4, 215 n.5
subtlety 73, 128, 131, 139, 195–97
Sun O))) (band) 106
surnaturalisme 96, 111, 141–2
Surrealism 7, 16, 153–4, 171, 183, 220 n.5
Surrealist Manifesto (Breton) 16
Swearingen, James 215 n.3
symbolic 37, 86, 119, 173–4, 209, 220 n.2

symmetry/asymmetry 100, 117, 164, 176–7
    see also appropriateness
System Shock (Looking Glass Studios) 106

Taccone, Stefano 159, 182
Tallemant des Réaux, Gédéon 26, 30
Tanizaki, Jun'ichirō 110
taste 1, 8, 44, 46, 58, 93, 129–30, 174, 189, 198, 205, 207
Tatarkiewicz, Władysław 36, 128, 132
techno hardcore music 105
Tel Quel (journal) 15
Tempo presente (journal) 15
Tetsuo: the Iron Man (Tsukamoto) 106
Thales 113
thing/s
    alienation 214 n.2
    as artworks 7, 177–81, 197
    Baroque imagination 130–1, 183
    beauty 37, 94
    becoming 6, 90–2, 94
    and clothing 102, 110, 144–8
    consumption 85–6; see also commodity
    and feeling 14, 96
    hybridization 95, 214 n.3
    indifferent 125
    inorganic 101, 105, 199
    Internet of Things 94
    living 8, 203–5
    Marxist view of 5–6, 86–7, 111, 214 n.2
    neutral 90–1, 209
    and objects 85–7
    radiation 84, 95–6, 103, 178
    religion 55
    sex appeal 84
    storiette 29
    that feels (*cosa che sente*) 6, 83, 102–3, 110, 121, 185, 197, 200, 214 n.4
    and transit 114
    uncanny 96–8
    virtual 107
thing theory 85–88
thingness 5–6, 83–6, 90, 199
Thucydides 168
Tiresia (Perniola) 6, 11, 28, 114–16, 198, 215 n.9
Tiresia contro Edipo (Perniola) 6, 11, 122, 216 n.10

Torres Ruiz, Miquel Á. 215 n.4
totality 156–7, 163–4, 168, 181, 200
trance 35
transit (*transito*) 3, 4, 84, 88, 94, 112–15, 118, 131, 165, 180, 183, 204–5, 208, 215 n.8
Transiti (Perniola) 49, 113–14, 126, 180, 215 n.10
transorganic 95, 178
Traverses (journal) 34
Trione, Vincenzo 182
Trump, Donald 25
Truth of Masks, The (Wilde) 189
Tsunetomo, Yamamoto 149

ukiyo-e 113
uncanny 88, 96–7, 178, 183–4
unconscious 21, 119, 121, 153, 176, 204, 220 n.2
Unheimliche, Das (Freud) 96
Unnamable, The (Beckett) 19, 21, 25
Ussama, Yaqub 25
utilitarianism 101, 108, 135, 150, 200, 207, 211 n.2
    see also bourgeoisie
utopia 113, 164, 200, 208, 212, 218

value 57–60
vampire 112, 204, 215 n.7
vampirism 84, 108–9, 112
Van Gulick, Robert H. 215 n.6
Van Sevenant, Ann 129
Vattimo, Gianni 2, 65–6, 212 n.3, 220 n.1
Velotti, Stefano 182
Verdicchio, Massimo 2, 215 n.5
Vincentini, Isabella 192
Virgil 169
virtue 124, 126, 145, 147, 159, 216 n.3
vitalism 6, 8, 13, 90, 93, 101–2, 106, 127, 168, 175–6, 181, 211 n.3, 214 n.2
Vogt, Erik M. 2, 179, 184, 213 n.2, 220 n.3

Wahbeh, Farris 220 n.4
Warhol, Andy 173
Warner, Daniel 106
warrior 129, 132, 138–9, 149
weak thought 65–7
    see also anti-intellectualism

Weiwei, Ai 205
Westworld (Nolan) 106
White, Hayden 211 n.1
Whitley, David S. 88
Wilde, Oscar 2–3, 8, 150, 187–97, 199–205, 207–9, 221 n.1
will to power 120
wit 77, 128–9, 195, 209
Wit and the Art of Inventiveness (Gracián) 128
Wittgenstein, Ludwig 6, 84, 96, 178
Wittkower, Margot 160
Wittkower, Rudolf 160
Witz 118
Woelfel, James 216 n.3
Woolf, Virginia 30

Wordsworth, William 77
Work of Art in the Age of Mechanical Reproducibility, The (Benjamin) 173

xenomorphs 107
Xingjian, Gao 30

Yoshioka, Hiroshi 85
Youngblood, Gene 182

Zappa, Frank 105
Zen 6, 92–3, 104, 142, 144–5
Zeno of Citium 123
Zeran, Aurie 1478
Zhou, Xian 211 n.1

www.ingramcontent.com/pod-product-compliance
Lightning Source LLC
Chambersburg PA
CBHW062127300426
44115CB00012BA/1840